The Ten Commandments

Other books by Dr. Laura Schlessinger

Ten Stupid Things Women Do to Mess Up Their Lives

*How Could You Do That?! The Abdication of Character,
Courage, and Conscience*

Ten Stupid Things Men Do to Mess Up Their Lives

THE TEN

Commandments

The Significance of God's Laws in Everyday Life

Dr. Laura Schlessinger

and Rabbi Stewart Vogel

A Cliff Street Book
from HarperPerennial

References

The two versions of the Bible referred to in this text are:

Old Testament: The Stone edition of the *Tanach,* part of the Artscroll series, published by Mesorah Publications Ltd., 1998.

New Testament: *New Jerusalem Bible,* published by Doubleday, 1990.

A hardcover edition of this book was published in 1998 by Cliff Street Books, an imprint of HarperCollins Publishers.

THE TEN COMMANDMENTS. Copyright © 1998 by Dr. Laura C. Schlessinger. All rights reserved. Printed in the United States of America. No part of this book may be used or reproduced in any manner whatsoever without written permission except in the case of brief quotations embodied in critical articles and reviews. For information address HarperCollins Publishers, Inc., 10 East 53rd Street, New York, NY 10022.

HarperCollins books may be purchased for educational, business, or sales promotional use. For information please write: Special Markets Department, HarperCollins Publishers, Inc., 10 East 53rd Street, New York, NY 10022.

First CliffStreet/HarperPerennial edition published in 1999.

Designed by Jessica Shatan

The Library of Congress has catalogued the hardcover edition as follows:

Schlessinger, Laura.
    The Ten commandments : the significance of God's laws in everyday
life / Laura Schlessinger and Stewart Vogel.
        p.   cm.
    ISBN 0-06-019138-4
    1. Ten commandments. 2. Conduct of life. I. Vogel, Stewart. II. Title
BM520.75.S35 1998
296.3'6—dc21   98-223559

ISBN 0-06-092996-0 (pbk.)
99 00 01 02 03 ❖ 10 9 8 7 6 5 4 3 2 1

For Lew and Deryk, who have shared the journey. (L.S.)

For my wife Rodi, who is my true partner in life:
"and they shall be as one flesh" (Genesis 2:24);
and my children Talya, Eliezer, Ari, and Avi:
"Children are a heritage from God." (Psalm 127:3). (S.V.)

Contents

Acknowledgments

This month marks the fourth anniversary of my radio program's international syndication. It has been a fascinating broadcast journey from a local program on KFI, Los Angeles, with a format some termed "shrink-talk" to what I have termed a "moral health" program. I "preach, teach, and nag" about morals, values, ethics, and principles. The evolution of this format followed my personal religious journey. I began on air some twenty-three years ago, first as a civilian, then later as a trained and licensed marriage and family therapist. Religiously, a product of an "inter-faithless marriage," it took most of my adulthood to work my way into a profound belief in God.

Rabbi Stewart Vogel provided my first guidance and support for this effort. At our first meeting, he gently chided me that "feeling Jewish" was no substitute for education and practice. My son, Deryk, and I formally converted to Judaism through the Conservative University of Judaism program in Los Angeles headed by Rabbi Neil Weinberg, a wonderfully enthusiastic and knowledgeable teacher.

After hearing my program in Ottawa, I received a delightful

fax from Rabbi Reuven Bulka, an Orthodox rabbi, prodigious author, and fellow radio broadcaster. After developing a phone and fax friendship for a number of years, he mentored my family's Judaic studies, culminating in a family (Lew, Deryk, and me) conversion to Orthodox Judaism in 1998. We accomplished this Herculean feat with the tutelage and support of Rabbi Eli Schochet and his wife, Penina.

I have been encouraged by the strong and touching support I have received from the Christian community for my program as well as for my personal religious growth. The number of nuns, priests, pastors, ministers, lay teachers, and Christian folks who have corresponded with me over these four years has been inspiring; I am moved and grateful. It proves that people sincere about their love and awe of God are ultimately of one mind.

Since it is largely through my radio program that I have the opportunity to communicate and "nag," I am, of course, grateful to those who make it possible: Premiere Radio (Steve Lehman, Kraig Kitchin, and Greg Noack); Multiverse Networks (David Landau and Ken Williams); my personal, magnificent staff (Keven Bellows, Lisa Medel, Amir Henrickson, and DeWayne McDaniel); and my on-air support (Carolyn Holt and Dan Mandis).

I forgive Diane Reverand (aka "The Reverand Diane"), my editor and publisher, for putting in so many commas and taking out so many parentheses. This is our fourth book together—imagine! I appreciate her patience, insight, criticism (most of the time), and enthusiasm.

My gratitude to my husband, Lew, and son, Deryk, for being the loves of my life is something I tell them personally . . . so, enough said. Blessings to my dear friend, Patti Edwards, a spiritual soul-sister.

And infinite gratitude to my audience. Thank you for struggling with me . . . for, besides God, we are all we have left.

—Dr. Laura C. Schlessinger

There are many paths in life I could have chosen. It was the love of Judaism demonstrated by my grandparents Abe and Betty Jabkowski (of blessed memory) and my early experiences with them that planted the seed for my later commitment to a religious life. Dr. David Elcott recognized my potential and taught me how to be a passionate and committed religious school teacher. Later, rabbis Robert Wexler and Elliot Dorff awakened a sense of purpose through their encouragement to become a rabbi. I am indebted to their wisdom and friendship.

I have been privileged to serve synagogues with loving and committed congregants who have made being a rabbi a fulfilling experience. My work at Temple Israel Center (White Plains, NY) and Valley Beth Shalom (Encino, CA) allowed me to be part of model synagogues and learn from the best. As spiritual leader of Temple Aliyah (Woodland Hills, CA), my relationship with the congregation can only be described as ideal. With excellent professionals and dedicated congregants, we are creating a synagogue that emphasizes community and Jewish commitment. Every day brings the blessings of people who share their lives with me and enrich mine in the process. Much of my contribution to this book evolved from the sermons and teachings that I shared during the past several years.

This book has been a labor of love. Collaborating with Dr. Schlessinger brought us together for many hours of learning, sharing, and writing. Her insight and friendship have been an important part of my life during the process. I am grateful to Dr. Elliot Dorff and Leslie Gilbert-Lurie for their comments and to Rabbi Naomi Levy for her encouragement. Their friendships have been instrumental in my life. Many clergy responded to questions on the Ten Commandments and helped us understand their diverse interpretations and applications. I am particularly grateful to Monsignor Paul Dotson for his wisdom and friendship. One of the most important people who brought sanity to my life during the writing of this book was my secretary, Barbara Schwartz. Without her my life would be a primordial chaos.

I have always been taught the importance of family. My parents, Pearl and Bill Vogel, make it easy to fulfill the Fifth Commandment. With love and encouragement they have always been there with support and shared in my successes. It takes an entire family to raise a child, and I am indebted to my entire family who has given me a lifetime of love and friendship. With my four sisters, aunts and uncles, cousins, and all their offspring, life is a series of large family celebrations. I was fortunate in my marriage to not only gain a remarkable wife but also another wonderful set of parents. Shirley and Eric Mauer are always there for family and are the most nonintrusive in-laws one could ever hope for.

I am most grateful for the blessing of my wife, Rodi. Life with her is a wonderful journey that gets better every day. Her intelligence, zest for life, and remarkable parenting skills are an inspiration to me. She brings balance and meaning to a hectic professional life. My children, Talya, Eliezer, Ari, and Avi, teach me so much about life every day. It is remarkable how such diverse children can be created from the same genetic material. I can only hope that the values espoused in this book will guide their lives.

And finally I am grateful to God for giving me a life that has exceeded all my expectations.

—RABBI STEWART VOGEL

Preface

Everybody knows the Ten Commandments, right? Let's see: There's something about stealing, lying, murdering . . . ahhh . . . that's only three . . . ahhh. More people claim to live by the Ten Commandments than seem to know what they specifically are, let alone what they really mean. Well, why should they? How important are they anyway? This is the modern world, and those biblical events, ideas, and stories are from an ancient time—how could this possibly be of much value in this jet-propelled, nuclear era?

Each day we make innumerable, seemingly minute decisions about things that don't really seem earth-shattering. So what if we broke a promise? Lots of promises are broken, and people get over it and get on with it. So what if we find passion in another bed while we or they are still married? We're entitled to derive pleasure and self-fulfillment. So what if we are too focused on work, TV, or clubs to spend time with family? No one has the right to tell us what to do. So what if religion is not a big deal in our lives? Religious types are all hypocrites, and God is a silly myth for the weak.

When one adds up all the "so-whats," one ends up with a

life without direction, meaning, purpose, value, integrity, or long-range joy. What too many people haven't learned about the Bible is that it's filled with wisdom and direction for all ages to elevate our lives above mere frantic, animal existence to the sublime levels humanity is capable of experiencing.

I first met Rabbi Vogel in 1995 when I began my religious journey, culminating in my whole family's conversion to Orthodox Judaism in 1998. Our decision to write about the Ten Commandments stems from our common passion for the Bible and our desire to share the Judeo-Christian values derived from it. Although this book has been a collaboration (we argue over Scripture with panache!), I have used the first-person singular in order to avoid the confusion of multiple voices and, in some cases, to distinguish issues that are of particular importance to me.

This is not meant as a biblically exhaustive, academic tome. This is a modern update and popularization of the words of God. In *The Ten Commandments,* we will take what seem like straightforward and succinct expressions ("You will . . ." and "You will not . . . ") and expand them to their fullest conceptualizations to demonstrate how, through their application, your life can be made more satisfying, meaningful, directed, moral, and even holy.

This book is filled with ideas, emotions, and humor. It will touch, move, enlighten, inspire, sometimes frustrate, educate, and entertain you. You won't be able to look at even mundane moments in your life in exactly the same way. After reading this book, you will stop and think about the right thing to do. Although you might, at that moment, feel annoyed at the challenge coming from your soul and psyche, you will ultimately feel enlightened and elevated. We promise.

—Dr. Laura C. Schlessinger
June 1998

Introduction

"God, I'd Like You to Meet Laura; Laura, This Is God"

Believing in God is a relatively recent experience in my life. My father, born a Jew in Brooklyn, New York, never mentioned God, religion, or Judaism—except for one all-encompassing criticism of the Jewish Passover service. He said how, at a very young age, he walked out of his parents' Passover seder celebration screaming that he "wouldn't celebrate the wholesale slaughter of Egyptian children."

"Boy, that *is* terrible!" I thought, and that subject, or anything about Judaism, for that matter, was never discussed again.

Imagine my surprise when, some forty years later, while attending a Passover seder in a synagogue, we got to the part where the Ten Plagues are recited, culminating in the death of the firstborn of Egypt, and we dipped a finger into red wine and dropped onto a plate those symbolic tears of compassion, sympathy, and anguish from the Jewish people in response to the suffering of the Egyptians. Imagine my anger at my father when I came to learn that the Exodus experience was a story of re-

demption of a people from bondage into a covenant with God
to bring to all peoples His character and desire for universal love
and ethical behavior *and not,* as my father had negatively and
summarily condensed a four-thousand-year magnificent history,
a study in barbarism.

My mother was born in Italy to a Catholic family, met my
father as he participated in the U.S. military's liberation of
northern Italy, and married him at the end of the war in 1946.
Her only contribution to my religious training was that American Catholics take it all more seriously than Italians and that
she hated the priests because, as they walked around well-
garbed and fed, the people starved.

Once, when I was an adolescent, my parents asked me if I
believed in God. "Of course not," I said with assuredness.
"That's *Twilight Zone* stuff." Remembering back now, they
seemed surprised. I have to wonder why when one parent told
me God is a sadist and the other parent that men of God are
selfish and greedy. There was no conversation about God or
prayer, no worship, and no observances.

Probably realizing that they had made a mistake, or because
they felt they were missing something in their own lives, my
folks decided to do something religious when I was about
sixteen-years-old. "Compromising" their different faiths, backgrounds, they signed us up at the local Unitarian church. I remember my confusion between the weekly service literature
extolling the virtue of "no dogma" or commandments while the
choir sang beautifully about Jesus Christ. The Unitarians taught
that there was beauty and truth in many traditions and believing
in God or Jesus as divine was optional. I had the same reaction
to this smorgasbord of tradition that I had when a restaurant
would overfill my plate with food I couldn't really identify. I lost
my appetite.

It is not that I led a life without morals and ethics. My parents taught me what was right and wrong. Wrong was sassing
your mom or dad, using bad words, lying, cheating, stealing,

disobeying authority types, coming home late or misrepresenting where I was or what I was doing, hurting someone's feelings, smoking, drinking, doing sexual things, and so forth.

What was the authority behind these rules? I could be arrested by the police, be hated by friends, or get spanked by my father. The authority behind the rules was the consequences, which would eventually cause me pain, regret, and unhappiness. Fear is very motivating . . . but only for a while. As I grew older, the influence of literature about heroes and ideals, the reinforcement of concepts of virtue at school, and the reminders by my parents that goodness and decency are their own reward supported my rising above most temptations that the freedom of living in a college dormitory provide.

I wanted my parents to be proud of me, and I wanted people to like me. These were my motivations to be "good." Now for the complications. Even many nice and popular people don't always like you when you won't *"go along"* with cheating ("It's no big deal, Laura; it's not a subject in your major—it's just an elective . . . "), drugs ("Come on, Laura, it's a great feeling—don't be such a drag . . ."), sex ("You're not going to be popular with the guys, Laura, if you're such a prude . . ."), cutting classes ("Oh, Laura, stop being so compulsive—learn to loosen up and have some fun . . . "), or protesting ("We have a right to stop the university from functioning if they're not doing something our way or giving us what we want . . .").

Consequently, I wasn't "in" much with the in-crowds. It wasn't as if all or even most of my college chums were "bad." The freedom afforded by being away from home gives opportunity for experimentation away from parental authority, mostly out of view of university authority and in the company of others who are supporting the notion of *individual* choice, taste, preference, desire, values, and decisions. Yet, somehow, mixed into this brew is the notion that the folks before us just didn't know what we know or have the ability to appreciate life as we do. Talk about perpetually inventing the wheel.

The next complication was the realization that my main authorities, Mom and Dad, were imperfect, inconstant, sometimes troubled, and oftentimes very difficult. This weakened the notion of concerning myself with their pride in my activities.

Nonetheless, I was still fervent in my determination to be decent and good. For me, this was an internal status symbol. I used the basics as a format (no cheating, stealing, and so forth)—with the caveat that my intelligence permitted me leeway in interpretation and execution of these ideas.

In other words, I discovered rationalizations. Rationalizations include:

➤ Notions of superiority ("*I* know what I am doing").

➤ Arrogance ("I can handle this—it won't be a problem").

➤ Elitism ("I should have this leeway because I do special things").

➤ Stupidity ("This is really no big deal—it's just an experience").

➤ Foolishness ("This really has no impact on who I am").

➤ Shortsightedness ("My future will not be impacted by this").

➤ Selfishness ("If *you* can't handle it—it's your problem, not mine!").

The universal experience of youth is to struggle between acceptance of authority with its rules, regulations, and attitudes and the energy and excitement of what seems to be the first and only discovery of the true essence and meaning of life. In "pre-" maturity, that essence is focused on the self and sensuality, limitless freedom, perpetual want and desire, impulsiveness, confusion over personal identity, and painful ignorance about the *meaning* of it all.

Although the scope of my upbringing afforded me more than enough discipline to not cross over that often or that far, I do have regrets and shame. To some extent, the heavy, uncomfortable presence of those regrets in my soul and mind, together with my deepened appreciation and reliance on godly authority, helped focus my radio program during the last half dozen years. I am especially trying to help young folks minimize the occurrence of such historical self-disappointment, and the sometimes terrible or difficult consequences, by introducing and reinforcing the morals and values they ought to have received at home. These values aren't reinforced in general society, and they are unassailable by rationalizations: God's commandments.

I am still trying to figure out when and how I took that leap into an acceptance of God. Even yesterday, I asked my husband, who has known me for a quarter-of-a-century, if he ever would have guessed that I would have become "religious." He said, "Never!" In fact, I'd always been slightly condescending, but polite, to anyone on or off the radio who professed a relationship with God. I would never permit God or religion, especially Bible quotes, to be mentioned on my program!

That had left me with the question of who or what is the authority behind my positions and answers. That authority would come from a combination of:

➤I'm the one with a microphone.

➤I'm smart.

➤I'm a licensed psychotherapist.

➤I'm a college professor.

➤I'm an author.

➤I'm the one they're calling up.

➤I'm insightful.

➤I'm right because it's the way I think I'd do it.

➤I'm speaking divinely commanded behaviors without realizing it.

➤I'm rational and can figure stuff out.

➤I'm confident in my positions.

➤I'm older and experienced in life.

➤I'm into the literature of philosophy and psychology.

➤I'm successful with what I'm doing; therefore, it must be right!

This is all worthy. This is all necessary. This is not sufficient. I felt something was missing personally and professionally. I came to what that was through my son, Deryk. When Deryk was born, neither my husband (Episcopalian background—no religious practice or belief) nor myself (you already know this part) was religious. We worried about that for our son—but figured that he was too young for religion to matter and we had time to figure something out. Of course, we did nothing.

One rainy Sunday, Deryk, then about six or seven, and I were channel-surfing. My finger froze on the remote turner when the visual image appeared on our TV screen of scores of naked women, holding their equally doomed babies, huddled along the ridge of a deep pit in the earth, waiting for the Nazi soldiers' bullets to end their fear. My son's mouth opened in amazed horror. He and I heard Elizabeth Taylor's voice as one of the young children calling out to her dead mother that she couldn't breathe because her dead mother's body was squashing her in the pile of bodies. I was in shock, as I was every time I saw Holocaust footage, but more intensely so because my son was witnessing something incomprehensible to him—to anyone of conscience.

"Momma," Deryk screamed out, grabbing me, "what is happening?"

"Honey," I tried to say calmly, "those are German soldiers in World War II, murdering mommies and their babies."

"Momma, why are they doing that?"

"They're evil."

"Who are those women?"

"The women and children are Jews."

"Momma, who are Jews?"

"Deryk, the Jews are our people. You are a Jew."

"What is Jew?"

"You know, Deryk, I really don't know. I'm going to study up and tell you as I find out."

We spent the rest of that weekend crying and holding each other. That was some way for my son to be introduced to religion.

Now, according to Jewish law, neither myself, born of a Jewish father but not a Jewish mother, nor Deryk were Jewish. We did have Jewish blood through my father. Through some inexplicable emotion, I had always felt a Jewish connection—I just didn't know what it meant. To me, my son and I were Jews, and those were our people. Jewish law may not have accepted that, but Hitler would have.

I made my promise good to my son. I started studying. Study, prayer, and practice were my eventual movement toward God. The first time we entered a synagogue, I had to leave because I was overwhelmed when they took out the Torah and held it up for the congregation. I stood in the parking lot, not quite understanding why I was crying my eyes out. It seemed to be incredible that I was part of a four-thousand-year history of something so magnificent and special: the world's introduction to God's relationship with people.

My son started Hebrew school. My husband and I went through a conversion course at the University of Judaism, Los Angeles. Deryk and I converted through that Conservative program. After my husband finished his studies, he, Deryk, and I converted together in an Orthodox ceremony. We're planning on Deryk's Bar Mitzvah in Jerusalem in 1998. I can hardly stand the wait to touch the soil of Israel and to link our son to the "nation of priests."

If there was one moment of revelation that awakened me to God and Judaism, it was the reading of Exodus 19:4–6. The Israelites are camping out at Sinai some three months after leaving Egypt. God calls Moses up the mountain and tells him, **"You have seen what I did to Egypt, and that I have borne you on the wings of eagles and brought you to Me. And now, if you hearken well to Me and observe My covenant, you shall be to Me the most beloved treasure of all peoples, for Mine is the entire world. You shall be to Me a kingdom of ministers and a holy nation. These are the words that you shall speak to the Children of Israel."** Reading this virtually took my breath away. I had spent my whole life trying to find *meaning*—in being the "good kid," in doing well in school, in being intelligent, in being successful. Though it was all important, it didn't fill some special empty space, where meaning needed to be. Realizing that I had a God-mandated responsibility to represent His character, love, and ethical will was the meaning I'd been searching for.

Rather than as metaphor, I take the covenant at Sinai as real and true. This does put me at odds with some contemporary Jews, for whom Judaism is more a people and a culture than a people of "the covenant." However, without my firm faith and belief of a *whole people* experiencing God *directly*, I wouldn't be able to believe in God at all or accept God's authority over the world and me. I am moved to *faith* because the covenant between the people of Israel and God is *evidenced* by the continued existence of the Jewish people in spite of thousands of years of almost continuous attempts to eliminate them by great and powerful cultures, which have themselves become extinct.

This covenant, making Jews the "chosen people," has been misunderstood throughout the ages. The Jewish understanding of "chosen" does *not* mean favorite child or a teacher's pet—to be chosen is not an issue of specialness, it is an issue of accepting serious responsibilities.

The Israelites were basically given an assignment. By their adherence to a unique way of life, with laws of holiness, justice, generosity, mercy, ethics, and compassion, the whole world would come to know, love, and obey the One and Only God. The Jews were to be role models, and their behavior in personal and public life, as commanded by God, would draw others to follow: ultimately resulting in God's kingdom on earth. God loves all people. We are all made "in His image." The task of the Jews was not and is not to make Jews of all the world's peoples but to bring to everyone the knowledge of the presence of God and the basic values commanded by God as a blessing: "**. . . and all the families of the earth shall bless themselves by you . . .**" (Genesis 12:3).

Once I had absorbed the significance of this religious purpose, my lifestyle, level of happiness, satisfaction, and state of mind and heart changed dramatically. When interviewed recently for a newspaper magazine section, the journalist commented that my friends all said I was a hard worker and were pleased at my doing so well. I found myself silent, which confused me for a moment, since, after all, that was a compliment—I should show pleasure. Instead, after about twenty long seconds of cogitation, I said that "before I became a serious Jew, hearing that I was doing well would have been a wonderful compliment and relief. But now, with my motivation coming from quite a different place, I would only feel complimented by the phrase 'doing *good*.' "

Being successful is something I've worked hard at and earned, and it is gratifying. The respect, opportunity, and financial compensation are wonderful. If I felt I were successful without doing something of meaning or value, it would be an empty victory, indeed. Going up a rating point is of little interest to me compared with the joy I feel when I meet a family in public who gives me some credit for their joy in staying home with the children, saving the marriage, or giving up a bad habit like drinking. That is my new, nonsecular measure of success.

My new joy comes with major obligations and responsibilities. Even the most noble ideals of thoughts, words, and deeds are meaningless when they stay philosophical or symbolic in nature. It is in the *everyday* that we give meaning to ideas and ideals. That's why rituals are so important. For example, Jews are to put a mezuzah on their front doors. Inside this small, tubular, artistic case is a small scroll of parchment on which are written two biblical passages: (Deuteronomy 6:4–9) **"Hear O Israel, the Lord is our God, the Lord is One . . ."** and (Deuteronomy 11:13–21) **"And if you will carefully obey my commandments. . . ."** Now, you might wonder, what is the point of bothering to hang up this object? Although they are often pretty, they are not for decoration. Although they house the words of God, they are not good-luck charms. Though I do not have the arrogance to presume knowledge of God's reasoning or purpose for each of His commandments, my humble guess would be that the mezuzah's purpose is as a *reminder*.

Tipping your hat to a lady is a reminder of respect. Saying "please" before each request is a reminder of humility. Saying "thank you" after each gift or blessing is a reminder of gratitude. Blinking your car signaler before each turn is a reminder of your concern for the welfare of others. Saying grace before and/or after each meal is a reminder of your love of God, and God's for us.

Without these reminders we can too easily become crass and self-centered. These ritualized acts give us the opportunity to become more holy in our purpose and closer to God. That's why I keep kosher (special dietary laws explained in Leviticus), observe Shabbat (the Sabbath), have our child in Jewish day school, attend services, support my synagogue, read religious materials, pray, and try my darndest to *obey* God's commandments. Now, I always say that I'm a serious Jew, not a perfect Jew. I worry about people who get so into the *form* of rituals that they stop living the *meaning* of the rituals. The *meaning* behind the rituals is to aspire toward holiness, in the image of God, not perfection, for God is quite well acquainted with our human imperfections and occasional accidental or intentional misuse of free will.

I have always considered myself a rational, scientific, intellectually oriented, and independent person. It may seem an odd leap for someone like me to accept external authority, especially without specific explanations from God on His motivation for each commandment. I have discovered that although we do gain wisdom from the exercise of analysis and discourse on God's commandments, we gain character from our decision to obey in spite of our limited human capability to understand.

Science can explain the "what"—only religion gives the "what" meaning. Perhaps pure reason will never be able to demonstrate scientifically the existence of God and the immortality of the soul.

When Moses (Exodus 19:3–8) put before the Israelite elders the concept of covenantal relationship between God and His people, the response is *not* "Wait a minute, what's the deal?" The response *is* **"Everything that God has spoken we will do!"** (Exodus 19:8) The immediate and unequivocal reaction is the acceptance of divine authority based upon the love and gratitude of the Israelites for their redemption from Egyptian bondage.

In life, a higher idealism and a more profound, just, and consistent morality is only found through the commandments. My life has focus, purpose, and meaning. I feel a part of something more important than my daily experiences might indicate; that is, that my actions and being have significance past my personal joy and/or pain. I don't feel so alone anymore. I feel as if I am part of a bigger picture—even if I don't always "see it" or "get it." I feel more able, actually, to help folks who call in or listen to my radio program, where I "preach, teach, and nag!" I can offer them a plan, God's purpose; a way, God's commandments; and a goal, God's holiness. My family life has a focus above and beyond creature comforts, needs, and desires. I have some deeper friendships because of shared, though different, religious interests and involvements. I have a more fair, just, and consistent framework upon which to make moral decisions. I have discovered the inherent peace in that acceptance.

—DR. LAURA C. SCHLESSINGER
June 1998

There Are Many Roads to Rome . . . Oops . . . I Mean . . . Jerusalem

I could have written the above paragraph, although my religious journey was quite different from Dr. Schlessinger's. I was born into a family who practiced some Jewish observance. We did not observe the fundamental commandments like Shabbat and the dietary laws of keeping kosher, which are part of the overall call to holiness, but I grew up experiencing the warmth and joy of celebrating major Jewish holidays and life-cycle events. I did not have a "Jewish awakening," since Judaism was the assumption of my existence. To ask "Why am I Jewish?" was to ask "Why do I breathe?" I was proud to be Jewish and proud of my history.

The downside of being born Jewish is that Jews often take their Jewishness for granted, whereas converts like Dr. Schlessinger virtually explode with enthusiasm and serious commitment, sometimes making an uneasy relationship between the groups.

In our society, an example of our taking Jewishness for granted occurs at the Bar (or Bat for girls) Mitzvah. A Bar

Mitzvah, literally meaning "son of the commandment," is the Jewish rite of passage indicating the adult status of responsibility celebrated at age thirteen. The newly designated adult is obligated to observe the laws. Whether one celebrated a Bar Mitzvah ceremony or not, the status of obligated adult was automatic. The ceremony is simply a public statement that the man/woman-child was old enough to know right from wrong and was accountable to the law.

For most American Jews, the Bar Mitzvah does not have this significance and is instead a social-religious ceremony representing the successful completion of religious studies and a public demonstration of Jewish pride. The truth is that thirteen is actually too young to understand the significance of religious responsibilities, and that this ceremony is too often viewed as the honorable discharge from Jewish study and involvement. That is how I celebrated my Bar Mitzvah: a ceremony of Jewish pride but *not* religious commitment.

In the Jewish tradition, understanding the reason for specific laws, customs, and rituals helps to make their observance more meaningful, but that background is not essential for the observance itself. My great-grandparents, who were very religious, did not know the reasons for all the things they did. It didn't matter to them. They did "Jewish things" because that is what Jews did. Was it their deep faith in God that motivated this attitude, or was it blind obedience to the only way they knew? I would like to believe that it was their faith in God and a way of life that had been part of the Jewish people for four thousand years. Theirs was a generation that did not challenge authority.

I am a product of a generation that challenges all authority; a generation for which doubt and rebellion have replaced faith and belief. These powerful forces, which helped a nation question and overthrow that status quo of racism and openly protest a questionable war (Vietnam), have also led to a general decline in organized religious affiliation. Instead, we live in a country yearning for "spirituality," a search for comfort and meaning. We want the benefits of God without the obligations. Ultimately, the modern New Age movements are simply placebos, feeling better without necessarily being better.

My Polish-born maternal grandparents demonstrated a great love for Judaism. I have vivid and beautiful memories of attending prayer services with my grandfather. I had learned the words of the prayers in religious school and I could see the devotion of my grandfather's praying, but I could not feel the prayers. The words of the Psalm (51:17) **"O Lord, open my lips, that my mouth may declare Your praise"** did not make sense until I began my search for God. Only then did I realize that this was an appeal to God to help us transform a "prayer of our lips" into a "prayer of our hearts."

Through literally hundreds of informal surveys with Jewish audiences I have discovered that most Jewish families do not talk about God. Sure, parents must answer the questions of their young children like "Where is God?" or "What does God look like?", but the answers are brief and tenuous. As a rabbi, I have come to learn that many Jewish adults are uncomfortable with their own views of God, and hence the subject has become taboo. I grew up in such a house—and in their turn, so did my parents. This was the culture of theological dysfunction that defined my prerabbinic life.

Given this, how or why would I ever become a rabbi? I became a rabbi because my passion for Judaism compensated for my theological uncertainty. I believed in a God of Creation, but not much more. It was a beginning. During the ten years of functioning as a rabbi, of seeing God at work in my life and the lives of my congregants, I have come to believe in a more personal God. Whereas most people see life through their own eyes and those of a select group of family and friends, as a rabbi I experience life through the eyes of almost one thousand families, from birth to death, 365 days of the year. By virtue of being a rabbi participating in the lives of all those individuals and families, I have the distinction of seeing more of life than the average person. I believe that God is active in our lives. I cannot see the hands of God at work, but I can *see* and *feel* His presence in the creation of the unfolding design of the infinitely complicated and wondrous nature and experience of life.

To believe in God is to believe that humans are more than accidents of nature. It means that we are endowed with purpose by a higher source, and that our goal is to realize that higher purpose. If each of us creates his own meaning, we also create our own morality. I cannot believe this. For if so, what the Nazis did was not immoral because German society had accepted it. Likewise, the subjective morality of every majority culture throughout the world could validate their heinous behavior. It comes down to a very simple matter: Without God there is no *objective meaning* to life, nor is there an *objective morality*. I do not want to live in a world where right and wrong are subjective.

At age fifteen, after a youth trip to Israel inspired me to begin my Jewish journey, I began to observe some of the basic commandments. I did so with little support from my Jewish friends, since for them their Jewishness was a cultural-ethnic identity more than a daily experience or format for holiness. I finally understood the purpose of religion is to lead us to holiness, a relationship with God, and an aspiration of living up to being "made in the image of God."

With that goal in mind, I came to realize that observing the Sabbath, kosher laws, ritual prayers, and other obligated observances were not a burden of prohibitions but a way of developing godliness in all my words, thoughts, and deeds.

During my admission interviews for rabbinical school I was asked why I wanted to become a rabbi. Though I do not remember my exact answer, it involved demonstrating to Jewish youth that Judaism could be a vibrant, dynamic, and integral part of one's life. Not until several years after my ordination did I understand the internal drive that led me to be a rabbi was of a more personal nature. When I began to share with congregants my love of Judaism, I realized that the times in my life when I felt most complete, fulfilled, and connected to family and community were the Jewish moments. My "Jewish growth" and eventual ordination were simply a desire to fill my life with these Jewish moments, sharing them with others, in our communal as well as personal efforts to connect with God.

The choice of a rabbinical school forced me to resolve another religious conflict. What was the nature of my obligation to God? Could I choose which of the commandments I wished to observe, or was I obligated to all of them? Were the commandments actually God-mandated behaviors or meaningful folkways?

I was uncomfortable with some Jewish denominations' philosophy of appointing the individual with the right to be final arbiter. I had faith in the human ability to reason, but I also knew the human tendency to rationalize unethical behavior. After a great deal of personal struggle, I eventually accepted the authority of the commandments as binding. I could now celebrate God—not the stern, judgmental God often emphasized in religion, but rather the Judge from whom authority and all goodness emanates. In my personal spiritual evolution, I finally was as Jacob awakening from his dream sleep: **"Surely the LORD is present in this place, and I did not know!"** (Genesis 28:16).

As a rabbi, I am the spiritual leader of my synagogue and a religious representative of the Jewish faith. I preach and teach to many people who have the same sense of theological dysfunction as I had fifteen years ago but have yet to take religion seriously enough to resolve their conflicts. Although people come to me for answers, most often they are not interested in what God has to say through the Bible and rabbinic writings. After ten years as rabbi, I find myself talking more and more about God and less and less about "feeling good about one-self." I hope to inspire them to search out God; not just a God who can make them *feel* good, but a God who can help them *do* good.

It was a long journey, but I am now more at peace with God than ever before. I still question the *ways* of God. It is in my blood. From Abraham, who argued with God about the fate of Sodom and Gomorrah, to Job, who could not understand why his life was filled with tragedy, my faith has taught me to challenge God. When a child struggles to understand the ways of a parent, the struggle turns into a dialogue once the role of the parent is accepted. Although there are still many more questions than there are answers, it is possible to find God in the questions as well as in the answers.

—Rabbi Stewart Vogel
June 1998

1

The First Commandment

**"I am the Lord your God who brought you out
of the land of Egypt, the house of bondage."**

According to numbers published by the *New York Times Magazine* (December 7, 1997), 96 percent of Americans said they believed in God; the words "In God We Trust" decorate our money; and a depiction of Moses and the Ten Commandments adorns the courtroom where the Justices of the Supreme Court often pronounce the Ten Commandments unconstitutional when placed on the wall of a schoolroom. Our founding fathers in America acknowledged God as our creator and source of universal, unalienable rights and moral standards. Why do we now appear threatened by that assertion?

Judge Roy S. Moore, the Alabama jurist who is locked in a legal battle to keep a handcrafted replica of the Ten Commandments on his courtroom wall, said he is at the center of a debate about Americans' acknowledgment of God. "Are we still one nation under God? Do we still acknowledge a higher law?" he challenged. (*Jewish Times,* October 24–30, 1997). It would seem that we suffer from ambivalence about believing in God, acknowledging God as our ultimate authority, and publicly teaching that belief and authority to our children.

Jim Senyszyn, a self-proclaimed atheist, wrote in the Greensboro, North Carolina, *Record* (November 2, 1997) that "since the Bible's basic cosmological model is monarchical, any rights that do occur are by the sufferance of the monarch," and that "Religious symbols [e.g., displaying the Ten Commandments] intimidate and give false authority." An op-ed column by John Tuouy, appearing in the same newspaper, countered that "Nothing in the Commandments prescribes a Gestapo-like authority to enforce compliance. Human beings have free will whether or not to comply."

Universally, people struggle for freedom from despotic domination to determine their own destiny. Personally, adolescents struggle for freedom from parental power, so they can do what they want, when and how they want. Freedom from external control allows for self-determination, self-expression, self-fulfillment . . . oh, oh, too much "self" . . . opportunity, diversity of opinion and ideas, experimentation—clearly a chance to explore the farthest reaches of human individual possibilities. As far as it goes, that is not a bad thing. But should there be limits? How do we judge whether what we are doing is right or wrong? Is all individually desired behavior fair or good for others or society as a whole—and should that even matter? What ultimately makes life purposeful and meaningful?

For many folks, "believers" or "non," the issue of "outside and ultimate authority" is a touchy one. Many people call my program and describe a relationship with God as one in which God loves and comforts them or sometimes does them favors. When I question them further about their sense of obligation *to* God, there is generally an uncomfortable silence, followed by protestations that churches are manmade and so are the rules, therefore there is no obligation other than their personal prefer-ence. When I suggest that the Scriptures clarify God's will for our behaviors, they often dismiss me with arguments like: "The Bible is written by a number of different authors over a long pe-riod of time and 'after the facts' and therefore isn't necessarily literally the word of God," to "There are many ways to interpret the passages," to "That was then and this is modern times," and finally, "My situation is different." Yet, many of these same peo-ple will turn to the Scriptures in times of pain or challenge. As somebody once said, "There are no atheists in a foxhole."

As Donna, one of my listeners, wrote, *"I heard something on TV last night and I thought of you. It was on a new show about a priest called* Soul Man. *The priest asks an acquain-tance if she goes to church. She says, 'No, too many rules.' The priest replies, 'Do not steal, do not murder . . . who can take that kind of pressure?' "*

While it is noble for human beings to aspire to freedom, if there is no flip side to that coin it will inevitably collapse in on itself. A *Frank and Ernest* syndicated cartoon strip (January 14, 1998) depicts Moses holding the tablets and asking God, "This isn't one of those 'Take responsibility for your own ac-tions deals'—is it?" The flip side to the freedom coin is re-sponsibility, without which you have the logic given by former Washington State Bar Association president Lowell Halver-son, who had sexual affairs with several of his clients whom he was representing in divorce and child-support cases. Asked if his conduct was "inappropriate," Halverson called that a "value-laden word." "What is inappropriate for one person is not for another," he said. "I respect other people's values, but they don't have to be my values." (*Seattle Post-Intelligencer,* December 13, 1997).

The oft-quoted line from Dostoevksy's *The Brothers Kara-mazov,* "Where there is no God, all is permitted," comes to mind here. There are those who think that adult sexual activ-ity with small children is morally correct; there are those who think that eliminating the weak and ill (Hitler) or the educated (Pol Pot) or the different (Hutus, Serbs, race supremacists) or the dissenting (Stalin or Mao) is correct.

Can the human population survive if it tolerates no standard of values for what is correct? Can we tolerate the concept of absolute values without thinking our freedom has been usurped? Can we find more value, meaning, direction, and gratification from a life with absolute values than without? And whose values will they be?

If the values are not God-derived, they come from fads and favorites (these days, single motherhood by choice is idealized, but moving an owl from its nesting place to make way for construction is real bad—huh?), laziness (if you actually admit that something is "wrong" you'd have to give up your comfortable life and do something about it), selfishness (what I want is automatically defined as good), and a personal desire to get away with anything under the protection of nonjudgmentalism (it's my life!).

Values inform our conscience, which influences our behavior. Our behaviors determine the quality of our lives and the meaningfulness of our personal contribution to others, to life, and to history.

Perhaps we need to stop thinking in terms of blind obedience and subordination to an invisible authoritarian. Perhaps we need to start thinking in terms of an inner need to be and to do good for the sake of a special, only human, inner moral imperative—that moral sense being God, that which desires us to be as He, defined by goodness, justice, compassion, and holiness. When individual people come up with "the rules," it is fair and smart to ask, "What's in it for them?" When we acknowledge God's rules, we know what's in it for Him—our well-being and grace. For some, this may not be as seductive as power, greedy consumption, and constant stimulation. However, those folks find themselves humming the tune to "Is That All There Is?"

The First Commandment challenges us all to take our relationship with God seriously. Once you release yourself into the assumption of faith and say that you are willing to honor God's commandments, you will create an environment in which to feel God's presence.

What *Is* Required by the First Commandment?

For the Jews and some Protestants, the first of the Ten Commandments reads: **"I am the Lord your God who brought you out of the land of Egypt, out of the house of bondage"** (Exodus 20:2). According to Catholics and Lutherans, that commandment continues with the words **"You shall have no other gods before me,"** which clearly reads more like something *is* commanded: an exclusive relationship and an implied prohibition against polytheism. For Jewish and Protestant traditions, for which those words appear as the Second Commandment, what is being commanded by this apparent "statement"?

To understand the answer to what is being decreed by **"I am the Lord your God . . . ,"** one has to recognize that this is a statement—not a "Thou Shalt/Not" standard form for a commandment. In fact, the more accurate translation of the original Hebrew declaration by Moses to the Israelite people in Deuteronomy (4:13), is not **"He declared to you the covenant which He commanded you to observe, the *Ten Commandments*; and He inscribed them on two tablets of stone."** The correct interpretation of *"aseret he'devarim"* is not "commandments" but "sayings" or "declarations." Moses reiterates that God has commanded obedience to ten particular statements. In this context, the "Ten Sayings," which we will continue to refer to as the Ten Commandments, are the ten essential *statements* of *faith* or *life* given by God at Mount Sinai.

It wouldn't make sense for God to command belief that **"I am the Lord your God . . . "** because, if you didn't already accept God as divine, then God wouldn't have the authority to command anything. After the Israelite people's miraculous redemption from Egyptian bondage, there was a profound basis for their respect and gratitude, motivating their acceptance of a covenant, or special bond and relationship, with God.

The First Commandment lays down the *authority* of the one God, more than commanding *belief* in one God. Without establishing the authority of God, the subsequent commandments become suggestions or folkways rather than commandments.

Since the correct translation of "Ten Commandments" is the "Ten Sayings," it might be tempting to slip into the more modern subjective-morality mode, considering these "statements" to be suggestions, open to your discretion—if you feel like it, if you think it's a good idea, if it wouldn't be too troublesome—rather than commandments, which you have a duty to obey because He is here for all of us.

Does God Demand Something Specific of Me?

In our extensive discussions with various groups, we have found that although many people are comfortable with the idea that humans have such general obligations to God as "Do unto others as you would have them do unto you," they are uncomfortable with the idea of specific obligations to God such as **"Remember the sabbath day and keep it holy"**— which puts a definite crimp in their shopping schedule.

The specific obligations may *seem* to require:

➤ Abdication of personal freedom (but not so—you always retain *free will*).

➤ Adherence to declarations that are probably only metaphorical, not literal (but is God not entitled to communicate concrete expectations in metaphorical styles?).

➤Acceptance of an anachronistic philosophy or way of life (but the power of traditional ways and mores is that they have stood the test of time).

➤Abandonment of personal will or power (but tapping into God's grace is the way humans have to generate and focus their potential to cope and do what's right).

➤Acquiescence of intellect to ancient mysticism (but imagining one's own intellect as the ultimate possible intelligence and power is supreme arrogance).

Even those people who espouse a belief in God still often resist and resent the notion of specifically commanded behaviors. People often want the benefits of having a God for personal requests or crisis interventions, and may use being a "believer" as a way to increase status, respect, or trust from others.

Entering into a relationship with God is not just about the rewards we receive in this world or the next but rather how we show God that we are serious about our relationship with Him.

We have had too many experiences with people in the hospital who tell about the bargain they have made with God, if only he would save them. "I promise to give money to the synagogue" or "I promise to keep more commandments" are common prayerful promises I hear mumbled by those whose futures are uncertain. We see the pain on their faces and sense their fear and are saddened when such prayers are the only time these people speak to God. Because their relationship with God has not been developed, they are too busy asking for miracles, when a long-standing relationship with God could have provided the comfort and strength necessary to deal with their illness and their fears. Our relationship with God, like any other healthy relationship, must be predicated on the idea of mutuality and obligations.

How do we know what God wants from us specifically?

The problem with the intangible nature of God (no direct e-mail or hot-line phone) is that people cannot always know with absolute certainty what God wants of them at any particular time. We attempt to discern and clarify "God's will" (expectations, obligations, rituals, etc.; in other words, what God wants of us) through the filter of our religious tradition (expectations, obligations, rituals).

One of my listeners, Pat, from San Diego, California, wrote the following passage, which describes a relationship with God: *"I see God in everything, every day. I believe He is in all of us all the time. All we have to do is learn to hear, feel, and pay attention to what and where God is leading us through our daily lives. It is true that God is love, but love is a verb and that requires us to show action. God does not exist for us if we are not open to his love by showing others love. We can choose at any point (there's that word 'choice' again!) to turn away from God or not to pay attention to His calling or existence in our lives. That is why so many people believe that God does not exist, they mistake power for God's presence. He is usually not that blunt. If you want to hear or feel and come to understand his call, you must first be in the right frame of mind and still enough to hear His voice."*

How Do I Love Thee?

In our struggle to understand a relationship with God, we often turn to more familiar relationship forms. The first obvious example is the model of husband and wife. One can view the Ten Commandments as the prenuptial agreement that stipulates the obligations we have to God. Commitment is demonstrated through action. Marriage is more than just a verbal commitment made during the wedding ceremony. It is more than a piece of paper: It is a sacred covenant.

The response "But, I don't feel like it" is no longer acceptable because we have marital responsibilities and obligations.

Love must be seen as a verb, and as a verb, it requires action; "...therefore love *is* the fulfilling of the law." (Romans 13:10). As Pastor Bill Miller (Caney Orthodox Presbyterian Church, California) wrote to us, *"The person who says that he doesn't need the Ten Commandments is silly. Because if he says, 'All I need to do is love God'—how does he know what to do unless God tells him. I would like to see a guy try that logic successfully on his wife. If I truly love my wife, she will tell me how to love her in the way she wants to be loved. I'm not smart enough to make it up as I go along."*

How can we know and trust in the love espoused by the lips if the actions do not prove and perfect the words? The commandments are the precepts of love. Words are not enough: **"Wherefore by their fruits ye shall know them. Not every one that saith unto me, Lord, Lord, shall enter into the kingdom of heaven; but he that doeth the will of my Father which is in heaven."** (Matthew 7:20–21).

To achieve a holy life is a common goal of Judaism and Christianity. But what is a holy life? The Hebrew word for *holy* in the Bible is *kadosh*. It means to set aside something for a special purpose directed toward God. When a union between a man and a woman is endowed with a godly purpose, it becomes "holy matrimony"—as opposed to "shacking up" or "getting some." When we fulfill God's will through action, we engage in a holy act. When we live each day conscious of the fact that we are one of the ways in which God brings goodness and righteousness into the world, we become holy vehicles.

For those who would "cherry-pick" through the laws of the Holy Scriptures by deciding what works for them, what seems relevant today, or what is convenient and comfortable, there is the temptation to categorize the laws simplistically, as a prelude to their dismissal. Even the most seemingly archaic of laws (as in the Jewish kosher law of not mixing milk with meat or wearing clothes that mix flax and wool) is God's recipe for holiness, the moral perfection of human beings.

Most people don't even stop to say grace before a meal because they weren't raised doing so, or because they're tired or in a rush, or because they've come to see human beings (farmer to grocer) as the ultimate provider. God provides the earth, sun, and water in which to grow the wheat. Man takes the wheat and transforms it into bread. It's teamwork—and, as in all teams, all the members are important. Each deserves respect from the other. When you take the time to demonstrate that respect, the relationship becomes deepened, your being is enriched, and there is more joy and fulfillment from the entire experience.

Because I'm Your Parent—That's Why!

The human-divine relationship can be compared to the child-parent relationship. To children, parental rules seem arbitrary, limiting, and annoying. Parents can try to explain their standards, but sometimes after exhaustive wrangling, the parent must decide to impose the highest of all reasons: their own first commandment, which is essentially, "Because I am the parent who brought you into this world, pays all your bills, and wipes your nose—and till God takes you or me back, I am the lord your god." In that simple statement, authority is established. Parental rules are binding because they are given by the parent—the more immediate giver of life, the intermediary between the child and God.

Parents feel responsible for their child's welfare, and with absolute responsibility comes absolute power, just as it was for God, who expressed responsibility for the Israelites and therefore took them out of Egypt: **"I have now heard the moaning of the Israelites because the Egyptians are holding them in bondage, and I have remembered My covenant"** (Exodus 6:5).

From Eden to present time, the God-human relationship demonstrates a subtle evolution, if not in power, then in responsibility. Noah, for example, when told by God of the impending flood terminating all mankind save him and his family, responds with the equivalent of, "Cool. It's You and me, God. Uh, how many cubits long did you say?" When Abraham was confronted with God's plan for Sodom and Gomorrah, he argued with God about the justice in that act, in spite of the fact he and his family would be saved. Abraham takes responsibility for the welfare of "his brothers." In the ten generations between Noah and Abraham, something special has happened.

As children grow and mature, they take within themselves the rules and morality of their parents. As every parent recognizes, their children yearn to be powerful adults, but parents sometimes waver in not wanting to let go of their protective power. The Israelites, freed from Egyptian slavery into the desert, had some second thoughts about the weight of responsibility and difficulties of "freedom": "Is this not the statement that we made to you in Egypt, saying, 'Let us be and we will serve Egypt'?—for it is better to serve Egypt than to die in the wilderness!" (Exodus 14:12). And God, in response, tells Moses to inform the Israelites to stop whining and get into gear: "Why do you cry out to Me? Speak to the Children of Israel and let them journey forth!" (Exodus 14:15).

As a parent must finally let go of the bicycle seat and allow a child to move and balance on his own, God gives us all we need and lets us go. We know what we need to do to balance life's earthly challenges with God's divine expectations. With free will, we choose each minute of each day between the sacred and the ordinary.

The Ten Commandments are binding because they were given by God, the parent of all humanity.

Typically, there are two parents. Who is really in power? Children, especially those from broken homes, know all too well how to play one parent against the other to get what they want (not necessarily what they need). At the time of the Ten Commandments (approximately 1300 B.C.E.), the idea of an obligation to *one* God was unique. Instead of allegiances to many gods who had conflicting roles in the world, and whose all-too-human moods and behaviors blurred the absoluteness of right and wrong, monotheism (belief in one God) posited a single, objective morality. The Israelites were told that they need not be confused like children with parents who cannot agree on consistent rules because they're battling each other for power and love. Instead, by acknowledging the One true God, what was required would be clear.

Ask Not What Your God Can Do for You . . .

Whether it is through the model of spouse/spouse or child/parent, covenants made with God represent a relationship of obligations and benefits. It is the nature of all-important relationships in our lives to have give-and-take. We express our love of God through the observance of God's commandments, and God reciprocates through his presence in our lives and in the world. The Ten Commandments are the foundation of these obligations.

To accept the First Commandment is to accept the idea that God is at least as demanding of us as we are in our relationships with each other. If God is the standard of bringing goodness and compassion to the world, and we wish to be partners in creating a "very good" world (the term used at the end of the Creation, Genesis 1:31), then we must acknowledge our respective roles. This is the true essence of the religious idea of a covenant. The First Commandment reminds us that our relationship with God is not *casual* but *covenantal*.

That Was Then, This Is Now

The ultimate motivation for the Israelites to accept these commandments was their appreciation for their *redemption,* their rescue from bondage and the anticipation of continued sustenance. This people-saving gesture was so great that it demanded a new relationship, a relationship in which the Jewish people entered into a *partnership* with God to help perfect the world (Tukkun Olam). Israel's continuous presence (in the Diaspora or in the homeland) serves as evidence that God is alive and well and has not abandoned his promises to Abraham, nor to all humanity—no matter how ungodly our behavior continues to be.

There is a commonality to the motivation of Jews and Christians to *love* and *obey* God: salvation. There are differences in the perspective of how and what that salvation entails. Both Jews and Christians see God as "Savior." For Jews, that saving grace is our survival in spite of *external* oppression and enemies. For Christians, that saving grace is Christ's sacrifice to save each Christian's soul from its own *inner* tendency toward sin. In the Christian view, the world is redeemed as each individual's soul is saved through Jesus Christ. In the Jewish view, we are redeeming the world by our own efforts.

Whether by the covenant at Sinai or by Jesus' resurrection, we are all charged, through a sense of duty and gratitude, to demonstrate appreciation of God's saving grace through the way we *act*. The quality and character of how Jews and Christians lead their lives becomes the ongoing *visible* recognition of God's presence and truth.

Religion Is Fine—It's God That's the Problem

Sadly, discussions of God are cautious or infrequent in our lives and homes. An obligatory, guilty, or habituated adherence to certain holidays or rituals reduces Judaism to obscure legalisms or a culture club, albeit with a profound sense of civic responsibility. But this is not only a Jewish issue. There are movements afoot to redo churches in the model of shopping malls, complete with food kiosks, so the folks won't be as *uncomfortable* as they would be in a *holy* place.

David Klinghoffer calls this "Kitsch Religion"; in other words, synthetic religion. He wrote in the *National Review* (June 3, 1996) that:

> In a religious system centered on an orthodoxy, the system asks the believer to subscribe to a set of principles, deriving from what it asserts as the Truth about God, from which also follow definite standards of conduct. After the believer has accepted these principles and sought to order his life by them, he gets the payoff: the experience, however fleeting, of God and His transcendence. . . . Kitsch religion reflects only the world: its political interests, its desire to be free of troublesome moral obligations. The relationship to the Ultimate, which the orthodox believer derives from his faith is derived . . . as a result of reflection upon the immediate impression left by the Truth about God. It is only then that the miraculous enters. Kitsch religion, by contrast, predigests orthodoxy for the church- or temple-goer and spares him effort, claiming to provide him with a shortcut to transcendence that detours what is necessarily difficult in genuine religion.

OK, You Can Preach—but Don't Nag Me

Even for the Israelites, who experienced the spectacular revelation of Mount Sinai, accepting the obligation did not come easily. Only forty days after experiencing the greatest divine revelation of all time (in person and in living color), some of the Israelites were ready to give their wealth to make the Golden Calf. This object they could worship was more tangible than the God of the Exodus. Also, it demanded nothing of them other than their adoration. More so, it gave them license to do as they pleased.

The tug of our animal side (self-centeredness and immediate

gratification), the temptations of life ("I love my wife, but oh, you babe"), the constant distractions of the mundane (too many things to do in too little time), make God a "bother." The truth of the existence of God is not dependent upon our individual attention or belief. However, the existence of God in our lives does require our open heart, mind, and soul. Part of our personal relationship to the ancient experiences is found in the text of the First Commandment when it says, "I am the Lord *your* God. . . ." Hebrew, unlike English, distinguishes between singular and plural forms of address. The "you" is not the collective, Southern *y'all* but rather the singular personal *You*. Although delivered to the people who stood at Mount Sinai, it is addressed to each individual of all subsequent generations. These words were not spoken just to the generation of Moses but are addressed to you and me today, because God continues to offer his covenant for those who hear the call and are *willing* to respond. In this context, Mount Sinai is not the first and only call. Mount Sinai is the metaphor for God's continuing presence in the world.

Oh, Yeah? Where's God Now?

We must each find the role of God in our lives. From the miracle of birth to the miracles we experience every day in our lives, once we can acknowledge the role of God in our lives it is easier to feel the comfort of not being "ultimately" alone. Unfortunately, many people are not able to *feel* God in their lives. The intangible presence of God can be compared to a radio signal. These radio signals are all around us; we just can't see them. How do you know the radio signals are there? Simply turn on a radio. You can hear beautiful music. We are the radios that must be turned on and then finely tuned to pick up God's frequency. Just as sometimes it takes extra effort and precise fine-tuning to find a particular radio station, it is not always easy to perceive God's presence in the world.

It is not enough to believe in the "historical God"; we must also believe in the "personal God." Feeling God's involvement in our own daily lives makes life meaningful and a difficult time bearable—and it is in the gratitude and love for God that we find our motivation to conform to God's expectation on our actions.

It is not difficult to imagine that a basically happy or satisfied person may find it easier to feel motivated to conform to God's expectations than one who is suffering, frustrated, or disappointed. The former is motivated in part by joyous gratitude. The latter's motivation is more difficult to understand since depression over the problems and anger with God for the apparent lack of blessings or imagined punishment may be the predominant feelings. If you are willing to trust God, then you will not see God as a "fair-weather friend" (or be one yourself) or an enemy when your life seems miserable and hopeless. If you are willing to trust God, then that optimism coming from a belief in ultimate meaning and purpose even to your suffering keeps you looking for the blessing and close to God.

According to Rabbi Reuven Bulka (*Judaism on Illness and Suffering*, Aronson Press, 1998, p. 171), "One of the major messages in Jewish thought on suffering is that it may be a blessing in disguise. But it is a blessing only if we translate properly from event to assumed meaning or challenge; otherwise it can be a debilitating curse. Suffering, then, with all its travail, is an opportunity. What we make of that opportunity is a defining component of our lives." Our commitment to life, to making every precious moment meaningful, and our commitment to God, to live our lives nobly and holy in spite of challenges, must be unconditional—without which even the good parts of life lose meaning.

How and when God actually intervenes in life are ultimately unanswerable questions. Nonetheless, many people feel certain that God specifically blesses and punishes. Here are some of the Website (www.drlaura.com) responses to the questions of "How active is God in life?"

➤ *God is very active but will not impose Himself against our free will. God speaks to us but in our business and stress, we sometimes fail to listen—for He can only be heard in the quiet of the heart. The more time you spend with Him . . . no matter what fills your day . . . the closer you feel. (Jayne M.)*

➤ *When I was in my early adulthood I spent a lot of time in counseling. All the counselors agreed I was "broken," but no one knew how to fix me. Then I came into relationship with Jesus Christ. All of a sudden, behaviors I had always despised but could not change were being transformed little by little. I saw that He is the Great Counselor. He gives instructions that changed my life forever, things I would not have chosen, but which have become the things I am most grateful for. (Beth K.)*

➤ *God is in everything. The beauty of a child to the sun rising in the desert. Most of all, God is within our choice that we make every moment of our lives to do what is right instead of what is not. Only then does He shine through us. (Kathy P.)*

➤ *. . . and I do believe that sick people can be healed and the lame walk if it is God's will to do so. Most often the world just happens and we cope. Those who turn to Heavenly Father in bad times and good are rewarded with inner peace and blessings. That is the daily miracle. (Michele L.)*

The pain of misery and the horror of evil typically challenge one's faith in God. As a listener wrote, "*. . . a specific, active God who tests us with things like my wife's breast cancer? Uh-uh. That's not something I want to believe in.*" (Jim S.) That's, of course, the rub—wanting God to be as a personal body-guard and tooth fairy rolled into one. Although God saved the Israelites from Egyptian bondage, they then had to endure forty years of wandering in the desert, pre–comfort stations. Was that punishment? Was that a test? We believe that it was a necessary part of spiritual growth and development.

In a recent *A&E Biography,* Teddy Pendergrass, the "Black Elvis," spoke of his life after the car accident that left him a quadriplegic. He was quite emotional and poignant when he spoke of the pain, frustration, hurt, fear, and anger. He was equally emotional and poignant when he spoke of becoming a "better person" since and maybe due to that event.

Ultimately, we cannot know and understand as God. That would make us God.

A World Without Thee

I've been asked whether nonbelievers in God can be moral. I suppose we can all call up a framework we call moral. Unfortunately, much of it has to do with culturally accepted mores (television programs that are nonjudgmental about unmarried sex and motherhood, or drugs), or personal desires and whims ("It's nobody's business but mine"), flimsy rationalizations ("Sex is okay as long as [l] I like him, [2] he tests negative for HIV, and [3] he uses a condom" is what one recent twenty-four-year-old female caller said), or what the immediate situation has to offer ("Yeah, why not? Who are you to judge?"), and lastly, by virtue of your feelings (the modern deity).

The morality of that world is subjective and therefore dangerous. If each of us designs our own morality, it would be to suit ourselves (that's the animal part of us). Actually, the most perfect world for each of us who desires independence from the authority of commandments is a world in which *everybody else is* God-fearing or God-obeying, we're safe from the animal in them, and we're then free to be the animal in us.

Ultimately, the decision of what is right or wrong has to come from somewhere. Human logic and rational thought or nature's laws do not fully provide that framework in a universally just way. Nature, for example, would allow the vulnerable, weak, injured, or sick to die ("survival of the fittest"), whereas human beings, valuing each life as sacred, would hospitalize, protect, and nurture. Human logic, for example, would be able to rationalize self-interest and survival over that of a stranger, whereas God's law reminds us that no one is to be valued less than ourselves: "... love your fellow as yourself: I am the Lord" (Leviticus 19:18).

In "civil law" things are right because they are commanded—by a legislature and judicial system. In "God's law" things are commanded; therefore, they are right. Man does not define virtue and vice; God is the arbiter of morality. To "be" in the image of God is by God's definition.

In a response to our "inventory" of Christian clergy on issues of the Ten Commandments, we received this input from Minister Ray McClendon of the Church of Christ of Hesperia, California, which addresses the issue of God's authority: *"What is wrong-headed about [a particular] remark on your [LS] web-site which stated, 'It's a scary thought that we need more religion . . . we need less, not more . . . if people are too lame to make their own decisions.' She goes on to describe her 'virtue' in respecting animals and not eating meat as not having [needing] anything to do with religion. . . . The problem with [that] is that as long as she is her own Deity, she will never be able to rise above herself. Which points out to us that when it comes to Deity, there are really only two possibilities. We either acknowledge our creation in the image of the objective God revealed in Scripture, or we inevitably MAKE GOD in OUR own image."*

What's in It for Me?

The Ten Commandments seem like an excellent formula for making one a "better person"—and if everyone were to observe them what a better world we would have. Seems logical with or without God, doesn't it? Except people do not always behave with their or anyone else's best interests in mind, nor are they altruistic enough to engage in self-sacrifice for the benefit of humanity. By accepting the idea that God demands things from us, we find the strength to accept the challenge—no matter how painful or confusing. The truth is that we are often unable or unwilling to change something for ourselves, but when in response to the pleadings of a spouse or child, people can often find the will or motivation to change.

There is a benefit of accepting a voice beyond us that reminds us that there can be no compromising on the most important values of life. This external voice of divine authority can help us do what is right for ourselves. For example: Chicken Parmesan is not *healthy* because of cholesterol and fat. "So what! I'll just cheat a little and I'll exercise (yeah, right) tomorrow and work it off." Now, if you're an observant Jew, chicken Parmesan is not kosher—not *holy*. "Oh, well. That's that." There are always rationalizations about the profane—there are none to get around the divine.

There is a connection between respecting what is holy and ultimately doing what is moral. The discipline of observing ritual laws provides the strength and conviction often necessary to do what is moral—especially under those difficult conditions of peer pressure, temptation, conflicted emotions, and great passions.

God's is a voice that says, "I care what you do." Sometimes the voice is so clear, and at other times it is the still, small voice that Elijah heard (I Kings 19:2) atop the mountain. Whether that voice emanates from Mount Sinai or from the cross, it is a call that beckons us, and it is a relationship that can provide strength and comfort in our own lives.

In the Beginning . . .

Does God care how we act? If so, what does it mean to God when we sin? If not, why does our behavior matter at all—if we can get away with it?

When we violate one of the commandments, we disappoint God. We must see every act, both good and bad, as *the one* that tips the scales of judgment. It is through each act that God evaluates us and we evaluate ourselves. A Jewish tradition states that the reward of a commandment is the performance of another commandment and the consequence of a sin is the performance of another sin. In our relationship to God, the observance of a commandment brings us closer to God, and every time we violate a commandment we become further estranged from God.

If we believe that God cares about us, we must also believe that God cares about what we do. The First Commandment is a reminder of this important correlation. Our way of reciprocating God's love is to acknowledge His sovereignty, and in so doing, we not only enrich our own lives, but also bring God's spirit into the world.

2

The Second Commandment

"You shall not recognize the gods of others in
My presence. You shall not make yourself a
carved image nor any likeness of that which is
in the heavens above or on the earth below or
in the water beneath the earth. You shall not
prostrate yourself to them nor worship them,
for I am the Lord, your God."

"Mommy, Daddy, what *does* God look like?" That's a question you probably remember asking of your parents or have had a child ask of you. Even if you have always deeply believed in God, even if you feel you have a close personal relationship with God, even if you do daily blessings and prayers, you probably have not been able to come up with an answer to satisfy the concrete thinking characteristic of children.

You can talk to children about *spirit, grace,* and *goodness* (actions and virtues)—but when you point upwards to indicate heaven, a child will be looking for the bottoms of shoes between the clouds as evidence. And so, children's imaginations will fill in the blanks left by our ultimately inadequate attempts to communicate the divine. What they use to imagine God turns out to be the authority model with which they're most familiar—their parents.

In a 1997 study published in the *Journal for the Scientific Study of Religion,* several psychology researchers found that the image of God that children have tends to be a reflection of their family experiences. For example, if young children had a difficult home life, they tended to conjure up an image of God as strong, powerful, and protective—an image to which they could cling for comfort. Additionally, when children were asked to rate their parents and God on the qualities of nurturance (warmth, patience, love, and caring—generally like a mommy) and power (protection, fairness, and strength—generally like a daddy), the connection was strong.

The Ten Commandments are inscribed on two tablets, five on each. The first tablet contains laws regarding man's relationship with God, while the second refers to relationships among people. It is significant that the Fifth Commandment, which honors parents, is the transitional commandment. What God and parents share in is the creation and nurturance of life. According to Jewish tradition, when people honor their parents, God regards the behavior as honoring Him. Parents are their children's introduction to godly love as well as authority.

When that parental authority is misused, as it was in my listener Pam's life, God is often the safest target for our hurt and rage: "*Unfortunately, my father used the church to justify his abusive behavior, which really messed up my thinking for a while. Dad used God's words to enforce his domination and sexual control. When I was old enough to understand that a daughter should not have a sexual relationship with her father, I felt evil and full of sin. This created a very confused and timid child out of me. Eventually, my confusion led to a hatred of God. I believed myself evil. I dropped away from my church and mostly*

*my God. Like Cain, I was very angry with God. . . . I am in my
thirties now and happy to say I walk closely with my (our) God,
knowing the actions of my dad were not caused by God—(my father made his choices of his own free will)."*

Our *image* of God is intimately related to our personal, familial introduction to authority with its benevolent (or not)
balance of power and love; that is the image we worship from
love, or hate from fear. Yet, this is all about the *spiritual aspects* of God. What of the physical attributes? What does God
look like, anyway? *And what does it matter?*

Why Can't I See You?

All the way through the Holy Scriptures we read about "the
face of God," "the hand of God," or "the feet of the Lord." Yet
no one in the Holy Scriptures actually "sees" God, even though
it is written, **"Never again has there arisen in Israel a prophet
like Moses, whom the Lord had known face to face . . ."**
(Deuteronomy 34:10). "Face to face" is clearly not literal,
since Moses' experiences of God are unconventional: **"He saw
and behold! The bush was burning in the fire but the bush was
not consumed. Moses thought, 'I will turn aside now and look
at this great sight—why will the bush not be burned?' The
Lord saw that he turned aside to see; and God called out to him
from amid the bush and said, 'Moses, Moses,' and he replied,
'Here I am!' "**(Exodus 3:2–4) and, **"The Lord said to Moses,
'Behold! I come to you in the thickness of the cloud so that the
people will hear as I speak to you, and they will also believe in
you forever.' "** (Exodus 19:9)

Moses, in his persistent attempts to convince God to send
someone else to Pharaoh, says, **"But they will not believe me
and they will not heed my voice, for they will say, 'The Lord
did not appear to you.'"** (Exodus 4:1) Since "seeing is believing," what did Moses have to present to Pharaoh, or the suffering Israelites, for that matter, other than the seemingly idle

threat of "My god is bigger and badder than your god, so let that be a lesson to you. Now, let my people go!"? Actually, after the Tenth Plague, death of the firstborn, the power struggle was over. It was clear that might was the element that set things right for the Israelites.

So what was the big difference between this "God" and all the other pagan gods other than "He won this round"? The difference is awe inspiring. This God was outside our prior experience of having a god *contained* by form and name. This God was a Universal God. This God said he fulfilled a covenantal promise to his people. This God said he had expectations of our moral, just, and compassionate behavior. This God was not manipulated by our desires or magical incantations but had a divine, eternal intent that depended on our participation. This God was not a tool for serving earthly desires; this God demanded **"Righteousness, righteousness shall you pursue . . ."** (Deuteronomy 16:20).

In a way, God's initial power struggle with Pharaoh was more of what we expect from nature—survival of the fittest, strongest, and most devious. That was only the prelude of the holiness to come, holiness, which, by its qualities of sacrifice, humility, personal discipline, commitment, and righteousness, runs counter to those brutal laws of nature. God's might is also a model that goodness must be prepared to fight evil rather than to acquiesce passively.

In pagan practice and tradition, the "gods" were a part of nature, representative of such natural forces as rain, wind, sun, fertility, and animal behavior. To the end of appeasing and manipulating these gods for personal gain or survival, even human sacrifice was permitted!

This God was unique. Having **". . . made the heavens"** (Psalms 96:5), God was not an aspect of nature but a reality greater than the universe, admonishing us not to drop our eyes down to nature for an "easy fix": **". . . lest you act corruptly and make yourselves a carved image, a likeness of any** shape; a form of a male or a female; a form of any animal on the earth; a form of any winged bird that flies in the heaven; a form of anything that creeps on the ground, a form of any fish that is in the water under the earth; and lest you raise your eyes to the heaven and you see the sun, and the moon, and the stars—the entire legion of heaven—and you be drawn astray and bow to them and worship them, which the Lord, your God, has apportioned to all the peoples under the entire heaven!" (Deuteronomy 4:16–19).

Our ears can only hear certain sound frequencies. Our eyes can only discern certain-size objects and certain wavelengths of light. We are limited, mortal creatures. To believe that only that which we can see, hear, or touch is the extent of what is possible is a product of our arrogance and our tendency to worship our own egos. God is greater than form and beyond our sensory abilities. That we finite beings cannot fathom either the divine or infinity does not give evidence against God's existence, only evidence that there is more beyond ourselves.

> "To whom, then can you liken God,
> What form compare to Him?"
>
> (Isaiah 40:18)

Finally, to see the face of God, one need only gaze into the mirror, for we are *made in the image of God* ("... when God created man. He made him in the likeness of God; male and female He created them..." [Genesis 5:1–2]). It is our responsibility to *live in the intent of God* ("You shall be holy, for I, the Lord your God am holy" [Leviticus 19:2]). What exactly is required here? What does God mean by "holy"? "He has told you, O man, what is good. What does the Lord require of you but to do justice, to love kindness, and to walk humbly with your God?" (Micah 6:8–9).

The Résumé of God

Since we normally challenge arguments with the phrase "Seeing is believing," believing in the One and Only God was and is a supreme challenge for people prone to the simple, visible, touchable, fathomable, scientific, and controllable. God doesn't reveal Himself; He reveals His way. Following His way is our means of sanctifying life. In Exodus 34:6–7 (called the Thirteen Attributes) the spiritual attributes of God are summarized: **"The Lord passed before him [Moses], and proclaimed: 'The Lord, The Lord, God, compassionate and gracious, slow to anger, and abundant in kindness and truth; preserver of kindness for thousands of generations, forgiver of iniquity, willful sin, and error, and Who cleanses—but does not cleanse completely, recalling the iniquity of parents upon children and grandchildren, to the third and fourth generations."** The One and Only God is a Universal God, whose sovereignty is all things and all people; a moral God who demands moral, ethical living, and justice from all mankind.

God's "Witnesses"

It is not difficult to imagine that human beings, who have become so much more technologically and scientifically sophisticated, would drop idle idol worship like a hot potato. Who needs to sacrifice to the sun god when you can just flip a switch and the electric light comes on (assuming you've paid the electric company!)? When people do not appreciate that our technical achievements and our increasing ability to control the physical world are blessings from God, man himself becomes his own god:

"The man who views God in disbelief is tempted to set 'Man' up as the object of his belief, to view 'Man' as the all-knowing creature who is subject to no laws or rules other than those which he himself sees fit to promulgate. To wor-

ship man in general, or to worship some special man in particular, is the height of idolatry. If man, with his endowed intelligence and spiritual capacities, is the most sophisticated
of all God's creatures, he is also the object of the most sophisticated form of idolatry.

To accept the yoke of the Kingdom of Heaven is to throw
off the yoke of human domination and dictatorship. 'You
shall be servants unto Me,' said the Lord, 'and not servants
unto My servants.'" [*To Be a Jew,* Hayim Halevy Donin,
HarperCollins, 1972].

Worship of God entails internal beliefs and external acts
that, frankly, most often run completely counter to our immediate moods, desires, personal plans, goals, and circumstances. When we do what is "holy" rather than what is
"expedient," we are living witnesses—proof of God. It is
much easier to be concrete and self-focused than to focus on
character, integrity, and righteousness. By nature, people prefer total comprehension and control of the outer world, with
the intent of serving ourselves. When we live with that notion,
we cease being a symbol of what is potentially so special
about human beings. We become our own idols with a disturbed sense of sovereignty, filling the world with selfishness,
hypocrisy, callousness, terror, and even death. Where there is
no acceptance of the ultimate authority, law, and goodness of
God, any evil is permissible: "I think that if the devil doesn't
exist, but man has created him, he has created him in his own
image and likeness" (Fyodor M. Dostoevsky).

What Makes This God Different from All Other "Gods"?

Was the God of the Israelites just another "chief national god"
much like Zeus, who was the head of the Greek Pantheon? Such
national gods would fight the enemy gods to protect their peo-

ple while simultaneously leading their people into wars. When nations were conquered, so were their gods. In enemy hands, the idols had no power. Defeated kings would beg for their return.

Part of the significance of the Exodus experience was the defeat of the Egyptian gods by the God of the Israelites. In the words of Exodus (12:12), "**I shall go through the land of Egypt on this night, and I shall strike every firstborn in the land of Egypt, from man to beast; and against all of gods of Egypt I shall mete out punishment—I am The Lord.**" From the worshipped Nile River, to Re the Sun god, and finally to the special status of the firstborn males, the Egyptians experienced the victory of the Israelites' God over those *things* that they worshipped. Was the new God that Moses brought from the desert of Midian to the enslaved Israelites simply another "chief god" like all the others of the ancient world?

The God of the Israelites was different in many ways. For example, he did not dwell in *things* but rather communicated through them. God did not live in the Burning Bush or at the peak of Mount Sinai. Immediately following the giving of the Ten Commandments, God tells Moses, "**They shall make a Sanctuary for Me—so that I may dwell among them . . .**" (Exodus 25:8). God does not say that He will dwell *in it,* but rather *among them.* If the Israelites build a tabernacle, God's *presence will be felt through the worship.* In essence, the sacred experience of Mount Sinai is transferred to the tabernacle and later to the Jerusalem Temple. God makes *all* places sacred through His presence. Perhaps in the designation of *places* to be made and kept special, God was responding to our human, therefore limited, ability to perceive the divine without yellow highlighting.

You Can't Ship God by UPS

Another indication that this "chief god" of the Israelites was *unique* compared to the pagans' god experience is expressed in I Samuel 4:11. After the Philistines' victory against the Israelites, they took the Ark of the Covenant (the most sacred object of the Israelites, a golden box with cherubic figures on top containing the two tablets upon which were inscribed the will of God in the form of the Ten Commandments). In the view of the ancient world, the military defeat was also a theological defeat: The God of the Israelites was conquered and captured, as though the Ark was equated with God. Even with the Ark in the possession of the Philistines, the God of the Israelites was still powerful. He brought illness and death upon the Philistines until they returned the Ark to the Israelites. This God was not to be contained by things or the actions of people.

Ultimately, the God of the Israelites was no "chief god." He was/is the Only.

What's in a Name?

It is difficult enough to worship an imageless deity. For ancient people, the idea of a God who could not be represented and worshipped in a physical form was unimaginable. God makes the job of Moses, and us all, even more difficult by His seemingly obtuse answer to Moses' question, **"Behold, when I come to the Children of Israel and say to them, 'The God of your forefathers has sent me to you,' and they say to me, 'What is His name?' what shall I say to them?"** (Exodus 3:13). God responds with **"So shall you say to the Children of Israel, YHWH [I Shall Be], the God of your forefathers, the God of Abraham, the God of Isaac and the God of Jacob has dispatched me to you"** (Exodus 3:15).

The letters *YHWH* represent the four Hebrew letters of the Bible used to spell God's name. While God has many names in the Bible, which are assumed to represent His many attributes, *YHWH* is the most sacred name. Attempts to figure out the pronunciation of this name, like *Jehovah* or *Yahweh,* are most probably incorrect. Given our current historical information, we may never know the true pronunciation of the name. It is as if to say God's true essence is unknowable even by name.

The nature of YHWH was such a revolutionary concept to the ancient mind-set that it took the Israelites forty years of wandering in the desert to even begin to fathom it. Idolatry is best represented in the disaster of the Golden Calf. The Israelites, after waiting forty days for Moses to come back down from Sinai, thought he was either dead or had deserted them. They fell back into old patterns by building themselves a god representation—a golden calf. Idolatry, with its physical representation of gods, was so enticing to the Israelites that the prophets had to chastise the people about it repeatedly. In fact, so does God; more than 50 of the 613 laws in the Five Books of Moses (the Torah) are directed against idolatry.

What's So Bad About Idolatry?

Idolatry is dangerous at a personal level because "gods," being created by man, are endowed with human characteristics. The baser human desires of *unrestricted* sex, violence, and selfishness achieve validity, permission, and company by being associated with the worship of that specific god: Bacchus and gluttony, Zeus and power, Aphrodite and love, for example. Goodness was a function only of desire and availability. Human beings never had to rise above themselves because these deities were merely extensions of human qualities. We simply needed to create gods to serve and justify our desires and weaknesses.

The God of the Israelites, while not condemning human desires, sanctified their expressions with laws concerning "who, where, when, why, and how," thus elevating the mundane to the holy. In the pagan world, "The gods made me do it," a variation on Flip Wilson's classic line, "The Devil made me do it," took precedence. In six words of seven syllables, human responsibility is reduced to an external force, eliminating the essence of humanity, free will, and accountability. The God of the Israelites demanded personal responsibility and promised culpability.

Idolatry was dangerous at a communal level. If the gods of the world were in conflict, then the natural order was for their followers to be in conflict. Wars were not things to be avoided but rather the way of the world. The ancient creation stories are filled with the violence and killing of the gods that supposedly brought about the creation of the world and humans. The *Imatateo Dei*—imitating God's ways—was accomplished by imitating the unconflicted ways of God: a God who is demanding, but loving; a God who is judging, but forgiving; a God whose ultimate image is a world of complete peace in which **"the wolf shall live with the sheep and the leopard will lie down with the kid; and a calf, a lion whelp and a fatling will walk together, and a young child will lead them"** (Isaiah 11:6). To imitate God is to bring about this kind of world.

The Torah acknowledges pagan societies as representing the worst possibilities of how a society might be ordered. One need only look at the violence of Sodom, the cruelty of Egypt, and the ruthlessness of the Amalekites (Deuteronomy 25:17–19), who attacked the Israelites from behind, presumably killing the women and children rather than the men who would have been marching at the front to protect their families, to understand the dangers of paganism. The Torah speaks of the horror of those who offer up their children as sacrifices to Molech (Leviticus 20:4), and God specifically tells the Israelites, **"Do not perform the practice of the land of Egypt in which you dwelled; and do not perform the practice of the land of Canaan to which I bring you, and do not follow their tradition"** (Leviticus 18:3). In other words, do what is right in spite of the surrounding unrighteousness.

A godless society, or rather one in which other gods reign, is a place where immorality and social instability will ultimately dwell. The many tens of millions of murders of the Stalinist era, the Third Reich, communist China, and the killing fields of Cambodia, to name only a few, are blatant testimonials to godless chaos and cruelty.

So serious is the Second Commandment that in Judaism it is one of the three sins for which one must be willing to die rather than violate. The other two are murder and the sexual prohibitions against incest and adultery.

Idolatry, in the classic biblical sense of worshipping foreign gods, is not an issue to most people today. So, how is idolatry relevant in our lives now? Let us count the ways!

The *Reader's Digest* Condensation of God

Even thinking about God as an old man who sits on a celestial throne is a form of idolatry. While the Bible must use anthropomorphic language to discuss God ("...I shall redeem you with an outstretched hand and with great judgments," Exodus 6:6), nowhere is there an attempt to describe what God looks like. The Torah is written in the language of man to describe the unfathomable. Instead, God is described by what He "does" and "says" as perceived through His interactions with humans. God is not described as good-looking but righteous. God is not described as being tall but loving. Definitively describing God as though God were "made in the image of man" is idolatrous—God is beyond the limits of a physical being. In a post–*Star Wars* world, God can be called "The Force," something that is real and tangible, but something that cannot be seen.

A Hassidic rabbi (Hassidism is a mystical form of Judaism originating in eighteenth-century Eastern Europe) once asked a group of his students, "Where does God dwell?" Thinking the answer quite obvious, one of them called out, "God is everywhere, of course!" Disagreeing with the answer, the rabbi said, "God dwells wherever people let him in."

Why is it so bad to envision God as a kind of celestial grandpa? Why is it that when we focus on God's physical nature, we engage in idolatry? Reduced to human description, God's true and ultimate power is made to seem limited, and his motives humanly frivolous and changeable.

Children often pose the best questions about God. One of the most common questions Rabbi Vogel gets from the synagogue nursery school children is, "If God made the world, who made God?" He explains, "That God is different from anything else we know. God is not like an animal who gives birth or was born. God is not like a human who makes things with His hands. God is so amazing because He is the only thing that has existed forever." For older children, he concludes by telling them, "The Hebrew name for God, YHWH, is a condensed form of the Hebrew words for 'was,' 'is,' and 'will be,' and that God's very name describes His eternity." In reality, these answers do not answer the mysteries of God. In truth, no words can. It is only by sharing experiences with God that we can understand Him.

We even acknowledge the deficiency of language to describe God every time we use the pronoun *He* to describe God. No pronoun is sufficient, yet to describe God as "It" is too impersonal.

While human language is insufficient to create for us the true image of God, God's words were power: **"God said, 'Let there be light'; and there was light"** (Genesis 1:3).

Superstition

Believe it or not, superstitions can be a form of idolatry. Some people observe them from unconscious habit, and others really believe that superstitions can protect them. Such superstitions as avoiding walking under a ladder or throwing spilt salt over a shoulder represent entertaining rituals that reflect our fear of the unknown. Such superstitions are a left-handed acknowledgment of "other gods" or spirits that have powers over our lives. When superstitions rule the lives of people so that they are afraid of going out on Friday the thirteenth, or obsess over a broken mirror, these beliefs can become dangerous. How pervasive are such superstitions? Imagine that some hotels don't have a thirteenth floor because many people would refuse to sleep there!

It is a sad fact that many people demonstrate more interest and ask more questions about superstitions than about religious law and customs. Rabbi Vogel has been asked questions such as, "Should I tie a red ribbon around the newborn baby's crib?" Newborns were imagined to be at special risk from the evil spirits.

I took a call from Debbie, twenty-eight, who was debating about having a baby shower for her pregnant sister-in-law. Debbie, her parents, and her brother were Jewish, but her brother married a Methodist woman. Nonetheless, her family was holding her to an ancient Jewish superstition about not having baby showers until after the baby was born. While we could make a case for having sensitivity about the possibility of such tragedy as a stillbirth, and not wanting to burden the grieving woman with returning gifts, this is only a superstition. I told her that there was nothing in Jewish law prohibiting a prebirth baby shower and reminded her that her sister-in-law did not share this heritage anyway. The real point of this story is not the argument over when to throw the shower. I asked Debbie if her parents and family were religious or observant. She said, "No." I told her to ask her family, using my name, why they were enthralled and concerned about superstition but not religious obligation.

This is an important issue. Some folks put too much emphasis on trying to control life via "old wives' tales" and not enough effort into the aspects of religion that actually require something of them.

In addition to reflecting our fear of the unknown, superstitions are an attempt to find some causality in events so that we might take control. Incantations or superstitious rituals are attempts to make God/spirits do our will and are contrary to Jewish and Christian values. The Bible is clear: **"Do not turn to the sorcery of the Ovos and Yid'onim; do not seek to be contaminated through them—I am the Lord your God"** (Leviticus 19:31).

What is so bad about superstitions for the many people who observe them as meaningless rituals or habits? Frankly, this is similar to telling your spouse that the affair was meaningless . . . hmmmm. Superstitions also trivialize true religion when superstition turns into a religion of its own. All the serious rituals and customs that bring a true understanding of God and lead us to living sacred lives are cheapened by putting superstitions on par with religious observances.

". . . do not let these or any similar fantasies fill you with either fear or gladness about your future. Be whole-hearted with the Lord thy God. Do not consult staff and dice, day and hour, beast and bird, the grave and the dead, heaven and earth about your actions and your future. Inquire of God in His law about your actions . . ." (*Horeb*, Samson Raphael Hirsch, Soncino Press, 1994) is the reminder of the Jewish sages that cause and effect as dictated by any other than God is a lie, a delusion, and a separation of man from God. Ultimately, what we are to do and be is gleaned from the Bible—and not the stars.

"Hi—Like, What's Your Sign?"

Many people begin the day by looking at their newspaper horoscope. Will it be a day for love or staying away from difficult decisions? And sure enough, during the day something will happen in which they say, "This is what my horoscope was talking about." Although many people are comfortable with using horoscopes for relatively trivial personal issues, they have quite a different response when the wife of a president of the United States (Nancy Reagan) uses an astrologer to give guidance on personal and national issues.

Astrology is just another way for some people to avoid taking responsibility for their lives. By consulting the newspaper or astrologer, people can place the heavy burden of difficult decisions on the answers given by the stars.

One of my listeners reacted to the ubiquitous "psychic hot lines" in the following way: *"I saw a commercial on television today that made my jaw drop to the floor. First of all, it was for one of those 900-number psychic lines, which should have clued me in to be ready for garbage, but it didn't. The ad states that these psychics have insights into the minds and ideas of the people closest to you. One of the callers stated that she wasn't sure if her relationship with her boyfriend was 'right.' She calls this 900 number, and a complete stranger halfway across the country tells her he is definitely her soul mate and that she should hang on to him. She hangs up and smiles and says something about how glad she is she called and that the psychic was 'truly gifted.' It cuts away and when they flash back to this girl she says (HOLD ON TO YOUR SEAT), 'My boyfriend is moving in next week, thanks to my call to the psychic network.' Can you believe that? What kind of 'dim bulb' would do such a stupid thing anyway, much less on the advice of a stranger who reads the stars."*

Is astrology kosher? There are numerous biblical references to any kind of "magic" that can predict future events or advise on decisions:

➤ "There shall not be found among you one who causes his son or daughter to pass through the fire, one who practices divinations, an astrologer, or one who reads omens, a sorcerer; or an animal charmer, one who inquires of Ov or Yidoni, or one who consults the dead. For anyone who does these is an abomination of the Lord . . . "
(Deuteronomy 18: 10–12). So much for Ouija boards.

➤ "... the astrologers, the stargazers, who foretell by new moons ... Behold, they have become like straw: fire burned them, they could not save themselves from the power of the flame ... " (Isaiah 47: 13–14). So much for an astrologer's retirement plans.

➤ When the Lord replied to a beleaguered Job, he said, "Do you know the laws of heaven; did you place its rule upon the land?" (Job 38: 33), implying, of course, that we do not.

➤ And finally, Job got it right when he acknowledged that "Who alone stretches out the heavens, and treads upon the crests of the sea; Who made Ursa Minor, Orion and Pleiades, and the southern constellations; Who performs great deeds that are beyond comprehension, and wonders beyond number" (Job 9:8–10).

To deny that anything is beyond God or to imagine that we can circumvent God is blasphemy. To allow the forces of nature to determine our behavior is as close to ancient idolatry as one can get. Not allowing God to be the prime motivator of our behavior is not being wholehearted with God.

Some scientists suggest that the gravitational pull of the moon affects not only the tides of the oceans but also influences our moods. To predict the future based on this would be contrary to Jewish and Christian values and ultimately disavow our unique potential in creating our destiny through our choices.

The *Catholic Encyclopedia* states, "It [astrology] was condemned in 1586 by Pope Sixtus V. ... Predictions based upon zodiac interpretations and the confluence of moons, stars and planets are a form of fortune-telling that denies the free will of humans and preempts the providence of God, who alone knows the future." We couldn't agree with this more.

Worshipping Another Kind of Star

We live in a society that preoccupies itself with creating false idols from sports figures, movie and television stars, rock stars, and the like. These celebrities, like the 900 numbers for psychic hot lines or newspaper horoscopes that must declare in writing, "for entertainment purposes only," are for our entertainment. Instead, we wear what they wear, talk as they talk, and focus on their personal lives and doings as though there were something "personal" about our relationship with them (instead of risking pursuing healthy relationships?); as though we become special by an association with them ("identity" by association?).

Of course, since we don't have a true relationship with them, we have to be satisfied with "seeing everything they do," buying everything they endorse, and consequently, by reading every single bit of gossip we can find, feeding the indecent tabloid industry. It is our own gratification we're really after, generally not true respect, admiration, or affection. At first we see them as bigger than life, the image in which we wish we could in some way be re-created in terms of looks, possessions, loves, personality. At some point, when that "picture perfect" becomes more realistic, we generally have one of two reactions: blind defense, blaming someone or something other than our idols for their disappointing behavior, or rabid offense, in the form of relentless public humiliation and banishment. Either way, we don't take the loss of our fantasies without a fight.

An op-ed cartoon in the December 27, 1997, *Los Angeles Times* by Darrin Bell highlighted the typical reaction of destroying the once elevated icon: A pro athlete is shown balancing on about a dozen pillars of stone that spell out hope, quest for relevance, need for a hero, lost dreams, and fear, while an adoring audience member shouts out, "If you topple it, we kill you."

The accompanying problem is that whether they want to be or not, athletes and other celebrities become role models. While reaping the incredible financial and celebrity benefits, those who are immature and/or insensitive to that reality can take on an arrogance that propels them into behavior and risks that undermine their own lives and what they could have contributed to society. According to *Newsweek* (December 15, 1997), "The NBA generation gap was on full display last season when Dream Teamers Michael Jordan, Magic Johnson and Charles Barkley all criticized the lack of respect young players show the game—and pretty much everyone and everything. This lack of respect for authority appears endemic to all of today's big dollar sports." As if in support of this reaction, fourteen-year-old Joshua Powell wrote in the *Los Angeles Times* (December 27, 1997), "I know it's not the athletes' fault that kids look up to them. But kids do. When Tyson bit Holyfield's ear, some of my friends pretended to bite each other's ears and nicknamed one another Bite Tyson."

What is ironic is that we elevate them and then enjoy their downfall. We relish their collapse and humiliation, because it restores to ourselves the sense that they aren't better than us after all. Therefore, there is no need to feel bad about ourselves, and we are relieved not to have to grow at all.

Ultimately, the Bible reminds us not to find ourselves in things and the actions or personae of others with, **"I proclaim how you should be righteous and what deeds you should do, but they shall not avail you. When you cry out let your cohorts rescue you! But the wind will carry them off; nothingness will take them. But the one who trusts in Me will have a portion in the earth and will inherit My holy mountain"** (Isaiah 57:12–13). Ultimately, the ideal is godliness.

We would all love to live in a world in which cards of righteous people are traded, rather than professional athletes or mass murderers. Imagine cards of all the people who have received Nobel Prizes, and others who have made contributions to humanity, with a list of their achievements on the back. The cards would be limited to those people who have made a difference in the world by virtue (no pun intended) of the way they lead their lives. Believe it or not, there are some Jewish communities where children collect and trade cards of great rabbis of history, teaching that education and virtue are to be revered over athleticism.

Unfortunately, we are more enticed to worship through our emotions rather than our righteous awe and respect. For example, for many weeks in December 1997 *A&E Biography* promised a year-end story of someone important and courageous, someone who changed the world. Considering the host of significant people who died in 1997, one thought the heralded biography might be of James Michener, Jacques Cousteau, Charles Kuralt, Mother Teresa, or some other individual who touched lives. With all due respect to her and her family, I was surprised to learn that the special was on Princess Diana—whose basic claim to fame was being a pretty young woman who married a prince in love with somebody else and who responded to this insult with eating disorders, suicide attempts, affairs, a divorce, and sundry lovers—the stuff of soap operas. Her charity work as a function of her position (AIDS and land mines) was admirable, but an April 1998 poll demonstrating that in ten years she would be more famous than Albert Einstein is disappointing.

As one of my listeners wrote about the nearly universal hysteria over Diana both in life and in death, *"The outpouring of feeling for famous people who have had tragic events can get to the point of idolatry; especially when such feeling is rarely directed toward family, the suffering of innocents, or worship of God."*

The Profane Trinity: "Me, Myself, and I"

With just a bit of literary license, one could read the Second Commandment as follows: "Do not make of *yourself* an idol." When we think too much of ourselves, like young children who think that the world revolves around them, we turn ourselves into idols. We all know people who take the credit for things in which they were helped by a co-worker or a spouse. Their overstuffed sense of self-importance leads them to believe they have done it all and owe no gratitude to the people around them. They often do not respect their "teammates in life," because they fail to see or acknowledge how these people have helped them. The most important CEOs recognize the importance of their colleagues. The most respected *anyone* should acknowledge the importance of his or her family in evaluating the successes of their lives. Although you ought to enjoy the pride of your successes, we must acknowledge that we are indebted to our spouses and children for all that we have achieved. Their love, support, advice, patience, input, suggestions, compassion, assistance, and soft shoulders have contributed as much to our achievements as our own singular efforts.

The idolatry of egocentrism also denies us the ability to see the role that God plays in our lives, which we sometimes only seem to admit when our "tush" is miraculously saved, or "luck" seems to go our way. Such an approach makes God into a rabbit's foot. Others do not understand the causality of life and how everyday events and opportunities affect their lives.

One of my listeners described God's presence in our lives: *"God definitely intervenes in daily human life. He is there for those who seek His wisdom and strength. We are given choices. With faith, God will help us to make the choices that affect those around us. This promotes a chain reaction throughout the world."*

And from another listener: *"God is involved moment to moment in every facet of His universe, from the smallest part of the smallest atom to the most complicated thought and action processes of His most incredible creation: man. God's plan for me is not predestination for my life, but a series of incidents and stimuli for me to respond to and grow from."*

Humility is not a sense of subservience, but a magnificent realization that you matter even more, albeit differently, than your egotism would lead you to believe. You matter to God, and to every person now on the earth and to be. You matter because your actions and your attitudes are the start of a cascade of events that reverberates to eternity. No, you are not the center of the universe. You are the mechanism by which God's plan unfolds.

Some pop philosopher offered the saying, "You are the architect of your own life." Perhaps the saying should go, "God is the ultimate architect, and you are the general contractor of your own life." Yes, you make the decisions, and yes, you take the actions. Yet, there are those eerie moments and experiences when you wonder about divine intervention—it seems so coincidental that you made an unusual change in plans and avoided tragedy, or unexpectedly connected with someone and benefited joyously. Just coincidences? We accept the words of the writer Doris Lessing, who once wrote, "Coincidences are God's way of remaining anonymous."

Feelings . . . Nothing But Feelings

"Our feelings were given us to excite to action, and when they end in themselves, they are cherished to no good purpose," Daniel Keyte Sandford stated wisely. An almost indiscriminate, idolatrous reverence for feelings has been one of the most insidious consequences of the field of psychology gone "pop." Though it can be therapeutic to plumb the depths of an individual's emotional confusion while "in session," having feelings become veritable temples of worship has proven disastrous for civilization.

The mere experience of feeling is given a respectability and significance beyond its logical due—feelings are irrational, changeable, unpredictable, and oftentimes incomprehensible. Feelings are also confused with moods, which are sometimes merely a product of indigestion, insufficient sleep, or a bad hair day. When major decisions and actions are taken based predominantly on a feeling state, much damage and hurt is generally the result.

This problem is so prevalent with callers to my radio program that I find myself correcting people who use the word *feel* (as in, "I *feel* that he/she . . .) interchangeably with *think* or *believe,* or *worry* or *guess,* and as though *feeling it actually made it so.* Feelings have been so glorified that facts, or proof one way or the other, are no longer required, because "feelings" are their own facts.

The idolatry of "feelings" becomes evident when we revere and bow to our feeling state as the ultimate authority and our ultimate identity. Pop psychology has provided a dead end for too many people who see their "pain of victimhood" as the throne upon which they helplessly reign, sometimes for a sad lifetime.

Lorna, one of my listeners, wrote, *"I was quite selfish in the past and only thought about my 'feelings.' I robbed my children of their father. . . . I just didn't 'love him anymore' so I left. But now, I see that my children lost so much more than I gained. Although I cannot turn back the clock, I can 'tell time' much better."*

Another listener, Arthur, a retired minister, reflected on how accustomed he'd become to people perpetually *"celebrating with pitiful cries a wrong done to [them] years before. I was reminded that back in my bad old days, I would help them celebrate by giving them the metaphor that they had built a memorial to the event and placed it smack dab in the center of the living room of their life, going there every day to worship!"*

And, as if to second the minister's words, this letter from another listener, Helene: *"When you first started commenting about sexual abuse survivors hiding behind that label, I was*

furious. You see I consider myself a survivor of childhood sex-
ual abuse. But I feel that I am a survivor because I am not
under the power of that abuse any longer. It got me thinking
that people who are still letting themselves be controlled by
abuse from their childhood are really not survivors, but per-
petual victims. . . . I guess what I want to let you know is that
I think you are right. Many people do hide behind that label
and use it as an excuse for everything that happens or doesn't
happen to them. We make the choices in how we want our life
to be. We can choose to live with the pain from our past expe-
riences, marinate in it as you say, or we can choose not to. I've
given up forty years of my life to this, I don't intend to give up
another day."

What makes this syndrome of marinating in feelings idolatry? Simply, whenever anything besides God and acting out of
godliness (kindness, charity, compassion, and so on) becomes
the actual *endpoint* of your attentions and activities, that is
idolatry. Feelings are a fascinating language, expressing curi-
ous internal reactions that bring alarm, joy, pain, fear, pity,
and so forth. They are a means of understanding something
within us and between people.

Too many of my callers live their lives seemingly energized
by melodramatic situations, which inevitably produce extreme
highs and lows of emotion. It is as though they have an addiction to intense passions. I believe that in most cases, the emotion is what fills their lives. Sadly, the turmoil produces
anguish, not meaningfulness. Maureen, one of my listeners, finally realized what she really needed to be doing with her life:
"The focal point of my life now is my religion. My focal point
used to be my problems. Since I have been back to church, I
have learned to live my life, not focus on myself. I enjoy my
life so much more and I enjoy the people in my life more."

Our lives become meaningful and more satisfying when we
allow ourselves to become the means to a much nobler end (a
holy life), and not an end in ourselves.

If I'd Only Esteem Myself . . . Only Then Can I Be Good

Whenever someone calls my program and expresses low self-esteem as the reason for making sad or bad choices or acting without character, I usually bring up the words of God in the Ten Commandments and ask him where God said it was okay not to do the right thing if "*you're* not up to it," or "nobody's been nice to *you* lately," or "*you* don't feel good about stuff," or "*you* don't have self-esteem," or any other such "self" something. Hint: God doesn't make your doing good or right contingent upon *your* feeling state or *your* state of mind. You are supposed to rise above your*self* and do what's right simply because God said it was right. We don't have to "rise above ourselves" to get rich or powerful; for that we basically have to rise above others. We must be deeply motivated to consider what we should do to and for others, even beyond our ego, needs, or moods. In this way, *our needs* don't become *ends* in themselves. To these ends, we must rise above ourselves.

". . . while shunning the idea of considering God a means for attaining personal ends, . . . there is a partnership of God and man, that human needs are God's concern and that divine ends ought to become human needs" (Abraham Joshua Heschel, *Man Is Not Alone,* Noonday Press, 1951).

Happiness and pleasure do flow from a love of doing what is good as defined by God. Does this mean that religion is just a better way of getting kicks? Is this theological hedonism? No, of course not. There is a special kind of joy and pleasure that comes from decency. Generally, it's even a different kind of sensation than, say, winning the lottery. Sacrificing or standing up for others, for example, is filled with a sense of loss or risk—certainly not glee—but there is a deeper satisfaction knowing that through your actions you bind yourself with the divine.

The credo of the self-esteem movements has been that if "kids could be *made* to feel good about themselves, the epidemics of depression, suicide, violence, drug and alcohol abuse, and pregnancies could be mitigated." The movements' promoters held that blaming, which includes holding anyone responsible for his behavior, was a psychological assault on self-esteem, leading only to destructive behaviors. Case Western Reserve University professor Roy F. Baumeister (Religion News Service, 1996) made a powerful point: "If we would cross out 'self-esteem' and put in 'self-control,' kids would be better off, and society, in general, would be much better off."

It is not a love of self that permits, stimulates, and inspires decency and righteousness, it is a love of God. Listen to Sharon: *"I was so pleased by your differentiation lecture on the radio between self-esteem and self-respect (external input vs. product of own actions). Many concepts you hit on ring true in my soul. This concept of self-respect is one of those concepts. I had always said I was a victim of low self-esteem because of my past. In my quest for self-development and health, the natural progression of therapy, books, and spirituality led to the discovery that taking responsibility for my life, that is, my choices past and present, led to a better 'self-image' (or self-respect, as you say). It was then a snowball effect. The more I did that was good and right, the better I felt about myself, and the stronger and more in control I felt, so the more I wanted the challenge of doing right in all kinds of situations. This particular phenomenon was the turning point in my life and growth. I am writing to say that earned-self-respect is the way out of the darkness. It is God's truth."*

Without the focus on God's *ends,* and how our lives are a joyous means to those ends, the focus on our state of mind as an end in itself is idolatry.

"As Long As You're Happy . . ."

The American public has turned the pursuit of happiness into a form of idolatry. It is a dangerous and sad trend that says,

"Feeling good is better than feeling good based upon what one does." We tell our children, "We just want you to be happy." A recent popular song reflected this preoccupation when it extolled, "... don't worry, be happy." This kind of giddy, feel-good happiness should not be elevated to a virtue, because it is fleeting and irrelevant to how we feel about life in the end.

We see other people who look happy, and we want what they have. We look at them only, of course, from the outside: nice family, successful occupation, money, popularity, and assume that these are the sole constituents of happiness. Often, these very people whom we see in our professional capacities privately admit not being happy with and in life. Possessions and privilege, nor their lack, do not have the inherent power to create happiness or sadness. The fundamental issue here is the presence or absence of *meaning*. In the sage words of Dr. Viktor Frankl (*Man's Search for Meaning,* Washington Square Press, 1959): "But happiness cannot be pursued; it must ensue. One must have a reason to 'be happy.' Once the reason is found, however, one becomes happy automatically. As we see, a human being is not one in pursuit of happiness but rather in search of a reason to become happy...."

What might be a reason to become happy? **"Praiseworthy is each person who fears the Lord, who walks in His ways. When you eat the labor of your hands, you are praiseworthy, and it is well with you"** (Psalms 128:1–2). The ultimate human happiness is in relationship to God. When we spend the time to create a healthy family, when we act in just and righteous ways, when we act compassionately, when we act in a godly way, we feel the happiness that is found as we bring meaning to our existence and to life in general. This is what the Bible means when it says, **"Light is sown for the righteous; and for the upright of heart, gladness"** (Psalms 97: 11).

The moral person is one who has come to enjoy the love of

doing and being good. Any sense of moral *obligation,* as an internally experienced necessity to do good whether or not it brings immediate compensation or happiness, must find the power to transcend self-centered interests. That power of transcendence is the acceptance of the belief that divine ends ought to become our means of living our lives and that this is the ultimate source of meaning, therefore of happiness.

But, I Waaaant it!

After the miracles of the Exodus from Egypt, the "presence" of God at Sinai, and manna from the heavens, **"The rabble that was among them cultivated a craving, and the Children of Israel also wept once more, and said, 'Who will feed us meat? We remember the fish that we ate in Egypt free of charge; and the cucumbers, melons, leeks, onions, and garlic. But now, our life is parched, there is nothing; we have nothing to anticipate but the manna!'"** (Numbers 11:4–6). **To which the Lord told Moses, "To the people you shall say, 'Prepare yourselves for tomorrow and you shall eat meat, for you have wept in the ears of The Lord, saying: Who will feed us meat? For it was better for us in Egypt! So The Lord will give you meat and you will eat. Not for one day shall you eat, nor two days, nor five days, nor ten days, nor twenty days. Until an entire month of days, until it comes out of your nose, and becomes nauseating to you, because you have rejected The Lord Who is in your midst, and you have wept before Him, saying: Why did we leave Egypt?'"** (Numbers 11:18–20).

The desires of people are often put before their gratitude, morality, values, and sense of personal responsibility and obligation to one another. When desires become an "end," the quest for fulfillment of desires becomes the focal point of important life choices. This is a self-centered life. For as soon as self-fulfillment becomes the object of your life, you no longer see yourself as belonging to the world, but you come to perceive the world as belonging to you. You then know no law other than your desires and impulses; any sense of a more profound destiny is pushed aside as your laws of behavior are ratified only by your own desire.

Even "doing good" can be an extension of a self-centered desire to suck at the breast of life without truly giving for the love of goodness. As a "faithful listener" wrote to me, *"I've been looking for a reason to fax you and when I heard your comments today about some 'nice guys,' I knew I had found my topic. I am exactly what you described as a 'nice guy': I constantly do things for people, falling over myself, putting myself out, etc. Most of the people who know me will put their hand on a Bible and swear that I could very well be the nicest guy on Earth. But little do they know, it's all a sham. Yes, I will go out of my way for almost anyone, but it is excessively self-serving. And when I'm in top form, doing and being everything for a certain someone, I expect something in return. I never say it outright, but when I don't get what I expect (which is usually the case), I throw a tantrum and find myself extremely rejected and hurt. After this happens, that particular friend usually catches on as to how I am and quickly becomes less friendly. The motivation for goodness is not always honorable."*

I have begun to hear more frequently on my program the justification for breaking up a child's home, that one or the other parent, usually the mother, has decided that she is "not happy" or "not fulfilled." Is it a spiritual quest? No, it's generally just a new sex partner. The steps that follow include the father and children losing contact with each other, and the children being exposed to the sexualization of their lives by the hypererotic dating behavior and/or shacking up of their parents. In the tradition of "iniquities visited upon further generations," research shows that children who are exposed to the sex lives of their dating parents are more likely to be sexually active at an early age. "Girls who grow up in single-mother families have sex earlier than girls who live with both parents. More alarmingly, girls who grow up in single-mother households with a string of drop-in or live-in boyfriends are at a higher risk of sexual abuse and coercive sexual initiation than are girls who grow up in intact families" (Barbara Dafoe Whitehead, *Los Angeles Times*, August 25, 1994). And if not, it would still be wrong.

The desire for new sexual partners, adventures, and experiences, combined with the societal philosophy of the last twenty years or so that personal desires are more important than obligations (bolstered by the psychological "trickle-down theory" of happiness) has been outrageously destructive for individuals, children, families, and society in general. The *fact* is that at least two-thirds of divorces are unnecessary; that is, not founded in violence, addictions, or infidelities. These divorces are more destructive to the children than two people staying together "for the sake of the children," in spite of a lack of desire, fulfillment, or happiness (*Wall Street Journal*, January 5, 1998).

I believe that another recent occurrence of unbelievable self-ishness derives from a basically healthy desire to have a baby. The trend of "using men" or a sperm bank in order to make children out of wedlock is taken to be a fundamental right. Sadly, we live in an era where rights are neither balanced nor recognized to be circumscribed by responsibilities. It's easy to see why. Rights are about "me," responsibilities are about "someone else." We may not want to temper our needs and desires, but we'll rationalize undermining the needs and desires of others. For example, "I want a child," therefore I should have one. "A child wants a dad," but he'll have to do without because of my desire, which should make it good enough for the child.

Marilyn, one of my listeners, no longer agrees with that self-focused attitude: *"I am a single mom who used a sperm donor chosen from a catalog. Now that you've picked yourself up off the floor, I want to tell you that if I had listened to you three or four years ago, I would not have chosen to have a child through that method, but I would have adopted a slightly older child, who needed a home and who would not have been adopted otherwise. Don't get me wrong; I'm very, very happy that I had the pregnancy experience and that I have my child. However, I'm not sure I was fully fair to her by doing this. Now I say to women who want to make or adopt kids without a husband, who think I could be their role model, that even though I had done it, it wasn't fair to the child."*

The state of New Jersey is the first state to allow homosexual couples to adopt children on an equal basis with married heterosexual couples (1997), as though gender was irrelevant and as though there weren't enough two-parent, married, heterosexual parents to go around. Both statements are false. This is an issue of the desire of some homosexuals to parent; homosexuals are probably more than capable of providing for and loving a child. But, do we allow the personal desires of any one activist group to deny the inherent significance and importance of heterosexual reproductivity and parenting? This is another incidence of personal desires being dominant over the ultimate welfare of children. I have taken many calls on my radio program from gays and lesbians about this issue. I beg them not to have or adopt a newborn but, as with heterosexual single folks, be available to take in older, harder-to-place children whose welfare would be increased by such a placement.

That we are turning into a society that devalues children and family is clearly seen by our determination to institutionalize our children from birth via full-time nannies, day care, and baby-sitters rather than make the preparations and sacrifices necessary to raise, guide, love, and spend time with our children. This is rationalized in innumerable ways, including pointing out that children need socialization (family and friends don't count?) and to learn independence (as babies?!). *U.S. News & World Report* dedicated an entire issue in 1997 to debunking the myths surrounding day care, including that the family needs the money to survive. Bottom line: Self-fulfillment is no longer served in the home, with children and family—it is only achieved by accumulating money, position, power, and independence from commitment, obligation, and covenantal vows. Certainly, where there are the tragedies of divorce, death of a spouse, or economic catastrophe, child care is often necessary in order that the custodial parent survive and provide necessities. The problem is that day care is not seen so much as a parachute as a benevolent necessity.

Sexual expression as a rightful desire (gratis the Sexual Revolution) has resulted in the mainstreaming of perverse activities: "S & M or B & D, for bondage and discipline—has been mainstreamed from deviant perversion to just another wacky lifestyle choice.... People don't think of it as perverse.... Are we that jaded? Is there no shame anymore?" (*Newsweek,* January 5, 1998). Adultery, promiscuity, multiple divorces, and shacking up are no longer met with judgment. We have become entitled to fulfill our desires and respond to any and all unfulfilled desires with the panic that some important experience has been missed. What is missed is the joy of commitment and connection, which sexuality serves but does not create.

All desires are not worthy of being fulfilled. Some desires of value may not be fulfilled because of other obligations. We have to learn to rejoice in the opportunity to fulfill any desires of merit. As Cindy wrote to me, *"When I face a struggle, temptation or problem with a Christ-like attitude, it has a profound effect on my husband, child, friend and even strangers. When I keep at the forefront of my mind the morality and wisdom God has set before me, I know I will make right decisions in my life, my behavior and my treatment of others, including those I love the most. When I lose sight of that, I easily fall into temptation where I rationalize with worldly wisdom. My focal point is like the center of a bullseye. The outer rings are built around that center circle. Without it, there is a hollow center."*

Desire is a gift from God. The value of your life comes not

in the fact these desires are all fulfilled, but that these desires are fulfilled with compassion and justice for others and for the godly ideals that lead to a holy, healthy expression of these human desires. A pursuit of the satisfaction of desire without the context of godliness is akin to idolatry.

I'm Not ALIVE Unless I Really Feel It . . . or Don't Feel Anything

When Rabbi Vogel and I were children, we found ways, things, and other kids to play with. Now parents seem to be frantically searching for ever more means of stimulating and occupying their children: high-tech toys, multiple sports teams, videos, computers, movies, TV, and more. The meaning of life for these parents and their children is stimulation. According to psychiatrist Dr. Ronald Dahl of Pittsburgh Medical Center (*Newsweek,* December 15, 1997), "Surrounded by ever-greater stimulation, their young faces were looking disappointed and bored. I'm concerned about the cumulative effect of years at these levels of feverish activity. It is no mystery to me why many teenagers appear apathetic and burned out, with a 'been there, done that' air of indifference toward much of life."

Once we seek stimulation as an endpoint of life, when it fails we can medicate to achieve greater stimulation, or to survive the disappointment and feeling of meaninglessness, or to create a designer mood. That's where addictions come in. Addictions are short-term answers to universal and timeless problems of understanding and coping with life. Addictions also create a mood, feeling, or state of mind that becomes the endpoint of that person's life endeavors. Laws, morals, commitments, obligations, values, relationships, and even love are sacrificed to create that feeling. And don't forget that addiction is a voluntary condition. The physiological phenomenon of addiction, while real, is not indentured servitude. There is no substance or behavior that thousands of people have not been able to stop taking or doing—often with the support or medical assistance of professionals for withdrawal, clergy, and support groups. The spirit has to be willing.

Kevin wrote to me, *"The focal point of my life at that time was mostly drugs and alcohol. I walked around with a burning desire inside. An all-consuming hunger to experience a sort of rapture beyond words. I thought drugs could reveal this to me, but they never did. Once I began to exercise, that 'raging storm' inside me began to subside and I realized that what I was looking for all those years had as much substance as an amorphous dream."*

Darla wrote about the natural "next step" after addiction: *"I did a lot of drugs and foolish attention-getting stunts to try to feel important. But I didn't feel it until I turned my life and will over to God. I feel confident that I am important and loved as a child of God."*

There is no question that for people with mental illness, certain medications or supplements are literal lifesavers. For the bulk of us yearning to be the thinnest, feel the most charming, intelligent, powerful, and happiest, important, and most loved, quick fixes of chemicals and stimulation are not the answer. A good life takes work.

In addition to drugs, alcohol, or cigarettes, addictions are said to take the form of gambling, working, Internet surfing, thrill seeking, collecting, hobbies, exercise—basically any activity taken to its extreme, in spite of obligations to family and society, is behavior that serves the self and is a form of idolatry. Here is one listener's commentary: *"My grown daughter is a very strong Christian, supposedly, but her children cannot get her attention when she is on her computer chat-line. I have known others who make card-playing, Bingo, or other activities that might be less than earth-shaking practices on a moderate level, something that would be an abomination to God because it is too important to us and takes us away from doing the things He clearly wants us to do. I would challenge your listeners and myself, Dr. Laura, to ask themselves, 'What idol do*

I worship?' None? How about the TV, the car, food, drink, sex, cigarettes or even infatuations? Enjoy life in moderation, but don't let it revolve around anything except the One who commands that we put Him in the center of it."

My Life Is One Big Commercial Break

The easiest form of idolatry to recognize is the love of "things" and "style." Though it is fine that you work hard to provide material comforts, you have to be careful about letting the accumulation of things dictated by trends and marketing schemes become too central. In that regard, the enemy is our advertising- and entertainment-drenched culture that, by means of glamorous seduction, inhibits the development of maturity, psychological strength, and spiritual focus by creating a false world of pleasure by possession of things, styles of dress and behavior, and even people.

This is exactly what Karen Karl discovered with respect to raising her children (*The Tribune*, August 12, 1997): "As they grew, we turned them [her daughters] into walking billboards for every current-release cartoon imaginable. Later we bought them designer clothes and fancy labels because it was the style. . . . Advertisers and the entertainment industry are selling a product that is not necessarily the American Dream. Allow them to develop the maturity and the psychological strength they will need to be the future of our nation—not immature walking billboards and fashion plates for the advertising giants."

A focus on how we are supposed to look and how we're supposed to behave in order to be considered "cool" is demeaning and demoralizing to our unique qualities. Such endeavors do not engender maturity, or intimacy or adult responsibility, nor is respect for character and spirituality fostered. Basically, such an external focus takes what is sublime and reduces it to the ridiculous.

When an individual worships his or her looks, it is a form of idolatry. Whether it is the physique of the body or the features of the face, many people are obsessed with their looks. We live in a society, much like the ancient Greeks, in which the body is worshipped. The body was considered a gift from the gods; therefore, the goal was to achieve perfection of the human form. Hercules, Adonis, Venus, and Aphrodite were the godly ideal. Ken and Barbie are the modern role models for appearance. While Ken's physique is obtainable by men, Barbie's proportional measurements are not for women.

Although it is appropriate to care for the bodies that God has given us by means of cleanliness, nutrition, and exercise, we should not disavow our unique creation in the sight of God by idealizing one specific form, either the anorexic appearance of most models or the surgically enhanced *Baywatch* babes. There are those who focus their lives on cosmetic alterations—attempting to make of themselves an altar at which self and others can worship.

On the other end of the spectrum are people who abuse their bodies by smoking, excessive eating, not exercising, abusing drugs and alcohol. These habits are not only destructive for our bodies, they negate the idea that our bodies are a gift from God, entrusted to us by God to treat with reverence and respectful care. Both of these extremes have the potential to disregard important aspects of God, distracting us from focusing on the greater values of life.

Volunteering for a Chain Gang

The pressure of competitive success, namely money, status, reputation, and power, is often too great a temptation for some who will cut corners on legality, ethics, morality, and common decency in order to "win."

Hard work without an ethical framework is self-destructive. According to business consultant Tom Morris (*News-Sun,* October 23, 1997): "We talk about what is quantifiable, but what we ignore is the relationship between people's deepest values and the work they do every day. There's a lot of pent-up stress in the workplace due to moral issues. . . ."

Lately, the legal profession has been scrutinized because of the sense that winning is above justice; politicians are seen as "expedient" in their promises; psychologists are viewed as bowing to the trends, and so forth.

When work for its own sake becomes the focal point of your life, when family is sacrificed at the altar of your workaholism, this is idolatry. It is often not until after the first heart attack that a man recognizes that he works to live, not that he lives to work.

We always have the ability to make choices, so excuses that lead with, "Honey, I can't help it right now . . ." are not necessarily genuine. I get many calls at the radio station from folks debating about moving their families—yet again—for a promotion, from men who query about moving away from their children for a better income opportunity, from women who consider bicoastal marriages because of a dream job, from both men and women who are married with children and still considering that dangerous job because of the excitement, or one which will keep them on the road, and from their children who just want an intact home with two parents at the dinner table listening to the events of their day.

We all have special gifts of creativity. We each have something special to give by virtue of what we can do with our hands, backs, and/or minds, but we are not to worship things of our creation as ends in themselves. When we rationalize in debating our priorities, recognize that we are only turning what we know we shouldn't do into a self-serving reason. That self-serving behavior is idolatry.

Susan came to that same conclusion: "*When I was working, which I did largely for myself since money was not an issue, our household was held together with staples and Scotch tape. The only time we were able to attend to the important issues in our lives was when they became emergencies. My son was having problems in school that I could not attend to. Because my husband traveled so much I was carrying the majority of the family life on my back. I was tired and depressed. Though I was very successful in a job I loved, I felt like a failure in my own home. I think money and material things were a big focus—they conferred status and success, and in Southern California, these are very important things. I have learned the simple things in life are much more worth having: love, God, family and most of all the self-respect that I am doing the best for the people I love."*

"The idols of the nations are silver and gold, human handiwork. They have mouths, but cannot speak; they have eyes, but cannot see; they have ears, but cannot hear, nor is there breath in their mouths. Like them shall their makers become, everyone who trusts in them" (Psalms, 135:15–18).

Humanity must not be in bondage to work; work is a means to a more spiritual end.

False Religions

When thinking of idolatry, most folks imagine historical objects of worship such as rock formations and totem poles considered sacred by cultures long gone. As you've learned from this chapter, idolatry is definitely a modern problem. Idolatry occurs when one holds any value, idea, or activity higher than God or morality. Even a godly mandated deed wrongly pursued can be idolatry—because it becomes its own end for the sake of the self (power, corruption, vengeance, control, domination).

Ideas can be idolatrous. Most recently there has been discussion that the Unabomber ought not to receive the death penalty for his premeditated murders because it would hurt the feelings of his brother, who turned him in to the FBI. What the brother did was decent and moral. He did not consider blood more important than justice, decency, and morality.

What those would do who want to hold the Unabomber to a more lenient standard for the sake of his brother is to put sentiment and feeling above justice, decency, and morality.

The same concept holds true for the "we protect our own" mentality within any group, such as physicians or police. Camaraderie is an important quality for group cohesion and effectiveness. When solidarity comes before justice, decency, the law, or morality, it is idolatry.

When we endow those with status, money, and power to make up rules as they go along—this is idolatry.

When members of religious groups decide that their perspective is above that of God—that is idolatry: "The Islamic terrorist groups believe that, before Ramadan or during Ramadan, they get closer to God when they carry out these terrorist acts," said Djamil Benrabah, a human-rights activist working with families of massacre victims in Algeria. "The only aim of these Islamists is to have a state based on Islamic Sharia (law)," he said. "They will use any means." State above godliness is idolatry.

In his recent book on Grigory Rasputin, the monk deviously and promiscuously active in the court of Nicholas II of Russia, Brian Moynahanis described, "His own attitude, in which sex and religiosity were easy bedfellows (so to speak), was that he was saving souls. The way to spiritual salvation lay through repentance: There could be none without sin to precede it, and he was merely supplying God-fearing women with this essential prerequisite" (review by Kyril Fitzlyon, *Los Angeles Times,* January 4, 1998).

A newly released Robert Duvall movie, *The Apostle,* portrays a Pentecostal preacher getting so carried away with himself that "his belief that he has a direct line to the Lord, is Sonny's sense that he's a law unto himself, a conviction that leads to a brutal act" (*Los Angeles Times,* December 17, 1997). When a man of God sees himself as God—that is idolatry.

Hypocritically professing belief, performing rote rituals,

calling oneself a member of a religion without attempting to follow holy prescriptions, participating in church or synagogue with a "social" country-club fervor—these can all be an evasion of holy duty, yet another form of idolatry, as practicing the "religion" becomes its own endpoint.

All of these "false religions and religionists" are false because they "use" religion to magnify their own person or personal beliefs. Religion as a quest for satisfaction of personal needs for power, salvation, immortality, or egotism is not true religion—it represents an attempt to reduce God to a valet, serving our desires, fears, and weaknesses.

The Second Commandment, **"Thou shall not make unto thee a graven image,"** provides a major frustration for people who look to religion to satisfy basic human needs (acquisition, opportunity, power, immortality, happiness, and personal satisfaction) as the end-all of their lives and who seek to exploit the forces of nature for their own gain and pleasure. This is not religion—it is magic, the antithesis of religion. Religion is a way to God. When we become interested in God, when God becomes our need and concern, when God's intent becomes our desire, when God's way or commandments become our way, our lives become holy. Religion is for God's sake, and it is God's blessings that bring meaning to our lives.

The goal of the Second Commandment is to negate all the vices that diminish our godliness and further estrange us from the true God.

3

The Third Commandment

"You shall not take the Name of the Lord, your God, in vain, for The Lord will not absolve anyone who takes His Name in vain."

What's in a Name?

"Sticks and stones may break my bones, but names will never harm me!" is a "So there!" response we were all taught by our parents as a defensive retort to be used against those who would call us names or make fun of us. Truth? We'd all probably have preferred a broken arm, since the other kids would definitely be in serious trouble, and we'd be the recipient of a ton of caretaking, sympathy, and ice cream. A broken arm doesn't make us feel ashamed or publicly damaged, the way having a bunch of kids yelling an embarrassing rendition of our last name does.

God clearly takes the issue of names and naming seriously. Consider that this, the Third Commandment, is the only one in which there is an immediate threat of punishment ("**For the Lord will not absolve anyone who takes His Name in vain,**" Exodus 20:7). Consider, also, that two of the Ten Commandments have to do with "good name" or "reputation." The Third Commandment involves God's good name or reputation, and the Ninth Commandment ("**You shall not bear false witness against your fellow,**" Exodus 20:13) involves our good names with each other.

Why is "good name" so important to God that 20 percent of the message of Sinai is concerned with ensuring God's and our good names? This God, unlike all the ancient, pagan gods of such things as wind, rain, and good fortune, is a God of "relationships," God's with us, and ours with each other. Through our relationship with God, we define and bring holiness to our lives and ultimately into all our other relationships. That which impedes, diminishes, or maligns the process seriously thwarts God's intent for a holy existence on earth. Giving God a "bad name" might diminish or demolish people's belief, respect, and awe for God, a tragedy for a world that needs holiness.

Names are generally used to define things. The difference between a *micro*scope and a *tele*scope is the difference between the two polarities of the infinitely small and the infinitely huge. You personally recognize that all of what you are cannot be contained in a simple description or specific name. When someone mistakes you for someone else, there is an uncomfortable sense of losing importance, or that all you have done and have become becomes discounted or lost. Moreover, when someone has or uses your same name, you feel threatened or diminished. Even though your name was the choice of your parents, somehow it feels *very personal*—as though it is shorthand for "you."

"Hey, God, What's Your Name?"

When Abram was ninety-nine years old, the Lord appeared to him and said, "**I am El Shaddai. Walk in My ways and be** complete" (Genesis 17:1). The usual translation of *El Shaddai* is "Almighty God," but that does not explain the fullness of its meaning. *Shaddai* is derived from an ancient language from Upper Mesopotamia and refers to mountains or open wastes. The implication might be to indicate vastness and greatness, conveying power. The Shaddai name indicates God's power to control; in other words, to limit. *El* means "God," the most widely used term for divinity throughout the ancient Near East. Therefore, we don't really have a name in the familiar sense—what we have is a description of grandeur, magnitude, and power.

When Moses was tending the flock of his father-in-law, Jethro, the priest of Midian, he gazed upon a bush all aflame, yet not consumed. God introduced himself to Moses as **"the God of your father, the God of Abraham, the God of Isaac, and the God of Jacob"** (Exodus 3:6). After listening to God's detailing of the "Mission Impossible" to Egypt to set the Israelites free, Moses wonders what he's supposed to say when the Israelites ask him, "What is His name?" **"And God said to Moses, '(Ehyeh-Asher-Ehyeh) I Shall Be As I Shall Be.' And He said, 'So shall you say to the Children of Israel, I Shall Be has sent me to you.' And God said further to Moses, 'So shall you say to the Children of Israel, The God of your fathers, the God of Abraham, the God of Isaac, and the God of Jacob, has sent me to you: This shall be My name forever. This is My remembrance from generation to generation'"** (Exodus 3:14–15).

When God clarifies His identity to Moses, he does so by stating His relationship to the patriarchs. God is also emphasizing His continual presence, concern, promise, and intent **"for all eternity."** Depending upon translations and interpretations, **Ehyeh-Asher-Ehyeh** could mean "I am that I am," "I am what I do," "I cause to become," "I shall be as I shall be" or "I am who I am."

The Bible uses several names for God. For the Jews, the Hebrew letters of the most sacred name of God roughly translate to *YHWH* (note the similarity to the name *Yahweh* often used to mean "Lord God"). It is possible that during the early biblical period the sacred name *YHWH* was readily known by the Israelites. Jewish tradition states that when the Temple stood, prior to 70 B.C.E., the sacred name of God was clearly forbidden to be recited except on Yom Kippur, the holiest day of the year, by the High Priest, the holiest person, in The Holy of Holies Within the Temple in Jerusalem, the holiest place. As written, the actual name of God is known as *Shem Ha Meforash,* or the "Ineffable Name." In respect for its great sanctity, *Shem Ha Meforash* is not pronounced as it is written. Instead, it is pronounced "Adonai" during prayer or when reading from the Torah. In ordinary speech, the word *HaShem,* "the Name," is substituted by some Jews.

This God is unknowable and beyond our finite perceptions. Ancient gods had specific names, usually denoting their specific, limited sphere of influence and power. By invoking their names in special rites, the ancient peoples could manipulate the gods to fulfill the will of people. The possession of a name was thought to imply control. From the time God has Adam give names to the animals symbolizing his dominance over them (Genesis 2:19–20), ancient people viewed names as powerful tools that allowed people to control the gods and the spirits of the beyond. The God of the Israelites was different from all other "gods." His name was to be used in blessings and not in magical incantations. By invoking His name, people could not manipulate this God to do their will.

This latter idea is highlighted in the biblical story of Balaam, the heathen prophet who is called upon by Balak, the king of Moab, to curse the Israelites (Numbers 22–24). Balaam was apparently well known in his time for being able to call upon the gods to bless and curse people. When he is called upon to curse the Israelites, even with a promise of a great reward, he can only say, **"I could not go against the order of YHWH my God in anything, great or small."** Even the great Balaam knows better than to try to work his magic against the God of the Israelites. It is interesting that Balaam says **"my God."** From the beginning YHWH is not just the Israelite God. He sent Jonah to the non-Israelite city of Nineveh, not to demand conversion but to establish righteous and just behaviors. YHWH is the God of all nations. He is concerned with all peoples.

Throughout the Bible God has many names, each of which represents the way in which He reveals Himself through His behavior toward the world. Throughout the ages, sages have used different names to describe His attributes of mercy, compassion, judgment, mastery over nature, timelessness, love, exercise of "miracles," and such. God is not limited. His names are limitless.

Is "God" God's Name?

In this book, you will recognize any *misuse* of God's name by the incomplete spelling of God: G-d. Some Orthodox Jews and Christians are most sensitive to misusing God's name, even in written form, and therefore always spell God's name "G-d" except in the context of a blessing or other sacred text. Those who write "God" for nonsacred purposes do so because they do not consider "God" to be one of God's *sacred* names. It is merely a reference to the Supreme Being. As we have already explained, there are also some Orthodox Jewish communities in which respect toward the name of God is demonstrated by saying *HaShem* ("the Name") instead of using any Hebrew or English name of God. Referring to God by *any* name, sacred or not, demands respect.

A Name Is Destiny

During the social and political upheaval of the 1960s, many people changed their names as a sign of rebellion, a new beginning, a new attitude, or a new value system. Many young people took on names of planets, plants, or animals. Some African Americans took on Muslim names as a way of connecting with another culture and another time. For the ancient peoples, a change of name meant a change not only in "what was" but "what it would become." A change in name could denote a change in destiny.

In Genesis (17), God changes Abram's name in preparation for fulfilling his destiny: **"And you are no longer to be called Abram; your name is to be Abraham, for I am making you father of many nations."** Furthermore, God clarifies to Abraham who his wife is now to be: **"As for Sarai your wife—do not call her name Sarai, for Sarah is her name. I will bless her; indeed, I will give you a son through her; I will bless her and she shall give rise to nations; kings of peoples will rise from her"** (Genesis 17:15–16). Just as Abraham's new role was signified by a change of name, so was Sarah's. The name *Sarai* means "my princess." One interpretation suggests that, at first, she owed her status to being Abraham's wife. Later, as Sarah, she is royalty to generations of royalty and, at the age of ninety, becomes fertile to fulfill this divine destiny. What a difference a name makes!

The Frivolous Use of God's Name

One of my listeners sent me this letter: *"I'll start by saying that I do not consider myself to be particularly pious. Having said that, have you seen the commercial for xxxxxxDrugs that is running on television? There is a man dressed in a white suit. He claims to be a 'heavenly photographer.' His job is to document our lives and report back to 'Him.' The voice-over claims that the only 4 × 6 photo lab that 'he' trusts is XXXXXX's. I find this use of a reference to God and judgment day to be in really bad taste. I know that there are cer-*

tain truth in advertising laws. Like a toy company cannot come out and say that 'Our toys are morally superior to the toys of some other manufacturer.' So why then can XXXXXX benefit from an endorsement that they have no proof of attaining? It just seems wrong to be using God's name in such a commercial way."

Clearly, there is no biblical evidence of God's using one particular drugstore's photographic equipment, or even needing a photographer to know what we're doing with our lives. Although the commercial simply meant to be humorous, the intent was also to connect the dots between a mundane product and our sense of reverence for God, hence adding to the value of that product.

We differentiate between that trivialization of the divine and recent billboards for a kosher hot dog that also humorously point out that their product conforms to the standards of a "higher authority." At least this claim is documented in Leviticus by the laws of Kashrut (kosher)!

We are certain that few are truly offended by the commercial described. It was probably considered cute. Although we don't want to appear overly sober and not able to see the playfulness intended, one should be conscious and careful about not crossing the line from playfulness to insult.

Mainstream media casually uses terms such as "G-d-dammit," "Oh, G-d," and "Jesus Christ" as simple exclamations. (And as one of my listeners wrote: *"And instead of 'ohhhh G-d' during sex—how 'bout they have the actors just say nothing and just groan and moan and scream?"*) Although most people don't mean anything disrespectful by these expressions, most religious folks understand this type of usage of God's name as the sole or main issue of the Third Commandment. This is obviously a ubiquitous form of profaning God's name, but the true translation of this commandment from the Hebrew points to "carrying the Lord's Name in vain." That means that actions, behaviors, and positions we take in God's name must not defame Him. History is pockmarked with episodes of torture, murder, rape, and plundering all in "God's name." This, of course, is a deeper profanity.

It's an Issue of Respect

This is really all about respect, something at least one administrative law judge in New Albany, Indiana, appears to know little about. It seems a Kentucky Fried Chicken worker, who quit over her manager's explicit sexual remarks, was denied unemployment benefits by a judge who said the talk may have been an attempt to boost morale. "Use of vulgar and obscene language and terms can serve to promote group solidarity," wrote Charles Schaefer, the judge who hears unemployment cases. "To the extent that it was intended to promote this end, it would have been an effort to achieve a legitimate business goal" (*Courier-Journal,* September 26, 1997). Unbelievable! And since when do business goals (profit) come before values, ethics, and decency?

When we use God's name frivolously, as in the drugstore commercial, we dishonor God and display irreverence—we ultimately malign or diminish God's reputation. We aren't showing the proper respect for God. When we use profanities in general, even when God's name is not invoked, we aren't showing the proper respect for people—which is one of God's oft-stated desires as indicated throughout the Bible. We show disrespect to people when we either direct profanities toward them or even simply use profanities in their presence.

Language is our way of communicating what we want and reflects who we are. By using bad language, we diminish the divine spark within us that defines our humanity. This certainly is not an emulation of God's ways.

It is God who gave humanity the gift of speech—a gift not bestowed on any other animal with the complexity with which we were endowed. **"Who gives man speech? . . . Is it not I, the Lord?"** (Exodus 4:11). It is to be appreciated and used with reverence and caution.

Never Curse at God

In Judaism, the traditional understanding of blasphemy is derived from Exodus 22:27, which states, **"You shall not revile God, and you shall not curse a leader among your people."** It is not only God who cannot be cursed but also our community leaders, though this is not the same as rebuking or holding them accountable. It is an issue of disrespect and undermining, something in which international journalism seems to revel.

What are we trying to accomplish when we "curse" or "revile" God? Basically, we are blaming God and making Him responsible for our own actions and behaviors and the sometimes bitter consequences of our choices. Other times, we are displaying our anger at God for our pain, disappointment, ill fortune, losses, and frustrations. Sometimes we are lashing out at God because of our inability to understand the meaning of seemingly senseless atrocities, because we cannot believe that He could let these things happen to us or anybody. How can we understand the killing fields of Cambodia, the Holocaust, a jihad, the Bosnian "ethnic cleansing," the Iraqi use of chemical warfare on civilians, or the drive-by shootings of innocent children?

God gives us free will, and we must take responsibility for all aspects of human action. To blame God for our problems and evils is a form of scapegoating that allows us to avoid responsibility for the courage it takes to be willing to stand between evil and the innocent. Adam, for example, blamed God for giving him Eve who, in turn, gave him the apple. God hates the evil that *we* do: **"The Lord hates these six, but the seventh is the abomination of His soul: haughty eyes, a false tongue, and hands spilling innocent blood, a heart plotting iniquitous thoughts, feet hastening to run to evil, a false witness spouting lies; and one who stirs up strife among brothers"** (Proverbs 6:16–19). God created man and woman, blessed us, gave us free will, and we, while not inventing sin, discovered sin when we resorted to evil.

Sin is an option, not an inevitability. In Genesis 4, Cain and Abel, the offspring of Adam and Eve, each brought the fruits of their labors before God. Cain offered God the produce of the soil, and Abel presented the firstborn of his flock. When God looked with favor upon Abel, Cain became angry. From the subtle contrast between the simple description of Cain's offering and the more specific description of Abel's offering— "... brought of the firstlings of his flock and from their choicest ... "—the assumption is made that Cain did not bring his best.

God asked of Cain: **"Why are you annoyed, and why has your countenance fallen? Surely, if you improve yourself, you will be forgiven. But if you do not improve yourself, sin rests at the door. Its desire is toward you, yet you can conquer it."** Cain *chooses* to appease his hurt and sibling rivalry by killing his brother in spite of God's understanding and warning.

Judaism teaches that God created in man the inclination to good and the inclination to evil. Without freedom to sin, there is no freedom to act righteously. Animals have no evil inclination—they fight, steal, or kill instinctively as a means of survival. Human beings have evil inclinations for survival and personal advantage that can be tempered or used for good— for example, when the inclination to conquer is transformed into the international competitiveness of the Olympic Games.

Don't Test God

Unfortunately, it is not unusual for insecure people to test the love and loyalty of friends, family, spouses, and other loved ones. This distrustful behavior is disruptive and destructive to relationships and does more to move people apart than to bring them closer together. People of faith often say, "It is in the hands of God." This does not mean that we should become passive or create situations that we know are contrary to goodness. There is a rabbinic teaching that states, "Do not stand in a place of danger and pray for a miracle, lest it not happen." Though God may have some grand plan for us, He has also given us free will to determine our fate. When we hold God responsible for the problems we have brought upon ourselves, we effectively take God's name in vain.

In fact, in Deuteronomy (6:16) Moses makes an appeal to the people for a clear display of their loyalty: **"You shall not test The Lord, your God. . . ."** Testing God to protect, provide, or reward you for some action or to punish you for an ill action is an insult to all that God has already provided and continues to provide. This is a profane attempt to challenge and manipulate God's will and to make God over into the tooth fairy.

Think about how often in your relationships you humiliate yourself and others by attempting to derive from them immediate simplistic proof of their love or loyalty without realizing that by that very action you demonstrate your lack of both. Think about how often in your relationships you deny the ongoing beauty of the interaction because of some misunderstanding, confusion, personal insecurity, and neediness. Think about how often you insult the depth and breadth of your commitments by straining to squeeze out one more feeling or action.

Profaning the Name of God

Since it is our duty to emulate God (**"You shall be holy, for I the Lord your God am holy,"** Leviticus 19:2), a clear way to sanctify God's name is to behave in holy ways, even and especially under threat and coercion. Historically, this has included martyrdom—a willingness to die—before denying God through our lips or our actions. According to Jewish law, only transgressions involving idolatry, incest, and murder require the individual to suffer death rather than commit the transgression. Additionally, if an "Israelite" is being coerced into committing any transgression other than the above three, and he is not in the presence of ten other Israelites, he is to commit that transgression rather than be killed. In the public presence of the ten Israelites, he is to endure death rather than commit the transgression even if it is a breach of a commandment other than the three pertaining to idolatry, incest, and bloodshed.

Although God's commandments are the standard for our behavior, God is understanding about our possible inability to carry them out under duress. With the exceptions of idolatry, incest, and murder, we must be aware of how, as professed godly people, our behaviors even under duress have an influence on the respect, awe, and faith others might have for God. By what you do at any time, you have the power to inspire others to goodness. Use that power wisely and bravely.

To put all this into a contemporary context, certain sins are not to be committed, even under duress. The Nuremberg Trials of the German World War II war criminals reiterates this ancient understanding: Even under orders or for fear of one's own life, one is not to murder. It is bad enough to do something wrong or evil, but when that wrong is performed in front of other people, it provides a degraded, negative influence that diminishes morale and trust. Additionally, the display of weakness and self-centeredness badly represents someone who "walks with God."

These kinds of behaviors profane the name of God because it is through our actions that His will, intent, and character is made evident on the earth for all peoples.

Making God Look Bad

Few of us will ever have a gun to our heads to force us to do evil or sinful deeds. Yet many of us have faltered under such everyday influences as peer pressure, a desire for popularity, a yearning to "fit in," a fear of derision or rejection. How far have you gone in doing things you know you shouldn't—

breaking commandments, promises, and the expectations of parents, teachers, and clergy—to gain acceptance? Isn't this version of coercion a more insidious type—a coercion of your choice? The mob mentality, a special kind of peer pressure, which resulted in the savagery at My Lai, Vietnam, and the beatings and murders in Los Angeles after the Rodney King verdict are examples of voluntary acquiescence to evil.

In Hebrew, *Hillul HaShem* describes such a desecration of God's name. The term refers to any time a Jew does something that brings the Torah or the Jewish faith and people into disrepute in the eyes of the outside world, desecrating God's name.

For all people, there must be the understanding that any time we behave badly, we bring shame and pain to our families, our community, our country, etc. I remember a PBS special on China I saw some twenty years ago. There was a scene of a man in a small village caught for some misdeed and brought before the village judge. The first thing that was said to this man was that he had brought shame to his ancestors, his family, and his neighbors. I was struck by how devastated the man appeared upon hearing this! You'd have thought the firing squad had raised their rifles waiting for the order to shoot. It was impressive to observe how meaningful the notion of his impact on people for all time was to him. His reaction actually encompassed a visceral understanding of "inequities visited upon the generations."

Even behavior without specific evil intent, emanating from indifference, laxity, or character weakness, has the power to profane God. Ultimately, we are each responsible for our actions and for the impact our behaviors have on history and the rest of humanity, for we are all a tangled web.

A sad example of the destructive impact of such behavior appeared in the following comments of a schoolteacher, published in the January 26, 1998, *Los Angeles Times* in response to the allegations that President William Clinton may have perpetrated even more infidelities and the possibility that he may have asked a woman to lie about this under oath: "It just saddens me so much that we've lost a lot of class and integrity to the office of the president," said Lynn Gorman, a nursery school teacher. "It's really upsetting. I think politics in general, whether it's a perception or a reality, is now seen to be sleazy and full of half-truths." The dignity of the office must be supported by the dignified behavior of the officeholder. The office outlives the individual inhabitants—and the tarnish stays with it.

"But to the wicked, God said, 'To what purpose do you recount My decrees and bear My covenant upon your lips? For you hate discipline and you threw My words behind you. If you see a thief you agreed to be with him, and with adulterers was your lot. You dispatched your mouth for evil, and your tongue adheres to deceit. You sit and speak against your brother, you slander your mother's son. These have you done and I kept silent. You thought that I was like you; I will rebuke you and lay it clearly before your eyes! Understand this now, you who have forgotten God, lest I tear you asunder and there be none to rescue. He who offers confession honors Me . . .'" (Psalms 50:16–23).

We owe God gratitude for all that is in life, and we are to behave in holy ways. Putting aside that gratitude is to dishonor our gifts and to profane God.

In the book of Genesis, when Joseph is sold into slavery and is working as a servant at the house of Potiphar, the wife of Potiphar attempts to seduce Joseph. The young Hebrew could have had many reasons for not succumbing to her overtures, including the fear that he would be put to death by his master, who just happened to be the captain of the guards and probably one of the biggest and meanest men in Egypt. When she corners him again, in addition to reminding her of his duty to Potiphar, Joseph says, **"How could I do anything so wicked, and sin against God?"** (Genesis 39:9). Joseph offers two different motivations: he could not betray someone who has trusted him, and he could not sin against God. Not only is Joseph an honorable person, but his belief in God helps to mold his character.

"God" Made Me Do It!

I have had several calls to my radio program from spouses or family members who are dealing with the selfish and destructive behaviors of people close to them who claimed that God told them to do the awful things they were doing. Now, the behavior in question was never to give to charity, to give up material things, to sacrifice for someone else's good, and so on. No, God has spoken to them about doing some unconscionable act, which they try to justify by making divine intervention responsible. After all, who can argue with God?

There are few things more demoralizing to us than people who use God and religion as a co-conspirator to defraud or to manipulate people. Sometimes it is a clergyperson who is more committed to living the good life or to having power than to truly helping his/her parishioners. A prominent religious leader some years back publicly stated that God would take his life if a specified amount of donations did not come forth from the audience. Talk about a marketing ploy! The money did not come in, and he did not get divinely taken out in the literal sense—but his credibility was destroyed, and along with it went the respect of innumerable followers, some of whom may have, by association, also lost their taste for God.

When the CEO of a company misuses corporate funds for personal use, he has committed a crime that directly affects employees' and shareholders' bank accounts. When a religious leader or charity misuses funds, he hurts people spiritually as well as economically. Such leaders place themselves in positions to be judged more harshly because their connection to a religious organization demands a higher degree of honor. Unlike businesses, in which people invest money for profit, religious organizations are run for the express purpose of doing good. When someone who claims to do God's work to help others is in fact helping himself, he deserves the public scorn that comes his way because he has violated more than a legal trust—he has violated a sacred, holy trust. Those who take upon themselves the task of spreading God's word will ultimately be judged accordingly by God as well: **"But the prophet who willfully shall speak a word in My name, that which I have not commanded him to speak, or who shall speak in the name of the gods of others—that prophet shall die"** (Deuteronomy 18:20).

Scandals by religious leadership perpetuate the misguided idea that religion is hypocrisy and all religious people are hypocrites. The arrest of a minister, claiming a worldwide ministry, for defrauding donors, or of a rabbi for money laundering is an act of blasphemy because it belittles God and estranges not only the perpetrators but also their followers, people who lose their faith as a result of the disillusionment over their fallen leader. Rather than asking the question, "Does religion bring more goodness to the world than conflict or hypocrisy?", they choose to prove that their lack of religious affiliation is warranted.

Such a Blessing!

To bless is to consecrate or sanctify; that is, to make holy, distinct, and special. The Hebrew word for "blessing" is *berakhah,* which, according to one interpretation, is a derivative of the word for "knee," suggesting a bending or bowing of respect toward God.

Ultimately, all blessings come from God: **"And God created man in His image, in the image of God He created him; male and female He created them. God *blessed* them . . ."** (Genesis 1:27–28). And God's blessings confer effective and irrevocable destiny: **"I will bless [your wife, Sarah]; indeed, I will give you a son by her. I will bless her so that she shall give rise to nations; rulers of peoples shall issue from her"** (Genesis 17:16). God also gives people the "power" to confer His blessing in this, one of the most serious and famous biblical blessings: "The Lord spoke to Moses, saying 'Speak to Aaron and his sons, saying: So shall you bless the Children of Israel, saying to them: "May The Lord bless you and safeguard you. May The Lord illuminate His countenance for you and be gracious to you. May The Lord lift His countenance to you and establish peace for you"'" (Numbers 6: 22–26).

In turn, human beings bless God, praising His greatness and goodness: "Then I bowed and prostrated myself to The Lord and blessed The Lord, God of my master Abraham . . ." (Genesis 24: 48). When people speak blessings, they are prayers of gratitude, longing for spiritual connectedness and good favor, and so forth. Jewish tradition includes a large number of blessings concerning food. The ancient rabbis, interpreting from the Scriptures, held that eating a meal without first blessing God was a form of stealing. Food is a gift from God, and the payment for our meal is acknowledgment and gratitude. For example, the most widely recognized meal blessing is that over the bread: "Blessed are You, Lord our God, King of the Universe, who brings forth bread from the earth."

Such blessings over seemingly mundane, daily experiences serve the wonderful purpose of reminding us of God, the source of all things, thus elevating the mundane to the sublime—elevating what is everyday to a special, even holy, realm.

Blessings are very serious in all religious traditions. In Jewish tradition, when God's sacred name, Adonai, is used in the context of a blessing, the words take on a sacred significance and are not to be taken lightly. If a blessing is recited in error, the Hebrew phrase *Barukh Shem kevod malkhuto l'olam va'ed*, "Blessed is the holy name of His sovereignty forever and ever," is immediately recited. This emphasizes the idea that God's sacred name should not be taken in vain.

Prayers are ways in which we speak to God. Sometimes we praise God, and sometimes we ask things of Him. Unfortunately, many people only speak to God when asking something of Him—as though he were a fairy godparent. Although we all do it at times, asking for inappropriate things is also a form of taking God's name in vain. Did you ever wonder about the prayers offered by football teams huddled together before the beginning of the game? Will God help the team with the best prayer? If their prayer is asking God to help them win, it is a vain prayer. When we turn God into a coach who can have an impact on the outcome of a game, we belittle His essence and take His name in vain. If football players gather together and pray that they play to the best of their abilities and exhibit the highest standards of sportsmanship, they acknowledge the true role of God in their game.

Martha Williamson, the producer of the television show *Touched by an Angel*, a self-defined "committed Christian," was interviewed by the *Los Angeles Times* (December 31, 1997) about the unexpected success of her religiously oriented program. When asked whether she felt God had a hand in its success, she replied, "I certainly pray for the show, that God will help me do the best job I can, but I never prayed for ratings." In her statement Williamson expresses a distinction between an appropriate prayer and one that might trivialize God.

According to Jewish tradition, if someone is approaching home and sees a fire from the distance, he or she may *not* say, "God, please let this not be my house." Such a prayer could be misinterpreted as a plea that it be someone else's house. In Jewish tradition, asking God to change something that exists already is a vain prayer—that likens God to an assistant to our personal magical powers. This is a vain prayer, which is different from saying that this is taking God's name in vain.

While both prayer and blessings are addressed to God, they serve different purposes. In the practical sense, prayer usually involves asking God for some spiritual intervention (courage, for example), while blessings concentrate on praising and describing the glorious attributes of God, communing with the ever-presence and influence of God. The deepest level of prayer, more important than petitioning for God's service to us, *l'hitpalel,* is about self-judgment, self-evaluation, intro-spection.

By the way, we are permitted to ask for things from God, as long as we are aware that God may say no.

Without these intense and profound moments of personal honesty, one can become perfunctory toward God (even meal-time blessings can become an empty ritual) and lose one's no-tion of divine purpose (when we tune into God only when we want something, we become like the college student who only calls home for money). When we take the time to connect with God concerning our contribution to His world and ex-pectations, we stand a very good chance of becoming better in thought, word, and deed.

Who's Sorry Now?

The expression "I'm sorry" is perhaps one of the most overused in the English language. A genuine "I'm sorry" has the potential to heal a shattered relationship, while an insin-cere one can cause further estrangement. Children learn to say "I'm sorry" early on, because they realize it is the fast route to getting out of trouble. They may feel no remorse, but they hope those words will help them avoid punishment. Some adults use those words in about the same way. Though they have no true remorse, they try to dismiss the whole problem or episode with a quick "I'm sorry." Some folks will never use those words, in spite of their own recognition of wrongdoing, simply because they don't ever want to admit to being wrong. Ego, narcissism, arrogance, power, and position seem to be more important than spiritual and relational depth. Only a sincere "I'm sorry" can allow people to forgive and the wrongdoer to change.

All religious traditions allow for repentance. From the time of the prophets, no ritual alone, including the sacrifices of the Jerusalem Temple, could atone for the sins of an individual. The Jewish tradition assumes that forgiveness from God requires remorse and a commitment not to commit the same sin again. After all, there are many people who feel guilty about an adulterous affair or the physical abuse of a spouse but still continue or repeat the behavior.

We live in a society in which people think that feeling remorse is sufficient. The classic example is of an adulterous spouse who says to his/her partner, "You know . . . this isn't easy for me either." With such an outrageous statement, he/she is often looking for compassion because of the embarrassment and shame he/she has brought upon themselves. The adulterer is upset because he/she is "torn between two lovers," one of obligation and history, the other of newer infatuation and lust. Experiencing such emotional pain alone is not sufficient grounds for granting forgiveness. To seek repentance from God, we must be able to offer God and each other a sincere apology and a promise not to repeat the offense.

The Catholic ritual of "confession" is strongly rooted in ancient biblical prescription: **"Speak unto the children of Israel: A man or woman who commits any of man's sins, by committing treachery toward The Lord, and that person shall become guilty—they shall confess their sin that they committed; he shall make restitution for his guilt . . ."** (Numbers 5:6–7). Confession is to admit, to acknowledge, to say "I am guilty." In Jewish tradition, the admission is between the person and God, without the intermediary priest who designates penance.

Whether through a priest or directly to God, confession is a divine obligation. Confession is designed to help motivate true repentance, to cause us to improve, to mend our ways, and to become more in "God's image." Confession contains the two essential elements of repentance: regret over the sin committed and resolve never again to repeat the offense.

Rabbinic tradition holds that the power of true repentance

is so great that even when only a single person repents, the whole world gains pardon through him. The interpretation is that even one individual's change toward goodness ultimately affects the world.

Insincere confession and repentance is a vain use of God's name and compassion. There is a misconception among many non-Catholics that the act of confession in itself ensures forgiveness. In how many Mafia movies have we seen the murderer enter a confessional, receive absolution by the priest, appear to be a forgiven man, and proceed to go out to "do family business" the next day? An insincere confession is not valid and is considered sacrilegious. According to the *Catholic Encyclopedia* (1987), "Sacrilegious confession willfully fails in sorrow for the sin or purpose of amendment. . . . In such cases the Sacrament of Penance is made void, absolution is not effective. . . ."

True repentance is a return to God. **"Return to me and I will return to you, says The Lord"** (Malachi 3:7).

God Makes Promises

God is our teacher of promises and swearing of oaths. After the flood, God promised all humanity through Noah never again to "wipe the slate clean" by natural calamities: **"And I will confirm My covenant with you: Never again shall all flesh be cut off by the waters of the flood, and never again shall there be a flood to destroy the earth. . . . I have set My rainbow in the cloud, and it shall be a sign of the covenant between Me and the earth"** (Genesis 9:11–13). A more dramatic godly "swearing" occurs after Abraham's challenge to sacrifice Isaac: **". . . By Myself I swear—the word of The Lord—that because you have done this thing, and have not withheld your son, your only one, that I surely bless you and greatly increase your offspring like the stars of the heavens and like the sand on the seashore . . ."** (Genesis 22:16–17). Finally, God has a perfect memory for a covenant: "... so that I may fulfill the oath I swore to your ancestors, that I may give them a country flowing with milk and honey, ..." which is predicated upon "Listen to my voice and fulfill the commandments, according to all that I command you, so that you will be a people for Me and I will be a God for you ..." (Jeremiah 11:4–5).

We learn from the Bible passages above that God makes promises and gives everlasting symbolic proof, that God swears upon Himself for emphasis and seriousness, and that God recognizes covenants are reciprocal. God's name, in any form, imparts a seriousness above and beyond anything else we might attempt to invoke.

As God Is My Reference

"You shall not steal, you shall not deny falsely, and you shall not lie to one another. You shall not *swear falsely by My Name, thereby desecrating the Name of your God* ..." (Leviticus 19:11–12). This prohibition forbids us to invoke the name of God as *a reference* for our personal honesty, our product, our service, our property, and so on, when we intend to create a "pious" picture of those things that we know to be distortions or outright untruths.

I am amazed at the sorts of things I've noticed constantly around me relevant to this book, especially when I'm in the middle of writing about a particular idea. For example, after beginning this section, I was "surfing" through the TV channels to get to local news when I came upon the Montel Williams program. I would have kept going without investigation, but a woman was in the midst of saying, "I swear to God ... you're going to get pregnant next month," to an overly made-up woman, who became hysterical with joy, since she'd been through eight or so miscarriages and one recent stillbirth. Well, I was riveted! I watched for five or so minutes longer and was deeply saddened and disturbed to see this "psychic" simply turn from one woman to another in that audience to tell them the good news. It was the "swear to God" that worried me the most. Assuming that this audience was not filled with ringers, this so-called psychic was making promises "in the name of the Lord." What would happen when the dreams did not come true? Wouldn't the believers be angry at the Lord for not "coming through" for them? Or wouldn't they be worried that God was "punishing" them? This is obviously profaning the name of the Lord.

Rabbinic tradition suggests that you can distinguish a false from a true prophet not simply by waiting to see if his/her prophecy comes true. If a prophet portends of terrible things that *do not* happen, this is not proof that he/she is a false prophet, since God, in response to some change in us, could change "destiny" from bad to good. However, if a prophet tells of something good that does not happen, he/she is considered a false prophet, because God would not withdraw a blessing.

This TV psychic told everybody something "good." The dangers here are obvious: exploitation for personal gain, the opportunity to hurt people when she's "wrong," and even worse, to hurt their relationship with God because they might ultimately feel cursed by Him.

Unlike God, you don't always have the power to come through as you'd like to, mean to, or should. Using God's name to verify your outcome is setting God up for a bad name; thus, it is taking the Lord's name in vain.

Necessary Oaths

Twice in Deuteronomy (6:13 and 10:20), we are reminded that **"The Lord your God shall you fear, Him shall you serve, and in His Name shall you swear."** Just as we are admonished against making any unnecessary oath, so are we specifically reminded that sometimes it is necessary to take one. The first time this phrase appears is to ensure that if we do any swearing it is by God, and not by any other god. The second relates to swearing to fulfill a promise, when by doing so the person swearing, fearing his frail human nature, makes the oath to increase his own likelihood of compliance.

According to some religious scholars, God asks us with this commandment to swear by His name to lend gravity and dignity to declarations in affirming or denying a matter. To take oaths of office and swear to tell the truth at legal proceedings, both incredibly serious and solemn occasions, the public ritual includes an oath while placing one hand on the Holy Scriptures.

Most think that those who believe are less capable of evildoing. When alone in a dark alley, we all would feel more comfortable to be approached by a bunch of guys holding Bibles than a bunch of guys with their hands just hanging; unless, of course, you were a Jew or proclaimed "heretic" during the Crusades or the Spanish Inquisition. When God spoke to Abimelech, the pagan, nonbelieving king of Gerar, through a dream, he was kept from having sexual relations with Abraham's wife, Sarah, because he believed Abraham and Sarah to be siblings. When he asks Abraham why he didn't inform him of the truth, Abraham answers, "**'I thought there would be no fear of God here and that I should be killed for the sake of my wife'**" (Genesis 20:11). Later, Abimelech says to Abraham, "**'God is with you in all that you do. Now swear to me here by God that you will not deal falsely with me nor with my son nor with my grandson; according to the kindness that I have done with you, do with me, and with the land in which you have sojourned.' And Abraham said, 'I will swear'**" (Genesis 21:22–24).

Though Abimelech did not fear, serve, or cleave to God, he believed Abraham, who did. That is a major responsibility to represent God, which should not be taken lightly. Profaning God's name can elicit cynicism, distrust, or disgust for God.

We have too many examples in our public arena of elected officials abusing their positions of power, using drugs, making illegal deals for campaigns, having illicit sexual relationships, lying, and such, after taking an oath of office. Michael Ramirez's political cartoon in the *Los Angeles Times* (February 1, 1997) depicts the American flag unraveling, with the comment, "Our Moral Fabric." If we as individuals or a nation wish to lead, we need to do it by example. Unfortunately, too many of our citizens have become so materialistic that as long as their personal "issues" are gratified, morality is a non-issue.

In his column in the opinion section of the *Los Angeles Times* (February 1, 1998), William Schneider writes about President Bill Clinton: "His character problems are bad. And getting worse. Increasing majorities view the president as not honest and trustworthy, as someone who does not share their values and as someone who sets a poor moral example." In explaining why the President's popularity soared, despite the sex scandal and after his lauded appearance in his State of the Union address, Mr. Schneider wrote, ". . . performance trumps character. Only 41% said it does matter 'because the moral character is important.'" And *that* is the true "state of the union." As long as personal needs, wants, and desires are appeased, many of us seem to be willing to abdicate nobler concepts.

Contrast this acceptance reaction with the pain, hurt, and anger we hear from folks who thought they could count on a co-worker, friend, family member, or spouse—only to find out that promises and expected loyalties were simply tossed when it served the desires of the other person to do so. Suddenly, appreciation for the need to be able to believe and trust becomes crystallized. Morality seems to count only when you are on the receiving end of another's lack of morality. It's too late then, isn't it? It is surprising how many people engage in relationships with folks they know have misused or abused other folks—and that behavior is okay until it hits them personally.

Another form of blasphemy is committed by those who utilize God and religion in order to gain respect or prestige: politicians who appear in churches and synagogues, not for the purpose of prayer, but rather to appear religious to their constituents—especially after a particular embarrassing "news flash."

Which Vows Hold Water?

How serious is the issue of taking a vow using the name of God? In the Jewish tradition, the *Kol Nidre* service, a central feature of Yom Kippur, the Day of Atonement, observance, asks God's forgiveness for any of the vows made *to God* and not fulfilled. Hitler and others have used the *Kol Nidre* service to malign Judaism as a religion that permits the making of promises and then breaking them with a simple service. The opposite is true. God only forgives those vows that people are unable to keep or those they should not have made to begin with because the implications were not fully understood. God is quite clear: **"If a man makes a vow to The Lord or swears an oath to establish a prohibition upon himself, he shall not desecrate his word; according to whatever comes from his mouth shall he do"** (Numbers 30:3).

Jewish tradition holds that forgiveness can be sought from God only for transgressions of laws between a person and God. For transgressions between people, forgiveness must first be sought and obtained from the one who was offended. A person is not required to forgive if the offense is too egregious and the damage horrendous and irreparable. Even so, they are not supposed to be harsh in their reaction. Ultimately, the predominant theme is God's willingness to grant forgiveness to those who sincerely repent. The atonement for any ill one man has done to another begins with repairing the injury; then one seeks God's absolution. The devout Jew will seek out every person he/she could possibly have injured, apologize, offer repairs, promise no repetition, and then ask forgiveness.

Repentance, *t'shuva* in Hebrew, is a forward-looking concept. It means returning to the correct way. *T'shuva* requires accepting responsibility, having true remorse, ensuring no repetition of such actions, and doing whatever is necessary to repair the damage done.

A vow is not valid unless it is made with intention and uttered with the lips. If a vow is made in error, that is, uttered thoughtlessly, or not said out loud, Jewish tradition holds that this is not considered a vow. Though children under the age of twelve or thirteen (Jewish tradition historically considers these the ages for girls and boys, respectively, to take on adult responsibilities and know right from wrong) are generally not considered mature enough to assume the serious nature of vows and oaths, they should be taught not to be in the habit of making promises and vows and be reprimanded if they make promises a trivial matter. In fact, if the vow or promise is reasonable and doable and can be done without damage to the child, he should be ordered to fulfill it—or what kind of person will you have when he turns fourteen?

Obligations once assumed must be fulfilled. The fabric of relationships, community, and government unravel when individuals deign to disrespect, abuse, and forsake their vows. In fact, most religious traditions hold that "promises" are weak substitutes for concrete action: **"You must not break your oath, but must fulfill your oaths to the Lord. . . . All you need say is 'Yes' if you mean yes, 'No' if you mean no, anything more than this comes from the evil one"** (Matthew 5:33–37).

These thoughts are seconded by two of my listeners, Lauren and Igmar respectively: *"But it seems that the prevailing attitude toward vows today is that they are just words, and this is sad. The expression 'his word is as good as gold' accurately applies to very few people today. It seems that people do not hold any vows as 'sacred'—not their marriage vows, or their vows to God. This reflects a lack of commitment on the part of the person making the vow. Sometimes people make vows just because they think that is what the other person wants to hear, and they never have any intention of keeping the vow. We should all be careful about the vows we make, and we should endeavor to live up to a vow once we make it— unless there is some sound scriptural reason not to."*

And: *"Nowadays it seems like no one takes notice of an oath, or pledge, or vow, or promise. It's okay to say 'we promise to do this or that,' but if something comes up that we disagree with, or if times are tough, then it's easier to quit the promise."*

This degradation of oaths, vows, and promises is in contrast to God's "example": **"He eternally remembers His covenant"** (Psalms 111:5). Breaking your word is to not "walk with God" or be "holy like God." When you break your word, you make your word profane. And, since the making of vows and covenants comes ultimately from God, you profane the name of God.

Vows Worth Breaking

While each religious tradition has rituals and rules for annulling vows, here are some significant answers my listeners E-mailed me in response to the question I posed: "Under what conditions could/should a vow or promise be broken?"

➤MG from Ann Arbor: *"I believe that a promise or vow should be broken when you realize that promise or vow was* **a mistake**. *When I married, we set up a relationship of inequality, never establishing a partnership. I don't blame him for this, just that we were young and dated in a 'fantasy world,' we all know college isn't the real world. We have a lot of marital problems that I realize stem from* *different views, backgrounds, and beliefs. I think we made a mistake and should have looked more deeply at our views of life, money, religion, family, career . . . not superficially like we did thinking, naively, that love conquers all. Thus, if we do separate and eventually divorce, I won't have guilty feelings of breaking my commitment and vows with this person. So, I guess when you feel you've made a mistake and all avenues have been exhausted, then you have the right to break your vows and move forward. Realizing, however, that to never make the same mistakes, you need to never forget them. Keeping a sense of what you did wrong before and how you changed and will never do the same stupid thing again is the way to improve upon yourself and your character. I hope that I can do this and that whatever happens will be the best for both of us."*

Many might argue that a "mistake" is merely a challenge to be confronted and overcome, not a justification for breaking promises of fidelity, loyalty, and loving behavior, since the problems are not necessarily insurmountable. "Feelings" of wanting more, being disappointed, or bored, or wanting a sense of more romantic or sexual excitement are frequently used to justify the breaking of marital vows. Most religious traditions don't uphold this pop-psychology–supported justification for terminating a marriage and breaking apart a family. Sue from Bremerton wrote: *"I personally feel if you make a promise, you keep it. If you make a vow, say marriage, you keep it. I broke my vow of marriage after seven years. I am not proud of the broken vow, or of the naïveté of what I was vowing or promising to do. 'Til death do you part. If I had stayed, we would be dead. I broke this vow to save my children and myself from continued bodily harm and ongoing degrading abuse. I feel that children, a precious gift from God, are given to us to care for to the best of our ability. If they are in danger, you need to save them from it. Thus, I broke a vow, a promise."*

➤Murray from Canada contributed: *"Vows or oaths should be broken when it morally or spiritually goes against what our Heavenly Father would have us or want us to do. I personally experienced this in a former marriage. My ex-wife wanted me to go into business with her father. He is a white supremacist (Nazi) right off the boat from Germany (he has been here for about forty years now). His business ethics were questionable and his attitude stank when it came to the rights of others. I chose not to go into business with him, seeing that as **immoral**, and it cost me a marriage, not being to be able to see my child because my ex-wife's father forbade her from seeing me. After my former wife had left me I was very heartbroken. I have since become Mormon, happily married with three beautiful little girls."*

➤Tricia from St. Louis added: *"I believe that the only reason that you should break a promise is if the promise is a **danger/risk** to the other person. I broke a promise of privacy involving my sister who is sixteen years old. I promised that I would never go into her room or involve myself in her business. Lately, she met a guy who is twenty-two years old, never received a diploma from high school, and doesn't have a job. A real winner, huh? She met him over the Internet in a chat room. When she would get on the Internet she would always get mad at me and my parents because we would always keep an eye on the stuff she was doing. To make a long story short, I opened a letter from this guy from Canada, and found out that she has been messing around with Satanism (we're Christian), tried to commit suicide, and was planning to run away this summer to see him. Plus, the letter was very pornographic. I could never forgive myself if I didn't open the letters, and someday they would find my sister dead. To me, it was worth the risk of breaking my word."*

►Becky from Nevada offered another exception: "*I feel a vow or promise should be broken when the promise is made to ones who are hurting themselves. Twelve years ago, I was twenty-three, I promised my best girlfriend of eighteen years, the maid of honor at my wedding, that I would not tell her parents she was using drugs. I did give her 800 help-line numbers, sent her rehab information, begged her to stop, let her stay with us to 'clean up,' but I did not tell her parents—a promise I made to her. Her mother found her hanging dead in her garage: suicide. A promise I wish I never kept!!! It's been twelve years and I still cry at times when I think of her.*"

►Paul from Ontario, California wrote: "*I suppose the obvious answer is to point to history: the German generals who (they would claim) did not realize how monstrously evil Hitler was when they took their personal oaths of loyalty to him. These men would have been morally justified in breaking these oaths—although few did. In fact, the Nuremberg Tribunal specifically rejected their appeals to the oath as a defense for their carrying out of orders that resulted in crimes against humanity.*"

The above represent some legitimate cases where breaking vows was acceptable. In each one of these situations there was a higher value involved, or there was an effort to counter an outright evil.

Biblical Punishments for the Third Commandment

". . . and anyone who blasphemes the name of God will be put to death" (Leviticus 24:16) and ". . . but anyone who blasphemes against the Holy Spirit will never be forgiven, but is guilty of an eternal sin. This was because they were saying, 'There is an unclean spirit in him'" (Mark 3:28–30). Clearly, religious traditions particularly highlight the absolute importance of this commandment. Cursing God; profaning God's name; misrepresenting God; pretending a special relationship to God for personal gain; using God's name to manipulate; invoking God's name while engaged in evil (remember the Crusaders raping and murdering with the sign of the cross embroidered on their chests and banners); making vows, oaths, or promises you don't really intend to honor—all these defy the Third Commandment.

The care that believers take not to misuse God's name is a sign of love. We take care not to curse at a spouse, parent, or child, because every time we do, it diminishes the status in which we hold that person. Likewise, every time we misuse the name of God we risk estranging ourselves further from God.

When we step on a flag of our sovereign country, we show disrespect to our country, its values, and potential. When we mistreat a Bible or any religious symbol, we offend God. Religious symbols like a *tallit*, a shawl worn by Jews during morning prayers, or a crucifix represent a love of God. To deface or abuse such objects in any way is an offense toward God.

If the First Commandment mandates the One and Only God's authority, and the Second rejects the authority of all other gods, the Third Commandment comes to teach us about the holiness of God, the sacred nature of our relationship with God, and our responsibilities to each other in His name.

4

The Fourth Commandment

"Remember the Sabbath day to sanctify it. Six days shall you work and accomplish all your work; but the seventh day is Sabbath to the Lord, your God; you shall not do any work—you, your son, your daughter, your servant, your animal, and the stranger within your gates—for in six days The Lord made the heavens and the earth, the sea and all that is in them, and He rested on the seventh day. Therefore, The Lord blessed the Sabbath day and sanctified it."

Gimme More Time

The following poem, author unknown, is a poignant reminder of the value of time:

To realize the value of ONE YEAR
Ask a student who has failed his final exam.

To realize the value of ONE MONTH
Ask a mother who has given birth to a premature baby.
To realize the value of ONE WEEK
Ask an editor of a weekly newspaper.
To realize the value of ONE DAY
Ask a daily wage laborer who has ten kids to feed.
To realize the value of ONE HOUR
Ask a couple waiting for the wedding ceremony.
To realize the value of ONE MINUTE
Ask a person who has missed the train.
To realize the value of ONE SECOND
Ask a person who has survived an accident.
To realize the value of ONE MILLISECOND
Ask the person who has won a silver medal in the
   Olympics.

How many times have you said, "I wish I had just a few more hours in the day"? The assumption is that, given more hours, you would accomplish everything you need to with less stress. But there is just as much chance that, given this wish, it would only mean two more hectic hours to live through in a given day. Perhaps we should actually be wishing for a shorter day, in which the crazy pace of our lives is limited to fewer hours.

As Renay, one of my listeners, wrote: *"I feel like my problem with time is that I have gotten into a bad habit of filling every minute of my time with something I think absolutely must be done and now I will not allow myself down time without feeling like I should be doing something. I am always exhausted from overworking myself that I am cranky and stressed out and I am not much fun to be with."*

Ironically, this manic White Rabbit (from *Alice in Wonderland*) behavior and attitude has become more and more an issue as modern technology has become a ubiquitous reality. Technology promised us modern conveniences that would make our lives easier, but in the workplace, computers, faxes, and cellular phones have increased the pace of work rather than diminished it. It is no longer possible to delay a deadline by saying that the proposal is in the mail, because they can ask for a fax to be sent immediately. Prior to cellular phones, driving in a car could be a time for music, catching up on the news, intimate discussions, or hearing a book on tape. Lunch in a restaurant could not be interrupted by the ringing of su- persmall cellular phones. Working hours have now been ex- tended by many people to include commuting time. In the home, washing machines, dishwashers, and microwave ovens have, in fact, made life easier. Yet it seems as if time follows the rule that nature abhors a vacuum, because whenever time is saved, it is spent somewhere else. Though people may be spending less time on housework, they are spending more time schlepping their children from one activity to another. Children are also overprogrammed, with fewer hours of free time for play or contemplative quiet time.

One can only deduce that we avoid free time because we don't value it as worthwhile. If we are not busy doing, we must not have important things to do. Indeed, time has also become a way of evaluating a person's professional worth. The term "9 to 5 job" often refers to tedious, basic employment. During the last century, first "downsizing," then "rightsizing," posited that fewer people could do the same amount of work. What wasn't emphasized was that the remaining people would be working harder as the price for keeping their jobs.

We have bought into the idea that the busier you are, the more important your life is. A recent book, *Time for Life* (Pennsylvania State University Press, 1997), surveyed ten thou- sand people and found that, after tracking their true working hours, they actually worked fewer hours than they thought. The survey found that people tend to overstate the number of hours they work because it elevates their professional status, which elevates their imagined self-worth.

Another report from the "Americans' Use of Time Project"

at the University of Maryland (*Los Angeles Times,* December 11, 1996) agreed that there was a big gap between perception and reality in time use. If that's so, then why does it feel as if there's not a minute to spare? The report concluded, "A culture that promotes instant gratification also helps to explain why life seems more hectic than it is. 'We want everything fast—fast food, eyeglasses in an hour, drive-through banking. Internally, we feel rushed. And the more rushed someone feels, the more they feel pressed for time.'"

We live in a society in which the expression "time is money," credited to Benjamin Franklin, has come to refer to the importance of time. The only problem with this expression is that money cannot buy more time and cheapens the value of time. We forget that money can be replaced, but time cannot. We would be far richer as individuals and as a society if we were to say that "time is priceless." Then we might treat it with more respect.

During a Saturday-morning sermon I recently attended, Rabbi Eli Schochet described a freeway billboard sign that was promoting the sale of a particular brand of watch. The catchy ad phrase was, "There's no present like the time." Certainly all of us feel the most moved by someone giving us some of their precious time rather than some precious object. Intuitively, we do know that time is the essence to fill well.

If time is so precious, what do we do with our nonproductive hours? Where does most of our free time go? You guessed it, television. On average, Americans squander fifteen of their forty hours per week of free time on television. Why do we do it? Because it is so easy to do. Turn on the TV, stop thinking, and time passes before you know it. How do children learn about time? Long before they know the meaning of an hour or half an hour, parents tell their children that they will have to wait for dinner "about as long as a Barney tape."

It usually takes a death, fear of terminal illness, or other severe tragedy for us to recognize how precious time is. If time is

precious, why don't we take more advantage of the time that
we have? Perhaps it is human nature to misuse time—especially in three basic ways: hedonistically, frivolously, or com-
pulsively. We either seek constant gratification, avoid
challenge, or avoid obligations, emotions, and realities too
frightening to face, generally by frenetic activity.

By and large, humans live in a "time paradox." We must
not focus on our mortality for fear that we will become obsessed with the notion every day could be our last. Aside from
the potential neurosis, it could lead to a hedonistic lifestyle of
immediate gratification. By not emphasizing the precarious
nature of time, we sometimes don't put the time into relationships or meaningful activities because we think that we will do
it "tomorrow." The time paradox leaves us with the dilemma
of how to recognize and remember the precious and finite nature of *our* individual time, without stimulating "mortality
anxiety," with its potential to cause people to lose hope.

There is an old story that one day Satan gathered his assis-
tants to discuss the most effective method of destroying the
meaning of people's lives.

One suggested, "Tell them there is no God."

Another said, "Tell them there are no consequences to their
actions."

A third proposed, "Tell them they have strayed so far from
the right path they will never be able to change."

"No," Satan replied, "such things will not matter to them. I
think we should simply tell them, 'There is plenty of time.'"

Obviously, Satan's notion is that if we're given "all the time
in the world," any imperative toward goodness, righteousness, depth, or meaningfulness would be removed. Time
surely is of the essence.

How do we overcome this time paradox? How can we accept our finite portion of infinity without fear? The Fourth
Commandment offers a day each week that teaches us about
sacred time—the Sabbath. The Sabbath is a taste of the holi-

ness of "the world to come." It is a day when we are commanded to cease involvement in worldly efforts and concerns.
It is a full day set aside to help you struggle with your petty,
inner demons—to reconcile their power against what is offered you in a spiritual relationship with God. Holiness is
timeless. To celebrate that beautiful truth every week is to help
you focus your life the other six days on the concepts of meaning, character, and spirituality. "But the Sabbath as experienced by man cannot survive in exile, a lonely stranger among
days of profanity. It needs the companionship of all other
days" (Abraham Heschel, *The Sabbath*, 1951, The Noonday
Press). This speaks to one of the typical criticisms by those
who, we think, just can't/won't give up the profane, the ordinary: that too many folks who pray on the Sabbath do ugliness all week long anyway. The Sabbath exists as a truth in
spite of the faltering of some of its participants; it just demonstrates that those who are not godly during the rest of the
week lose an opportunity to touch the divine.

In the Beginning

**"By the seventh day God completed His work which He had
done, and He abstained on the seventh day from all His work
which He had done. God blessed the seventh day and sanctified it . . ."** (Genesis 2:2–3). From the very beginning of time,
the seventh day is endowed with sanctity. The pinnacle of
God's creation, a day of sacredness built into the fabric of
Creation. Did God have to rest because he was tired? Hardly!
God does not exert energy in the way we do, which explains
why "ceased" or "abstained" is a better rendition than
"rested." When the Fourth Commandment tells us to refrain
from work, it is not necessarily the exertion of energy that defines work. Since God created through the spoken word, even
words can be considered work, as we will discuss later. The
Sabbath is so important that it is the only day given a name at

Creation. The week has six days, each numbered accordingly, but the seventh day is called the Sabbath, and it was only this day that God blessed: **"God blessed the seventh day and sanctified it . . ."** (Genesis 2:3). The creation of physical things ceased; by sanctifying a "day," spirituality was created on this, the seventh day.

The bridge between the sacred and the mundane or profane is us. Adam and Eve were created between all other things on earth and the Sabbath day. The Sabbath is ordained for spirituality, but only our actions can bring that potential to reality or not.

The first mention of Sabbath *observance* is anecdotal. From Adam to Joseph, there is no mention of observing the Sabbath until the Israelites are told in the wilderness not to gather the manna on the seventh day (Exodus 16:22–26). It was a day upon which God provided food for them. In Egypt, they had to work for their meager rations, and nourishment was given to them only so they could serve as slaves. The manna, a miracle itself, was to be collected in double portion on the sixth day so that no work for food would have to be done on the Sabbath. On all other days the manna would not survive the night, but the Sabbath was a day of miracles. The manna survived and nourished a people who could rest as God did at the completion of Creation. It is at Mount Sinai with the declaration **"You shall remember the Sabbath day and make it holy"** that the full potential of sacred time is realized and concretized in ritual.

Holy Time

Cinde, one of my listeners, wrote, *"I consider the Sabbath to be a monument to time."* This is an important revelation. Historically, things, people, and places were designated holy. This unique God proclaimed time as holy. What is the significance of that? Human beings can make things, human beings can designate themselves as special, human beings can fashion

markers to designate places as important, but only God created time, the ultimate divine gift. The Sabbath is a clear reminder of God, of God's presence and importance. A day
apart reminds us that the ultimate meaning in life is to be in
God's service. The essence of religion is not just to have an
emotional and mystical feeling about heaven and God but to
understand that there are expectations and obligations from
God to direct our lives toward goodness. This time on earth is
not just a queue to heaven. It has its own purpose—working
with God to perfect His world. The Sabbath day, spent with
community and family in study, prayer, discussion, and peace,
reminds us how we should regulate and perfect our spiritual,
intellectual, physical, domestic, and social behaviors. Observing the Sabbath reminds and instructs us to sanctify our lives,
the way God sanctified the Sabbath day. The commandments
don't limit our freedom; they give us distinct guidance toward
holiness and, therefore, meaningfulness for our lives.

While the Jewish tradition retains the celebration of the
Sabbath on the seventh day, Saturday, Christians commonly
refer to Sunday as the Sabbath. Both groups find the source of
their practice in their Scripture. For Jews, it is primarily based
on the commandment in the Decalogue, which, in the book of
Exodus, portrays the Sabbath as a commemoration of God's
redemptive acts as demonstrated in the Exodus from Egypt
(Exodus 20:8–11; Deuteronomy 5:12–15). For Christians, the
Lord's Day is rooted in the Resurrection of Jesus, which took
place on the first day of the week (Luke 24:1; John 20:1). The
two celebrations express different theologies but ultimately
circumscribe the same concept of holiness or sanctity.

While there may be theological differences that define the
specifics of observance, the Sabbath is revered by many Jews
and Christians as a day dedicated to God, a time in which our
relationship with God is intensified, a day of distinction in
which life changes from the mundane to the holy.

W. Scott Davis (LCDR, CHC, USN), a United Methodist

navy chaplain, writes: *"I preach that, in order to function best and glorify God to the fullest, one must set a day aside in every seven if one is to intentionally refocus his relationship with God, a task which is done to some degree every day, but is done with intentionality at least once in seven. Why seven? The Bible says so. To be able to do this in a congregational fellowship gives such an act much greater power because of the sharing and accountability of people who share a common belief."*

Particularly powerful is the chaplain's story of how he came to have a deep respect for the Sabbath traditions of other religions: *"When I was growing up in Chattanooga, Tennessee, each Christmas, Jewish members of the community would take all the shifts for the Christians at the area hospitals. I think this practice is done in many places now, but to a ten-year-old child it made a lasting impression. So much so that as an adult I often do the same thing in reverse for friends in the Jewish and Islamic faiths. We celebrate different Sabbaths, but some tasks have to get done in the community. Once, when I had to spend two Christmases away from my family, and not wanting to be alone, I went to the local airport where I was stationed and volunteered to work for baggage handlers who had families. The stipulations I gave the respective airlines were (1) the person for whom I am filling in must have a family; (2) they must still get paid for the day; and (3) they must never know who took their shift. The experience was one of worship each time."*

What is remarkable and important about this story is the chaplain's ultimate respect for the precious time of Sabbath, family, and, therefore, God. His behavior clearly underlines the "holiness" aspect of the appreciation of time. Isn't it so that we often say the greatest gift we can give is the gift of *"our time"*?

The observance of Sabbath ritual differs among various Jewish and Christian communities. For example, Pastor Dennis Gundersen, Grace Community Church of Tulsa-Baptist, wrote: *"We are persuaded that the Sabbath commandment was a ... foreshadow of a blessing He offers us through Christ—rest from seeking to be justified by works, and thus that there are no holy activities or behavior required by God for a specific day."* In contrast, Howard Culbertson, a minister from an Evangelical Protestant denomination with ties to the Methodist movement, wrote, *"We see it (the Sabbath) as a day of rest for body, mind and heart, a day to be consecrated to the Lord. Through the weekly participation in a sacred rest, we look forward to the final peace and happiness in heaven. For us, that special weekly day is for deepening a sense of God's presence. It is a looking forward to the 'day of the Lord' spoken of by the Hebrew prophets. For the devout in my tradition, Sunday is a day for strengthening the inner person, combining repose and elevation of the spirit."* And finally, this from Pastor Bill Miller from the Orthodox Presbyterian Church: *"The Sabbath or Lord's day is to be sanctified by a holy resting all the day, not only from such works as are at all times sinful, but even from such worldly employments and recreations as are on other days lawful; and making it our delight to spend the whole time (except so much of it as is to be taken up in works of necessity and mercy) in the public and private exercises of God's worship; and, to that end, we are to prepare our hearts, and with such foresight, diligence and moderation, to dispose and seasonably dispatch our world business, that we may be the more free and fit for the duties of that day."*

No religious tradition *forbids* observance of a day set aside from all the rest to engage in only those activities that demonstrate respect and love of God and appreciation for the blessings we've been afforded. Unfortunately, in a world of constant stimulation, opportunities, temptations, and distractions, it is all too easy to become habituated to those pursuits and to lose sight of what makes life important and meaningful: God and family.

Day of Rest

The Sabbath is one of the Bible's revolutionary innovations, according to Rabbi Joseph Telushkin (*Biblical Literacy*, Morrow, 1998). ". . . ancient societies tended to regard people as worthwhile only while they were working. Leading Roman thinkers ridiculed the Sabbath, citing it as proof of Jewish laziness. . . . In the ancient world, the Bible's struggle to establish that human beings have value even when not producing was a difficult one. . . . Over three thousand years ago, the Ten Commandments forbade treating animals in the manner that workers were permitted to be treated just a century ago (in the United States)."

Yet, the Sabbath is much more than a humane day off so that cattle and people did not die prematurely and lose their usefulness. There are a number of philosophical and spiritual implications of Sabbath recognition, appreciation, and observance, not the least of which has to do with not being enslaved but being free to pursue a godly life.

That is why the Sabbath was given to the Israelites immediately *after* the Exodus. To this group of ex-slaves the idea of a day of rest was not only enticing, it spoke to the essence of their being. For generations, they had toiled under the whips of the Egyptian taskmasters. Who would not be moved by a day of liberation in which all people could acknowledge the freedom granted by God? This is our freedom from servitude under human masters, the ultimate freedom of the human soul from oppression, toward its true purpose: to serve God.

As you conquer and create all week long, it is all too easy to get an inflated and self-centered idea of your own power. Egocentrism often takes us away from doing and being for others and God in a way that brings our life meaning and serves a greater purpose than our personal gratification and acquisition. Having to stop is not just about recovering from exhaustion from a hard week's work. Sabbath is about standing back and viewing our life, in the way an artist stands back from his canvas to get a more encompassing view of his work. This gives us the opportunity to contemplate the merits of our contribution to others and the world—it is about resetting our spiritual clock. The kind of Sabbath "rest" that is of value is that which reconnects you to your ultimate purpose in life.

The biblical goal of the Sabbath is to create a day of physical nonproductivity. Creation was a combined process of dividing that which was, and creating that which did not exist. The water was "divided" to create the firmament, while animal and human life are "made." For Jewish and Christian religious traditions, "a day of rest" implies resting from the things we do during the week to create a day of distinction. The physical and emotional energy that we expend during the week should be directed toward other endeavors in our attempt to distinguish between the holy and the profane. We believe that the Sabbath as a day of rest should be minimally observed by:

➤Not working for wages or competing for awards.

➤Making some time to relax and do nothing. (Although not specified in Scripture, a Sabbath nap is certainly a divine gift.)

➤Reading and studying religious materials.

➤Playing with children, spouse, and family.

➤Taking leisurely strolls.

➤Enjoying wonderful meals and discussions with friends and neighbors.

➤Talking with children about their everyday lives, thoughts, and feelings.

➤Attending religious services, lectures, and discussions.

➤Praying and contemplating.

➤Lovemaking with your spouse (reconnecting in mind, body, and spirit).

According to the Torah (the Five Books of Moses), God *created* the Sabbath. It is not just a day on which nothing happened, but God *blessed* it and *sanctified* it. It is intended as more than just a day of rest or fun. Within the day that represents one seventh of the week, we are to go beyond the focus of life that preoccupies our weekly existence and explore the greater issues of life. Pushing aside our perpetual concerns for physical survival, we turn to the bigger question of spiritual survival. By creating sacred time, we are motivated to explore these issues when we otherwise might not. A medieval sage proclaimed that the first six days of creation provided a world without a soul; the world was given a soul on the seventh day. The first six days of creation He considered *good*; the seventh He made *holy*.

Although there could be argument that a Sabbath isn't required, that each day can readily be marked with godliness in our thoughts, words, and deeds, the truth is that in working under stresses and strains, anxieties and deadlines, obligations and errands, and responsibilities, we too readily become separated from our *spiritual center*. By virtue of how much we struggle against the concept of Sabbath and our resistance to giving up "worldly pleasures, conquests, and acquisition," it becomes more and more clear that we all too naturally cling to the familiar, gratifyingly concrete and sacrifice the spiritual.

Some people try to rationalize that a Sabbath spent golfing, shopping, or going to the beach is fulfilling the spirit of the Sabbath. Golfers, in particular, plead their case by saying that they do more real praying on the golf course than in church or synagogue. However, "Please God, give me a birdie," is not recognized as part of any accepted liturgy, nor does it substitute for a good Sabbath service.

Time Flies Whether or Not You're Having Fun

The longer you live, the faster time seems to go by. Remember those school days when a day was an eternity? We would count down the minutes until the end of class. Summers were huge blocks of time that separated us from the mature status of the next grade. Only later, when the days are not long enough to accommodate all that we need to do, does time fly by so quickly. Days roll into weeks, into months, and before you know it we are a year older. During our school days, we yearned to be older, waiting as those birthdays crept up to us so slowly. Now, it seems that with the blink of an eye another year passes. If life is like a downhill bike ride in which speed increases and becomes increasingly difficult to stop, the Sabbaths are regularly scheduled stop signs that bring us to a halt, making time pass a little bit slower so that we might appreciate it more.

I remember all too painfully my struggle with Sabbath observance. The first several Saturdays I just stayed in bed, depressed and upset. I couldn't imagine what I would do with the whole day if I didn't work on my writing, go shopping, watch our son do some competitive sport, turn on some television, etc. I realized that our lives were very focused on "doing stuff." We were always together as a family for each meal. From the time Deryk came home from school till bedtime was already only family time. We didn't feel any lack of family togetherness. What we were lacking was a spiritual focus. Slowly, I weaned myself away from worldly frenetic activities to attend services, to read Torah and other religious writings, to pray and to contemplate and to relax (another task with which I had little experience). Given my nature to be diligently productive, it was a struggle to give up the sense of being busy, in control, and in charge. I discovered the blessing of turning it all back over to God and godly pursuits in a more pious sense. At first, I discovered the joy of being able to stop working, and because it was commanded by God, I didn't have guilt about some downtime. That was psychologically liberating for me (there's that freedom-from-slavery concept again). Next was the long road toward a deepening spirituality—with the time set aside solely for that endeavor. I'm still learning, and I'm not nearly good enough at it. I still struggle with letting go of workweek frustrations, annoyances, and the like, but observing the Sabbath has changed me from being a gerbil on an exercise wheel to a human being *aspiring* to "walk in God's ways."

A Time of Re-creation

The Sabbath is a day of *re*-creation. The Sabbath is the time to re-create ourselves. By re-creating the seventh day of Creation, we return to our humble beginnings; **from dust were we created.** By refilling ourselves with God's breath that brought Adam to life (Genesis 2:7), we are born again each week, appreciating the newness of each day with its opportunities to grow in meaningful ways.

The Jewish focus on celebrating Creation is important because of its universal message. God created all things and all people. Adam was not Jewish. Abraham and Sarah are recognized as the first Jews. A Jewish tradition states that God made Adam as the father of all humanity so that no one could say, "My daddy is better than yours." We are all the children of God and share our unity through the experience of Creation.

"And God saw all that he had made and behold it was very good" (Genesis 1:31). With these words Creation is completed. At the conclusion of all other days God says of the world "it was good," but with the addition of humanity it becomes "very good." Each Sabbath we are reminded of our potential for doing good. It is our re-creation each Sabbath that helps us acknowledge our role in bringing goodness to the world. We are the bridge between the worldly and the divine.

Time Out!

The goal of refraining from work is not just a physical concern. So many professionals come home from their job only to *think* and *talk* about their work. The Sabbath is the time to break ourselves free from the chains that enslave us to our work. In our role as counselors, we continually hear the complaint from couples that spouses come home and talk about what happened in the office. While it is important to share what happened during the day, sometimes office talk can be an indication of a self-centeredness or a substitute for other meaningful discussion in the home. The Sabbath is the time for taking "a time-out" from that which consumes us during the week.

A good rule for the Sabbath is to avoid any discussion of people's jobs. It is neither a time to "network" nor a time to prepare for the work of the week. The Sabbath is the *time to find meaning in the moment.*

Perhaps you recognize yourself as one of those who constantly has a camera or video in hand, busily creating a permanent record to be enjoyed at a later moment. By looking through the lens of the camera, we do not experience the reality of life, but only its one-dimensional image. We become observers, no longer participants. So busy are we preserving the moment, sometimes we do not live it fully. Observing a Sabbath gives you the opportunity to be in the moment, appreciate the deeper truth of existence, and enjoy the taste of eternity in every morsel of this holy day.

Have you ever watched a play or movie only to be so preoccupied with other thoughts that you could not enjoy it? Have you not been able to make love to your spouse because your mind is consumed with worry and work? Have you pushed aside the insistent attempts of your children to talk because your mind is jammed with last-minute details? Have you not had the time to take care of your body and health because you are overwhelmed with scheduling conflicts? The Sabbath is the time for putting all mundane actions and thoughts aside so that we can live and appreciate the moment. The Sabbath experience is the great liberator from your fears of worthlessness without frenetic productivity. The Sabbath is *spirit* in the form of *time* (Heschel).

Quality versus Quantity Time

One response to the imagined and unnecessarily orchestrated time crisis of which so many folks complain has been the invention of *quality time*. Quality time suggests that any designated small amount of time with someone else, usually our children, can be made special simply by saying it's so or by concentrating attention. Spouses, parents, and friends can all claim that they may not spend enough time with the other person, but the lack in *quantity* of time is made up in the *quality* of time. Although quality time can be a positive concept—namely, that we should strive to bring as much quality time into our lives as possible—it is problematic because there is a relationship between quality time and quantity time.

The Sabbath challenges the concept of quality time. Based on long discussions with me, Rabbi Vogel asked his nine-year-old daughter whether she would rather have him home for one hour (quality time) in which he was undistracted by work and completely at her disposal *or* for three hours (quantity time) in which he was in his study, able to hear her play piano and available for small disruptions. To his surprise (and my vindication) she chose the three hours! She told him that she loves having him at home even if he is not completely hers. She instinctively knew that it is very hard to make quality moments. Quality time doesn't happen when you want it, simply because people are not always ready for it. It is in the quantity time of a whole Sabbath spent together that the most quality minutes will accumulate. Quality time requires quantity time the same way soup ingredients require broth.

This idea is supported by Mary, one of my listeners: *"I've heard you say that you don't like when people say they're so busy, but they spend 'quality time' with their children. I am my kids' mom, and I do spend quality time with my kids. However, it always comes when we least expect it. It usually happens spontaneously (like a ticklefest before story time) and almost never happens during some 20 minutes that we've set aside for 'quality time.' I guess what I'm saying is that I do believe there is such a thing as quality time, but it can't be forced or planned. We do have wonderful times on our planned excursions and activities, but it seems like most of our most memorable quality time happens when we least expect it."*

The concept of quality time has been the rationalization of those who want to justify the more self-centered and sometimes irresponsible choices made that cause someone else, usually family, to sacrifice for the sake of the chooser's ego, status, power, and wealth. I remember the blurb that appeared in just about every magazine aimed at working women/mothers (1997): A New York child psychiatrist—"childish" psychiatrist would have been more appropriate—proclaimed that approximately fifteen minutes a day of attention and dialogue between parent and child is sufficient! Wow! I wondered how many women would have accepted that argument from their husbands or boyfriends! Hypocrisy? You bet. Politically correct statement of a professional who wishes to follow rather than lead? You bet.

Talk to Me!

Whether it is a hard day at the office or a tough day with the kids, by the time evening arrives, husbands and wives usually want and need a little quiet time. It is so easy to turn on the television and become a couch potato. Dinners and evenings pass quickly with the distraction of television. Before you know it, it is time for bed. All too typically, very little genuine dialogue takes place. It is no wonder that couples complain they do not communicate anymore. Communication requires dialogue, and true dialogue requires concentrated attention. No one can have a meaningful discussion in front of the television. Personal stereos and video games, computers, and other technological toys, which can be taken anywhere and, through the miracle of headphones, can shut out the rest of the world, have decreased the amount of time we spend communicating with the most important people in our lives. The Sabbath is an opportunity to take a break from those activities that discourage connection and be involved in activities that encourage sharing and communing.

Interestingly, a whole new category of adultery has been created in cyberspace. I have received hundreds of faxes and dozens of on-air calls in this last year from folks who have lost the attention and affection of their spouses to a cyber-honey. Somehow, folks will find the time to type tripe to unknown "lovers" but won't give the gift of thoughtful attention to their real committed partners. It would seem that many people prefer fantasy to a deeper spiritual connection. In their fantasy world, it's all the way they want it—should that waver, just hit DELETE. Relationships are challenging because they require sensitivity, tolerance, and sacrifice. In a workaday, rat-race, self-fulfillment–centered world, that requires a stretch. The Sabbath is the weekly lesson plan for you learning to give yourself over to something greater than that.

Have You Hugged Your Kids Lately?

The Sabbath provides the opportunity for creating quality moments, as all that time is devoted only to family, community, and God. Without the parents working or the children doing homework, without the distractions of television or running to extracurricular activities, Shabbat is about a family spending a whole day together and sharing the most important aspects of family life.

We are not justifying Sabbath observance on the basis of its obvious psychological and interpersonal benefits—which, as we continue to describe, are numerous and profound. Sabbath observance, for the Jew, is a divine commandment. Modern mentality seems to require some specific motivation or benefit for the participant before an activity is to be considered or valued. In other words, if "what's in it for me?" is not answered to our satisfaction, we just won't do it! We realize that holiness doesn't seem too practical or immediately gratifying, therefore, not as seductive as buying a lottery ticket. What we are pointing out is that holiness, those things done for God, also gives us tremendous emotional and spiritual benefits.

Almost every parent has asked a child what he did at school or during the day and received the very explicit answer, "Nothing."

"What did you learn?"

"Nothing."

Question after question, all the parent gets is "Nothing." On the Sabbath, when ideally all meals are shared as a family, with all the time in the world, parents have the opportunity to get into a new routine of really talking to and, maybe even more important, listening to their children. The Sabbath routine affords the opportunity to establish communications that may sadly be unparalleled during the week. The practice and focus of Sabbath family time gives you the opportunity to make communications and bonding an everyday event.

Imagine a day in which family members know they are the most important part of each other's lives, because they give each other time. Sadly, there are just too many parents so self-focused that squeezing time out to pay attention to children and family seems an imposition. This is what Amy Weisberg, a second-grade teacher in Los Angeles, wrote about in the *Los Angeles Times* (December 1996) when she described the behaviors of most parents at a school holiday singing performance: "The parents were engrossed and listening with full attention—until their own children finished singing. Despite multiple pleas from the principal, parents got up and left. . . . How can parents proclaim to put their children first, yet be unwilling to take two hours to watch the entire holiday program? Many parents used their cell phones during the performance."

When our children see that we give so little of our time and attention to them, that we focus most of our energy and effort on our "work"—what do they think is most important in life and to us? How will they learn about commitment to people over things and success? The time we apportion to things is our declaration of their importance in general as well as to us. I get calls from too many folks with adult children who have no time for them. Remember the song "Cat's Cradle"? When the boy became a man, and the father wanted his attention and time, he had as little for his father as his father had had for him. And so it goes.

Kids See—Kids Do

Most parents want their kids to believe in God and be religious, ignoring that a godly life requires more than speech; it requires commitment, sacrifice, and time. As one Mormon listener of mine wrote: *"The key is, how we as parents view spiritual things will be how our children will. We hold the Sabbath sacred. The principle here is to set aside time (at least) weekly solely for the purpose of fulfilling our spiritual obligations to our Creator. We meet two evenings a week for formal worship/Bible education of some sort. These are spent as a family attending our meetings to worship and learn by listening with Bible in hand to reference Scriptures quoted. On all occasions we dress respectfully, knowing we are in the presence of the greatest Being in the Universe. By having this a part of our weekly routine there was little argument when it was time to go. If worship is educational and up-building, then going to church/synagogue/meeting is a pleasure. The benefits are obvious even to the younger ones."*

As evidence that these "habits" have long-term impact, here is a letter from Pam: *"As the parents of five growing (and grown) children keeping the Sabbath as a special day has always been a great challenge. With active children and limited time on the weekends, many sporting events try to infringe on our time together. We have worked very hard to impress upon our children the importance of worshipping together, as a family, and spending our Sabbath together. The fruits of our labors are paying off. Our children, even when away at college, worship regularly and we speak with them each Sunday to keep them in the family loop. As for those who are home and have come back home now that college is completed, we still worship together and enjoy taking Sunday as a day just to enjoy one another."*

Patience Is a Virtue

The Jewish expression of the Sabbath provides a return to simpler times. It is hard to remember how the world functioned without computers or other technology. Elaborate receipts have replaced simple handwritten ones, although most of the time, purchasing an item takes longer than it used to. Faxes, computer e-mail, pagers, and cellular phones have created a world of immediate need. "I need it yesterday," which is possible if you fax something from Europe to the United States, and "I need to speak to her *now!*" have become more common.

The virtue of patience is tested every time a new product can do something faster. Businesses are more aware of the fact that we want things faster. Televisions in waiting rooms and special previews on monitors for those waiting in line for amusement park attractions help time to pass more quickly. Ultimately, the notion of just plain quiet time to contemplate has been lost in the hysteria for stimulation and input.

The Sabbath is a return to the virtue of patience, a day on which we should not demand things immediately. The Sabbath is a good day to stay away from the technological marvels that bring things to us in an instant. In breaking free from our reliance on machines, we elevate the importance of the *human* factor in life.

Respect for Labor

The appreciation of a nonproductive day is predicated on a week of labor: **"Six days you shall labor and do all your work . . ."** (Exodus 20:9). During the week we emulate the creative side of God. The creativity of being productive workers makes us feel good. After a hard day, even the ditchdigger can say, "I did something today." The television show *Married with Children* can belittle shoe salesmen, but in truth each profession has the potential for being a sacred job. Aside from the opportunity to express divine productivity, values are demonstrated and tested in the workplace. Whether a shoe salesman or a lawyer, by adhering to the highest values of honesty and integrity a person can make any kind of work sacred. How often has a grumpy receptionist, dishonest workman, or rude waitress ruined your day? Simple civility, honesty, and cheerfulness demonstrated by professionals can bring goodness into the world.

The news is full of stories of dishonest employees who cheat employers and abuse customers. Their feelings (and we know how objective, rational, and reasonable all our feelings are) are that companies are so rich anyway and that customers are demanding—both deserve what they get. People further rationalize or justify their behavior by saying they deserve more. This self-proclaimed entitlement is based upon anger, greed, frustration, and laziness—obviously a bad attitude. Their mentality pretends to turn the crime of stealing and bad behaviors into righteous acts. Those workers who behave ethically, honestly, and with common decency bring godliness to secular work.

All people need to return to the work ethic that once existed in our country, when individuals and companies were interested in providing quality products and service. Six days of Creation, filled with workmanship that God was proud of ("... **and God saw that it was good** ... ") should serve as a model for our workweek efforts. The Sabbath is the culmination of a productive week, in which the nonproductivity can be appreciated only when it is preceded by creativity.

Respect for the Labor of Others

"Remember the Sabbath day ... you shall do no manner of work ... nor your servant ... nor your animal, nor the alien living with you." Everyone deserves a day of rest, even the servant. We live in a society that tends to devalue certain types of laborers. From fast-food employees to lawyers, jokes abound for certain types of professions. If self-worth is judged at least in some part by one's profession, then we should respect all types of labor. Anyone willing to work, at whatever type of job, leads the kind of productive life that God wanted us to have.

I get so many calls on my radio program, mostly from men, who imagine, in this materialistic culture, that money and property are enough to make one a true parent or spouse. "But," they stammer, "without us both working/without me taking this job that will have me travel away from home constantly/without this schedule of meetings, I won't be able to provide all the luxuries and stuff kids want."

First of all, kids are naturally indiscriminate and perpetual consumers. If all we do is cater to their whims and desires, we educate them to be takers, not givers, consumers, not creators. When we are working for their futures, we are being too shortsighted and superficial in seeing their futures only in physical terms. We need to be there to nourish their minds and spirits; we need to be there to direct and guide their ethics and values; we need to be there to love and hold them; we need to be there simply because they need us.

There is nothing wrong at all in amassing external goods and goodies, except when the pursuit of these riches replaces becoming richer in spirit, conscience, love, connectedness to family and friends, and a strong moral sense, and when none of these goods and goodies are used compassionately to benefit those in true need.

Community *Spirit*

Most religious faiths gather for communal prayers on the Sabbath, focusing on the importance of community in the social and spiritual life of people. Through this shared communal experience, the values of the community are taught and reinforced.

Many people who consider themselves religious feel they can be religious and/or feel God's presence without going to communal worship services. It is absolutely true that private times of prayer, study, and contemplation are significant and essential vehicles of spirituality. Although solitary worship does have its place, it should not exclude the importance of communal religious experiences, which remind us that, as important as it is to feel God's presence in our lives, making God's presence felt in the world is even more so.

It is far easier to be a solitary person than it is to be part of a group that reminds us of our responsibility to function within our values as a group member. As soon as you regard yourself as part of a community, all egotism, which knows only itself, is banished. When functioning within a group, you are reminded of your need for concern and action for the welfare of others. Without that attention, your spirituality becomes a dead end in itself rather than a motivator for bringing and doing good for the world.

When God saw that Adam was lonely, he created Eve. Even with the majesty of a new world, Adam needed someone else to share the wholeness of Creation. The Sabbath, as a re-creation of Creation, is more fully experienced with other people.

In the Jewish tradition, certain prayers, as well as the public reading of the Torah, are not permitted without a prayer quorum of ten people, which is called a *minyan*. The basis for requiring a minimum community for certain prayers comes from Leviticus 22:32: "... that I may be sanctified in the midst of the Israelite people, ..." suggesting that the sanctification of God's name is a public obligation. This concept clearly leads to the potential for developing strong interpersonal relationships and social ideals, a community obligated to mutual aid and aware of a responsibility to its own members and to all humanity. Community worship is an antidote to self-centeredness.

John Calvin, upon whose teachings John Knox established Presbyterianism, believed that the ideal Sabbath prayer was not personal but rather communal, because such prayer required a public confession of faith. So, for both faith communities, the Sabbath achieves fulfillment through community. Communal Sabbath prayer also offers an antidote for the ailment of loneliness.

Nature Doesn't Rule

The Sabbath is a time when we step back to admire nature rather than figuring out how to change it. The truth is we live in a world that tends to make nature worse than better, and the Sabbath is the reminder that our divine directive is to realize our interdependence with nature and to respect it.

Primitive cultures actually worshipped nature directly. This, of course, was man's attempt to control nature: earthquakes, floods, hurricanes, droughts, tornadoes, and such would cause much destruction and suffering. Assigning gods to these forces and attempting to appease or cajole them into doing man's bidding was man's effort to pretend knowledge and power in the midst of great ignorance and impotence in the face of nature. Even our biblical ancestors believed that human behavior was a causal factor in explaining major natural events. **"It will be that if you hearken to My commandments that I command you today, to love The Lord, your God, and to serve Him with all your heart and with all your soul, then I shall provide rain for your Land in its proper time . . ."** (Deuteronomy 11:13–14). Indeed, many contemporary fundamental religionists cry "Retribution!" when the elements of nature cause destruction.

Ultimately, this is about man's yearning to find a relationship between behavior and survival. Think about the times you have felt so helpless, vulnerable, and not in control, when events around you, be they from man or nature, became threatening. You were frightened, angry, and desperate. Ancient man turned to gods to intercede against the imagined gods who caused their misery.

While it may be tempting to think this God is merely the great ringmaster of all gods (pray and/or promise and He will do your bidding), it is wiser to look at a deeper, more philosophical level. What this God was telling us is that your behavior matters in a spiritual sense, even if you don't receive a specific, immediate reward or relief. (Do you really want to be a chicken pecking a button to receive a kernel of corn?)

Perhaps a more reasonable perspective than simple divine one-for-one retribution would be to appreciate that God created the universe and the physical forces like wind, moving earth plates, and tides, to name a few. Instead of blaming God for the pain and loss after an earthquake, perhaps we might think not to live on a fault line or build vulnerable dwellings once our technology has shown us the error of *our* ways. Certainly, even if God were coordinating certain natural events, it is in our response to these physical realities that we can show good sense and conscience—or not. For example, sometimes it's hard to understand folks building homes in the fire-prone Malibu hills or right on Malibu beaches. Certainly, we can't call the loss of these homes an act of God when we play the numbers.

We don't have to run, hide, avoid, or give up. We can use our God-given ingenuity to build dams, fire- and water-restraining areas, and so on. We can try to control ourselves by respecting the fact that God, while giving us dominion over nature, expects us to nurture, not deplete or destroy, nature for our shortsighted gains.

Respect for Human Freedom and Equality

The Sabbath, as a time of Creation, Exodus, and redemption, is a reminder that equality and freedom are part of the divine plan. Although the Bible recognizes the reality of slavery, it does not do so in the usual universal perspective of slavery, especially that found in the beginnings of the United States of America. The Hebrew Bible, with its strict, protective laws about servants (slaves), is the first document to give rights and privileges to those slaves; a fact that many theologians believe was to set in place slavery's ultimate abolishment. The relevance of this conclusion seems obvious from such passages as, **"If a man shall strike the eye of his slave or the eye of his maidservant and destroy it, he shall set him free in return for his eye. And if he knocks out the tooth of his slave or the tooth of his maidservant, he shall set him free in return for his tooth"** (Exodus 21:26–27). The significance here is that the master is not permitted to do his "slave" ill—and that any harm caused that slave will naturally result in the slave's freedom.

In fact, Leviticus 25:10 describes God's plan for the Israelites' ultimate actions once they arrived in their Promised Land: **"You shall sanctify the fiftieth year and proclaim free-**

dom throughout the land for all its inhabitants. . . ." This latter well-known passage from the Hebrew Holy Scriptures is what is carved on America's Liberty Bell.

Judaism has always rejected all the caste and race ideologies of the ancient world that discriminated against people. The notion of "chosen people" does not refer to a belief of superiority, perfection, or divinity. The phrase refers only to the acceptance of the responsibility to serve God as a "nation of priests" and a "light unto the nations," as the people by whose actions God's character was demonstrated on earth. Any notion of implied moral perfection is readily dispelled once one reads the admonishments and frustrations of the Prophets to appreciate how human the chosen people were, and how they required reminding. The almost universally hostile reaction to the Hebrews' presentation of God and God's ideals to the ancient and developing worlds certainly made the title of "chosen" seem a mixed blessing. Though it may seem amazing that principles of love, goodness, obligation, responsibility, ethics, and so forth could be met with such resistance, you must remember that, to this God, all people were His children, which broke down the notions of race, caste, king-gods, and entitlements to which so many cultures adhered.

Judaism was essentially a democratic faith, a people's religion. "Hitler, whose hatred of freedom and democracy was surpassed only by his hatred of the Jews, somewhere stated: 'Democracy is fundamentally Jewish, not Germanic'" (Abba Hillel Silver, *Where Judaism Differs*, Collier Books, 1956).

The Sabbath as a commandment was given by God to the Israelites as a reminder of God's freeing them from slavery—as a reminder of God and the sanctity of human freedom.

A Day of Prayer and Study

The Sabbath provides a day of unrushed activity in which individuals cannot say "I don't have time for prayer and study because I have something else to do." Prayer and even study are ways of experiencing God, but people make excuses, especially about why they do not attend services. Some people complain that services are not exciting enough. For some people, no matter how good it gets, it will never be good enough to come on a regular basis. The reasons offered for not attending services are just excuses. Like many other areas of life, the excuses are often a cover-up for laziness and indifference.

Immediately after my initial infatuation phase, I found the routine of going to services on the Sabbath difficult. Instead of feeling uplifted, I felt constrained and imposed upon. I would watch the clock, praying more for lunchtime than for enlightenment. I realized I was resisting on a number of levels because it was hard for me to

1. give up thinking, worrying, planning, and doing worldly, mundane things from work to entertainment to problems.

2. give up petty thoughts, angers, and annoyances.

3. focus only on spiritual ideas, thoughts, and feelings (because of 1 and 2).

4. accept giving myself over to piety, paying attention to God and godliness (I'm an in-control kind of woman).

5. sit still.

6. give up the activities I've become accustomed to (like big breakfasts, reading a bunch of newspapers, outlining and cutting out articles of interest for future reference).

However, especially when Rabbi Vogel instituted a postservice buffet lunch (kiddush) wherein we could sit around munching and argue about the day's Bible portion or the rabbi's sermon (sorry, R.V.), I began to feel a new routine coming into focus, with its own special qualities and benefits.

Additionally, I recognize that without the discipline of services and study, I would not be demonstrating for my son the kind of respect for spirituality that I hope he will always treasure.

The Sabbath should be a special time to study. God endowed humans with intelligence. When we don't engage in study, we deny this component of our divine essence. In addition, parents need to serve as role models for their children to demonstrate that learning is not just a childhood affliction that will be cured with graduation. It is especially appropriate to study the Bible and other religious books.

I Am Not God

For one day a week, the Sabbath is a reminder that we are dispensable to work and the world, but *not* to our families, community, and God. We begin to think that we are godlike and must remind ourselves of our true significance.

The experience of the Sabbath is supposed to influence our beliefs and behaviors when we go back to work. The Sabbath is a reminder to take ourselves seriously, but not so seriously that we think we are God. In a world where we judge people for what they have done, we should learn from the Sabbath to judge them for who they are.

We think of ourselves as being omnipotent during the week. Through our creative abilities, we emulate God. Once a week we must redefine our essence. We spend the week trying to understand the mysteries of the universe through science. We perform new engineering feats, we open the mysteries of the atom, and we search the heavens and the earth for signs of life. On the Sabbath we search for the essence of God. Shabbat is the antidote to the tendency toward self-idolatry. On this day, we are reminded that God is God.

During the week we are often too busy to consider issues of God and life. We get caught up in doing and only thinking of things that we have to do. On the Sabbath, sitting in worship services or around a leisurely meal, when no one is running off to an activity, we experience significant moments of thinking about God and talking with family.

For Rabbi Vogel, services are a wonderful time for him to leave his rational weekday mind-set to explore unlimited possibilities of what God means to him. Rather than just accepting dogma, he considers thoughts on such issues as the soul and afterlife and asks such questions as, "If God blesses my life, is He also responsible for the bad things?" In the special sanctity and serenity of Sabbath services, he always feels closer to God.

Like the stars that are difficult to see at night in a city where there are too many lights, but can be seen in all their magnificence in the countryside, we spiritually leave the boisterous life of the city on the Sabbath for the serenity of the countryside (synagogue), where we are more likely to experience the presence of God.

Appreciating Life

Judaism and Christianity have prayers to acknowledge our appreciation simply for being alive. At night, many Christian children recite the prayer: "Now I lay me down to sleep / I pray the Lord my soul to keep / If I should die before I wake / I pray the Lord my soul to take." A parallel Jewish prayer recited upon waking up in the morning is: "I thank you God, Ruler of the Universe, that you have returned my soul to me with compassion; great is your faithfulness." Both prayers acknowledge the gift of life and demonstrate an appreciation for the significance of each day.

The sixth day of Creation was a busy one. The first Sabbath was the first *full* day of life for Adam and Eve. It marked the first time they went to sleep and woke up with the discovery, unlike the mayfly, which lives but a day, of a tomorrow. They discovered that life went on! Every Sabbath, like the first one, we should awaken with a deep appreciation of what it means to wake up and live another day.

The Ideal Day

If the Sabbath is a this-world taste of the next world, then it is a time to demonstrate our highest values. Though it is difficult to *always* act virtuously, by removing many of the forces that cause us to respond with anger, resentment, pettiness, and other base attitudes, we acknowledge the potential of ourselves on the Sabbath. We learn that we can control these baser responses and become better people.

The Sabbath is also the perfect day to overcome our vices. Whether it is smoking, drunkenness, or gambling, the Sabbath offers us the opportunity to demonstrate that we have the ability to control our desires.

Aside from refraining from our less-than-admirable actions, the Sabbath also provides an opportunity to achieve further holiness in the way we talk to and act toward people. By engaging in holy talk, discussions about God, improving the world, and speaking kindly about others, we can increase the sanctity of the day.

The goal is not only to live these values once a week but to bring them into our everyday lives. Each time we live a day dedicated to holiness, we have the opportunity to bring some residual effect into our daily lives. There is no question that the observance of the Sabbath has enriched our lives. It is our goal to bring the dream of the Sabbath to the reality of each day.

The Sabbath is *not* about time off; it is about sacred time. "What is so luminous about a day? What is so precious to captivate the hearts? It is because the seventh day is a mine where spirit's precious metal can be found with which to construct the palace in time, a dimension in which the human is at home with the divine; a dimension in which man aspires to approach the likeness of the divine" (Abraham Joshua Heschel, *The Sabbath,* The Noonday Press, 1951).

5

The Fifth Commandment

"Honor your father and your mother, so that
your days will be lengthened upon the land that
the Lord, your God, gives you."

Don't "Dis" Me

Every generation complains that the youth of their generation
are disrespectful. The serious concerns of classroom teachers
in previous generations involved gum chewing, talking, and
ditching; they now worry about guns, knives, mass shootings,
and drugs. Although previous generations have had their rebellious kids, the nineties represent a time in which "dissing,"
or disrespect, has become a national pastime.

Beavis and Butt-head, South Park, and the sexually active
teens of such shows as *Dawson's Creek* have become the
media models for the youth of today, a far cry from the Beaver
from the television series *Leave It to Beaver,* who was always
respectful and usually had his heart in the right place, al-

though he often got into innocent kinds of trouble by today's standards.

Parents tend to blame the children and society. The children blame their parents and society. Society tries to blame itself, while not assuming any personal responsibility, or genetics, or television, or movies, or music. Frankly, they are interconnected.

Whose Fault Is It?

It is easy for parents to point the finger at society, because it removes any responsibility on their part. This is not to say that external influences are irrelevant. I cannot count the number of parents who have written and called, frustrated that the values and rules they were attempting to teach their children were undermined by the general lack of societal conformity and respect for their efforts. For example, many a parent has expressed feeling "stupid" or "impotent" for forbidding teenage party drinking in their home, teenage coed sleepovers, unsupervised overnights at hotels after proms, dating at thirteen to fifteen years of age, overnights at theirs or the home of the girl/boyfriend of their child, and more. These parents are amazed that there is no longer a consensus on what is right, permissible, healthy, appropriate, or moral.

Television shows depicting immoral sexual behavior between adults, between children, and between adults and children, without judgment, are now common fare in situation comedies and teen-oriented melodramas (*Friends, Dawson's Creek,* and even *Buffy the Vampire Slayer*). I'm amazed that TV and movie producers and distributors deny the influential, seductive impact of such media fare. If millions of dollars are spent on thirty-second commercials geared to influence us to buy a particular product, how can anyone say with a straight face that hours of programming and commercials geared specifically to teens don't have an influence? Of course, a TV can be turned off, but it is basic human nature for children, identifying with their peers, to be drawn toward what is considered cool, what provides an easily attainable sense of importance—which is so difficult a struggle through adolescence.

Yes, society matters. And parents are a part of that society—not only the parents of any one child, but what all children see all parents doing. Most often parents are not aware of the models they set for their children. Parents hear their young child say "damn" or other even worse expressions and wonder where he or she learned such language, only to realize that the child learned it from them. And that's the mildest part of it! In the span of about a quarter century on the radio and talking to people all over North America, I have been struck by the changes, the virtual epidemic of parental bad behaviors: divorce, affairs, multiple shack-ups, women having several children with as many different, generally uninvolved men, drinking, drugs, neglect, and abuse. Nothing much here to revere or respect. I still can't believe a call from a single mother of a ten-year-old daughter, shacking up with a guy who had a twenty-year-old daughter, whose question for me had to do with her annoyance at the apparently promiscuous lifestyle of the twenty-year-old. It was a stunner that she couldn't see the parallel!

But I'm a Busy Parent

"And you shall teach them thoroughly to your children" (Deuteronomy 6:7) is the Biblical instruction for parents to teach the commandments to their children, including those focusing on morality and ethics. Many parents are too busy to parent at all, so they settle for being a buddy to their child. They forget their responsibility to teach them. In Hebrew, the word *horim*, "parents," is related to the word *moreh*, "teacher." Parents are teachers of faith and morality. What

God is to the world, parents are to their children. Unfortunately, some parents become so focused on the element of friendship or their own convenience, comfort, self-fulfillment, happiness, or love life that they forget their job is to help mold moral character so their children will have the strength to do what is right in a world that sometimes encourages them to do otherwise. They blame the schools, but schools can only reinforce the values that are taught in the home. If there is no modeling of ethical behavior at home, there is nothing for the school to reinforce.

Kim, a schoolteacher, emphasized this issue in an e-mail to me: "*I just had a parent of one of my fifth-grade students ask me if we teach obeying/respecting their parents. I replied that I try very hard to help students see the way they should listen, obey and respect their parents, but in my ten years of teaching, I feel that children's respect for parents has only decreased. I try to explain it like I explain my teaching: I work hard to decide what is best, and every lesson or activity I do has an end result that should help them become a better student and person. But many times they don't listen to me either. I wonder if when they are disrespectful, their parents and even their teacher, me, don't make it uncomfortable enough or enough of a big deal. My husband and I are working hard to firmly discipline disrespect from our two children, even though they are toddlers. If they say 'no' or are sassy, privileges like TV or toys are removed and they are themselves removed for a 'time-out.' I also work hard to model honoring my mother and father by letting my children and even my students see me reflect and write thank you notes for when my parents do nice things. I fear that many of my students are not 'fearful' of disapproval or disappointment from parents as I was as a child.*"

She's right. As William wrote to me: "*Our culture seems bent on teaching us to dishonor and hold our parents in contempt. TV and movies are full of examples of kids being smarter than parents and of stupid, pitiful old people. It is easy to fall for this unholiness."*

Without respect, awe, and even appropriate fear of their parents' disapproval, and all adults, and legitimate authority figures, our children become lost in the moral and emotional chaos of a *Lord of the Flies* culture, which they construct out of their untempered desires and impulses, immature decisions, and reactions; in other words, they give in to the innate animal nature that has not yet been honed into honorable humanity by training, learning, and revering something bigger beyond themselves.

Proverbs 13:24 and 22:15 warn about that lack of parental discipline: **"One who spares his rod hates his child, but he who loves him disciplines him in his youth,"** and **"Foolishness is bound in the heart of a youth; the rod of discipline will distance it from him."** These words are not necessarily a prescription for beatings but a reminder to the parents to discipline, which requires instruction, reinforcement, and punishment—all as part of the loving obligations of a parent.

Sabra's letter demonstrates one parent's profound understanding of the necessity for parents to teach their children right from wrong: *"Even though honoring Father and Mother is the child's responsibility, it is the responsibility of the parents to REQUIRE [my note: "requiring" includes acting worthy] that level of respect from children. As a single mother of three boys, I have to constantly remind myself that they are immature (10, 8 and 7) and that I have a tremendous responsibility to set clear and fair boundaries and to require them to respect me. I anticipate that will result in their honoring me throughout their lives. I couldn't expect them to honor me if I didn't first fulfill my responsibility to teach them to do so."*

Whose Values Are Right?

The values clarification curriculum that was popular in schools a decade or two ago asked the students their views on certain ethical and moral situations. It was an attempt to emphasize the importance of values in making decisions. The only problem was that teachers could not tell a child he or she was wrong. If Johnny said, "I lied to my parents about stealing money," the teacher could ask him questions to clarify his view: "Why did you steal it?" "How did you feel when you stole it?" "Would you do it again?" Teachers were prohibited from telling Johnny that lying was wrong. The disastrous impact of the rebellious 1960s resulted in a make-it-up-as-you-go-along view of one's obligations and responsibilities to others, where "me" became the highest value, as well as a notion that right and wrong were subjective. This produced every child's dream: eliminating the worry of being judged and punished. The highest value became the self and its gratification, comfort, and glorification. "Who is to say what is right and wrong?" went the mantra. "To each his own."

I wonder if that mentality would be held in such high regard if those New Age thinkers woke up one morning in Algeria, where women are murdered in the streets for showing their bare heads, or in many other parts of Africa, where slavery and external genital mutilation is common practice for all female children. Spouting subjective morality has little meaning when you are safely ensconced in a country where the law of the land protects you against those who would do objectively immoral things with the permission of their own personalized value system.

God Is the Yardstick of Morality

The next level of argument is often that there can be no objective morality because who is to say whose morality is the best or is right? I came up against that challenge in a recent interview for a Canadian television news program. I was amused when the anchorwoman challenged me for saying I had a moral health radio program and that I was personally deciding what was right and wrong. She finally attacked me with, "And who died and made you God?" Needless to say, I was stunned. I replied, "Throughout history, as well as depicted throughout the Holy Scriptures, there have been many who have reiterated the word of God. And I, like all others who nag and remind, do not arrogantly imagine that I have reinvented the 'moral wheel,' so to speak."

What is interesting about such an interaction is that the challenger will inevitably attempt to negate God or God's significance in the 1990s. Which reminds me of an old Jewish story I once read about a rabbi sitting next to an atheist on an airplane. Every few minutes, one of the rabbi's children or grandchildren would inquire about his needs for food, drink, or comfort. The atheist commented, "The respect your children and grandchildren show you is wonderful. Mine don't show me that respect." The rabbi responded, "Think about it. To my children and grandchildren, I am one step closer in a chain of tradition to the time when God spoke to the whole Jewish people on Mount Sinai. To your children and grandchildren, you are one step closer to being an ape."

And that is one of the main points of this chapter. Parents and their children both need to behave with the recognition that they are parts of a chain leading straight to God, the Ultimate Creator and Power of the universe, upon whom we are all dependent and grateful. That is a far cry from a bumper sticker that reads, "Be nice to your children, they pick your nursing home," or "Humor thy father and thy mother, they haven't written their wills yet."

My Child, Myself

Instead of guidelines and moral modeling, we live in a society in which many parents abdicate their important responsibility to parents and sometimes treat their children like royalty, endowing them with papal infallibility. Children are believed before other adults and even teachers because "of course, my child would never lie." Acknowledging that the child really did "do bad" would be to face their own inadequate parenting, availability, commitment, and circumstances. Additionally, the "me generation" folks often only see their children as extensions of their own egos and defend against any assault on their self-esteem.

Rabbi Vogel once had a twelve-year-old boy and his parents in his office because of a scuffle in which the child and a friend had roughed up another child. The boy offered a version of the incident in which he was blameless and which contradicted the friend, who admitted his guilt and verified the story, and five other children who also corroborated the story. When the boy continued to deny his culpability and the parents defended him, Rabbi Vogel asked the parents, "So what about the six people who have told me a different story?" They responded, "The other children must be lying because our son wouldn't lie." This child is learning from his parents that his version of a lie becomes the truth.

Once ego self-defense becomes the parental first objective, then some parents attempt to protect their children from the consequences of their bad deeds to avoid looking or feeling bad because of the mess their children make of their own lives. Their children must be acknowledged or succeed like all the other children, or be emotionally scarred for life. Yikes! Awards for excellence are less common in schools, and even valedictorians and salutatorians are becoming extinct, because of misplaced compassion for all the children excluded by the recognition of superior accomplishment. Parents and schools end up taking away incentives and rewards for excellence. We will achieve the ultimate society in which no one has to challenge himself or herself morally or academically because everyone is the same no matter what you do.

Another parallel trend in the quest to preserve and protect self-esteem as the highest value is to give everyone an award. I believe that you should give all children appropriate compliments and support for their efforts and accomplishment. This is important in motivation and well-being. However, it is better to have medals and other awards mean something by only awarding them to those who truly qualified, because this offers a role model and incentive for all children to strive for, and a truer representation of the real world. If feelings are the main issue, not permitting the excellent to revel in, and be acknowledged for, their superior accomplishment hurts theirs.

Self-respect Is Not Supposed to Be Self-focus

We live in a society in which the term *self-respect* has come to mean, "I deserve more respect than other people." Consider the proliferation of fractionated groups (feminists, gays and lesbians, foreign ethnic group–American, adult child of some bad experience, disabled by addictions, and such) of people with individualized agendas, angers, demands, and expectations based upon the notions of oppressions, hardship, prejudice, and entitlement. These days, folks seem to be in an "Ask for what the country can do for you" mode, making unbelievable and excessive demands, focusing inward, supporting lies and distortions as long as they "serve the cause." This mode breeds discontent in those who would be better prepared to take on challenging opportunities with a dose of optimism, instruction, compassion for others, and the understanding that focus and hard work have built many a bridge over a seemingly impassible river.

One of the main functions of religion is to return our focus to the bigger picture, instead of supporting the myopic view that only what affects me or mine is important. In fact, "... you shall love your fellow as yourself—I am the Lord" (Leviticus 19:18) is God's commandment to ensure that we show respect and consideration to our fellow human beings. Godly self-respect is the product not of false compliments and trophies but of the goodness by which we lead our lives and treat others in spite of our own trials and tribulations.

Where Are Your Manners?

The loss of manners is a very important indicator of the disruption that has occurred in our society during the last two generations. There is no question that American society has lost some of the formality and etiquette that convey a sense of respect. Not only is chivalry dead, but so are simple manners.

No longer do we refer to people with the formal address of *Mr.*, *Mrs.*, or *Miss*. Remember when most of us were growing up, the idea of calling an adult by his first name was ridiculous? With the use of these formal forms of address, we learned that we did not treat adults in the same way we might treat other children. Part of the reason children demonstrate less respect is because they are not provided with the guidelines to help them determine when it is most appropriate. We would like our children to respect everybody, but different forms of respect help them distinguish special categories of respect.

A trip to a restaurant for a family dinner can be revealing. We would all love our young children to demonstrate appropriate behavior all the time, but when we go out to eat, a special plea is made that they demonstrate "restaurant behavior." In Japan, the custom to bow toward someone reflects a relationship of respect and helps delineate even among adults the respect due to important people and the elderly. Manners and social etiquette create distinctions that help children to learn appropriate behavior.

Some people would argue that we have carried the American spirit of equality and democracy to its logical conclusion. After all, we rebelled against the authoritarianism of the monarch, the social distinctions of aristocracy, and oppressive religious authority. Young people affirm that new social doctrine is in place, one that states "respect must be earned." No longer is respect presumed, but rather it is granted. In a country whose legal system asserts "innocent until proven guilty," we now proclaim "not deserving of respect unless proven otherwise." The problem is that few young people appreciate that the years of developing wisdom from experience, survival of hardship and challenges, and acceptance of responsibilities is grounds for respect.

The loss of respect, the emphasis on "self-respect," and the overempowerment of children are not positive changes. These factors, and others, have contributed to the overall social decay we are experiencing. There is a way to fight back. We can reclaim the respect and at the same time improve the quality of our families. The answer lies in the Fifth Commandment.

The Good Old Days

In the "good old days" children had a great deal of respect for their parents. Some of it might have been fear induced ("Wait till your father gets home!"), but most of it related to familial and social expectations. We would never advocate a return to excessively harsh or damaging physical punishments utilized by many parents of previous generations.

The word "honor," *kavod,* is the preferred term for demonstrating deserved deference in the Bible. In English, the terms *honor* and *respect* are synonymous. In many English translations of the Bible, the word *respect* is used to imply partiality. For example, **"You shall not respect persons in judgment"** (Deuteronomy 1:17) is a command to be unbiased when acting as a judge. Biblically, therefore, honor is a commandment of veneration and courtesy.

We will use the word *honor*, rather than *respect*, when dealing with the obligations of a child toward a parent in order to distinguish between holding someone in high regard and demonstrating appropriate deference in actions. We are not commanded to respect our parents, in terms of holding them in high regard. Instead, we are commanded to behave in a certain way toward them that reflects their status as parents, sometimes in spite of our opinions and emotions about them.

According to Jewish tradition, to honor one's parents meant to "serve food and drink, provide clothing and shelter, and lead them in and out" as long as the parent is alive. The command to honor parents is supplemented by another biblical verse that states we must revere (some Bibles translate this as "fear") our parents (Leviticus 19:3). Jewish tradition interpreted reverence as meaning that we should not "stand or sit in our parents' reserved place, nor should we contradict their words." Honor was demonstrated through acts of kindness and caring, while reverence meant to refrain from actions that diminished their role as parent or embarrassed them in public. These simple distinctions are just as relevant today.

Rabbi Vogel has been involved in weddings at which the bride or groom did not invite their parents because of personal conflicts between the adult children and their parents or because of nasty postdivorce conflicts of their parents. Many couples probably elope to avoid such parental conflict. Imagine the strong statement made when a parent is not invited and does not walk down the aisle. It is a public statement that this individual does not have parents. This is clearly a form of dishonoring parents, but, in fairness, it is not always the fault of the child. Some parents create so much tension with their children that they made it a matter of self-defense to be excluded, as is the case with an addicted, violent parent. When the parent is a disappointment or annoying, as is the case with an immature or self-centered parent, I suggest that the invitations be sent anyway—there are some circumstances that simply must be accepted and with which we must cope.

You'd Better Listen to Your Parents!

Some scholars interpret the first four Commandments as dealing with our relationship with God, while the rest involve our relationship with other people. The placement of honoring parents as the Fifth Commandment between these two categories suggests a special connection between our parents and God. Just as we must honor God, the creator of all life, we must honor our parents, who gave us life. In truth, parents are like gods to their children, especially younger children. Parents are an important connection to God. As mentioned earlier, parents can nurture or negate a child's spiritual relationship with God. By honoring our parents, we learn to honor God. By honoring God, we become decent human beings.

"A father can make Your truth known to children" (Isaiah 38:19) is an indication of the trickle-down theory in action with respect to holy obligations. Though the connection to God is sometimes not seen or acknowledged, the wisdom of parents is often acknowledged too late. One listener named Caesar e-mailed this message reminding children of the consequences of rebellion against parental teachings: "Years ago, as a teenager, I recall listening to a radio program, where the announcer asked this sports hero one important question. The question was in response to the life history of this sports hero who had made it to the top: money and the power that went with it. As time went on, he lost it all. So the question was a simple one, 'What did you learn from all that?' The sports star replied, 'I learned one important thing ... I should have listened to my mother.'

Well, as time passed, I went to the university and completed an education that my parents never dreamed of. I looked into the worlds of science, philosophy, theology, physics, and accounting ... but I look back to realize that the wisdom of my parents, especially my mother, a wisdom so simple yet so true, was years beyond the truths that were taught to me in one of the finest Universities. So, *to you teenagers out there: honoring your parents means respecting them and their advice. Parents have an interest in your well-being and a wisdom based on life-earned experience that is intended to make your life a lot better. Remember, you are a part of them."*

Sometimes you're not even aware of how much and from whom you've learned about how to be in life. Nancy, one of my listeners, wrote of this revelation: *"I do not want to thank you, I want to thank my mom. It was my mom who stuck and is still sticking by my dad. It was my mom who taught us a love for church, family and gave us a good work ethic. It was my mom who taught us right from wrong, kept us in school, and gave me the morals and values I still have today. Even today, my mom instills just enough guilt to keep me moving in the right direction.*

Ok, ok, here is where I thank you. It took listening to you and reading your books to realize my mother is to be credited for what I have accomplished in my thirty-eight years of life, fifteen years of marriage and in raising my two wonderful boys, ages twelve and ten. I credit her for my drive to work my way through school, buy my own cars and home. I credit her for my ability to work through the highs and lows of marriage. I've heard you talk about rekindling the flame and I take pride in having done that very thing more than once in fifteen years. Not because my mother stood over me and told me to, but because my mother gave me the standards by which to live my life and set me free to make my decisions."

Do What I Say, Not What I Do

I remember one incredible caller who tried to sell me the notion that parents can really teach by "what they say" versus "what they do." She was shacking up with a fellow while she was raising her ten-year-old daughter. I challenged her on what she thought this would teach the daughter, mentioning, for example, diminished regard for marital covenant, sexual relationships as casual, family structure as whatever you're doing at the moment. The caller agreed that she didn't want her daughter to make the same choices. When asked "why not?"—if she was making that choice, what was so bad that she wouldn't want her daughter to follow in her footsteps?—I could tell she was torn between answering that question honestly and having to face making uncomfortable changes, and avoiding the answer to avoid facing her own weaknesses, insecurities, and fears. Instead, she responded, *"But, I'm telling her every day not to do this!"* Unfortunately, that's not as effective as demonstrating the courage, honor, and dignity we know is right and best for ourselves as well as our children.

Thom, a listener, wrote about how much he learned by parental example: *"I am a thirty-three-year-old male, the youngest of nine children, and the proud father of a three-year-old girl, the first of twelve to come (only kidding). I was thinking about what was really important to teach my daughter when I had a rush of flashbacks as to what my parents taught me, and how I learned their lessons. I sat down and wrote it out in tribute form to my parents and thought you might like it."*

A Tribute to My Parents

As I ponder my life I can't help thinking of the gifts you have given me. I know we had very little money, but we lacked nothing of importance. I am as thankful for the things we didn't have as I am for the things we did. I often wonder if I will ever be able to provide for my children what you provided to me . . .

You taught me by example to do what is right when you made me return a penny item and explain my actions after I took it without permission at age five.

When I was ten, you taught me by example to treat others with dignity when you gave shelter and care to my friend who was beaten by his own family.

You taught me by example that respect was more important than grades when I had a conflict with a teacher in sixth grade.

You taught me by example that acts of kindness are natural outpourings of a loving heart when you shoveled every neighbor's sidewalk instead of just our own.

You taught me by example that one's child was the most important thing in the world when you peeled my orange and wrapped it in foil, and cut my cake in half and placed the icing in the middle so it wouldn't come off on the wax papers when you packed my lunch.

You taught my by example to value my faith by attending church with us weekly when it would have been more convenient to stay home.

You taught me by example the importance of giving when you placed your offering in the plate each week to help others who were less fortunate than we were.

You taught me by example that honesty and integrity were more important than fortune when you struggled to pay your taxes rather than cheat on your return.

You taught me by example to hold fast to my commitments by staying committed to each other for all these years.

You taught me by example that reading is more important than television, that laughing is better than crying, that time is more important than words.

You taught me by example what it means to be a good parent.

It is clear from all that Thom and other children can learn from their parents' words and deeds that this parent-child relationship is the learning ground for a relationship between each new human life and God. Jewish tradition holds that there are three partners who share in the creation of man: God, the father, and the mother. When children have the opportunity to learn goodness and righteousness from their parents, this is their introduction to the source of all things: God.

Who Is a "Parent"?

The obligation to honor parents does not just apply to a biological father or mother. Parents of adopted children and stepparents who fulfill the role of parents are to be treated no differently than natural parents. There is a Jewish tradition that anyone who raises a child as his or her own child is considered to be the parent of the child. Therefore, a person must honor a stepmother or -father as well as foster-care parent or legal guardian. There is something special in the commitment to nurture and raise a child without a so-called "biological imperative" to do so. I have been impressed with the many callers who have adopted, both legally and emotionally, their spouse's children as their own. It also is touching to hear from those folks who take in their mistreated or neglected nieces, nephews, and grandchildren. One cannot help being moved by those callers who, filled with compassion and generosity, embrace abandoned, born-drug-addicted, or mentally or physically handicapped children. When those teenage or adult "children" call to bemoan their history, or complain about some surrogate-parental quirk, I quickly remind them of their blessing in having found safety, love, and nurturance, and of their obligation to honor that, albeit imperfect, gift.

We must also honor our father- and mother-in-law, as we see with King David, who honored King Saul, his jealous father-in-law, by calling him "my father" (I Samuel 24:12), the same father-in-law who wanted him killed! That was an extraordinary example of tolerating a quirk. In spite of that problem father-in-law story, in-law strife more typically resides in tensions between the women. It is not unusual for a mother-in-law to have serious problems letting go of the primary relationship with her son, and for the daughter-in-law to demand distance, especially with the birth of a child, when she can feel insecure and threatened by her husband's close maternal ties. Small slights and misunderstandings too often become major wars of turf, power, and importance. This is more of an issue between women than men, because women generally are more personally invested in, and feel more responsibility for, intimacy. Men seem to be able to get along with the relationship on a longer leash and don't personalize events and moods as much as women do.

When counseling young women on getting along with difficult mothers-in-law, we try to clarify the underlying psychological issues but still enforce the notion that once one marries, the in-law is deserving of the same displays of honor and respect as one's own parents, or an "easier" mother-in-law. Aside from the commanded nature of this law, it is simply smarter to try to get along than win some battles and lose family cohesion. This commandment is not qualified. It does not mean:

➤Honor only if the person is personally perceived as deserving.

➤Honor only if the person always reciprocates.

➤Honor only if it is pleasing to you to do so.

➤Honor only if you get compliments for doing so.

➤Honor only if it "feels right."

➤Honor only if other people also do so.

The commandment says, just do it. It is often astonishing to see how much positive ground is often won by "being polite"—how seductive and low impact that lesson can be for everyone involved.

Honor Your Parents . . . or Else!

In the book of Exodus, we are told the one who strikes or curses a parent is to be put to death (21:15 and 17). If this punishment were imposed today, we would not have a population in our country. In a strong statement demanding parental respect, the Bible states that **"a stubborn and rebellious son who will not listen to the voice of his father and the voice of his mother . . ."** (Deuteronomy 21: 18–21) shall be put to death. Many religious interpretations admit that this is an extreme case of an incorrigible child, who possibly committed other crimes because he did not follow the wisdom and law learned from his parents. Jewish tradition claims that a child was never put to death as a result of this "wayward son" law. Although not ever enforced, the severity of the biblical law reflects a warning, emphasizing the importance of honoring parents. Proverbs (30:8) says, **"The eye which looks jeeringly on a father, and scorns the obedience due a mother, will be pecked out by the ravens of the valley, and eaten by the vultures. Anyone who strikes father or mother will be put to death. . . . Anyone who curses father or mother will be put to death"** (Exodus 21:16–17).

Invoking the death penalty seems extreme to us today, but the ramifications of out-of-control children—procreating, using drugs, and being violent—is as major a family and cultural disaster today as it would have been then. It is part of human development that children need to be taught to be disciplined and civilized. As children growing up, we yearned to be free and in control. By being the center of our own universe, virtually idolizing our whims and desires, and wanting to avoid consequences of our misdeeds, we were frustrated by who stood between us and that power: our parents. In our internal struggle between our animal and potentially human selves, it is easy to disdain and exaggerate parental faults, maximize negative moments, and so forth, in an attempt to eliminate the lessons, controls, and punishments that thwarted our attempts at supplanting God as the ruler of our universe. God's commandment of honoring parents is basically the message that parents are a conduit of God. Any profanity or harm to the parent is as if we've profaned God. Therein lies the seriousness of this commandment.

Though parents don't invoke the biblical wayward son death penalty, it is often necessary for a parent of an out-of-control child to invoke the power of the state. In situations where a child does not respect parental rules and directions and becomes perpetually truant, addicted, violent, and criminal, some parents have asked the police to arrest the child on a legitimate charge or, by petitioning to have the child become a ward of the state, abdicate parental authority.

Honoring Parents Gets You Lifetime Credit

The parent-child relationship is the only human relationship directly prescribed in the Ten Commandments. There is nothing about honoring spouses or even children. It is also the only one in which a reward is mentioned: **"so that your days may be lengthened."** How is that for an incentive? If you're good to your parents and still smoke—do you get to live longer? Does it really work that literally?

At the most basic level, honoring parents is a way to repay the care they gave to us as we grew up. The fact that our parents fed, clothed, and provided shelter for us means that when necessary we must reciprocate. In previous generations, before social security and retirement pension plans, children provided these needs for their aging parents. The extended family was a socioeconomic necessity. Grandparents would help care for the young and contribute to general household functions.

The obligation for each generation to honor their parents is for their own sake so that their children will eventually care for them. Perhaps this is meant by the promised **"lengthening of your days."** If we take care of our parents, our children will take care of us, helping us to live longer.

Since some people who abuse their parents live long and healthy lives, and others who care for their parents die prematurely, there must be other ways to understand the reward of **"lengthening your days."** The honoring of parents reinforces social order as a whole and enhances the quality of life for everyone involved. According to this view, honoring parents brings long life through the preservation of society. The ability to honor parents serves as the model for not only honoring God but also teachers, elders, and everyone in society.

"Lengthening our days" can also be reflected in the enrichment of the quality and meaning of our lives. Denika Gum, an elementary school teacher from Charlottesville, Virginia, sent me this composition from one of her students. The assignment was

How I Show My Parents I Love Them

We as kids don't realize how lucky we are. In fact, many of us take our parents for granted. We worry too much about "things" instead of what is really important in life. Things are desires, not requirements. Our possessions take up too much time and effort in life, but what we should really be doing instead is to show forth our love. We must try to consider the important things in life and don't worry about those "wants." Love, faith, hope and peace are to me the importance of life. Without these, we would be worthless. The dust in the wind. That is why we must try to never forget these things, the things that matter. So not all comes down to the kind and loving parents we all have. The ones who have put up with us for all of these years. They have given us so many

things needed. A roof over our heads, clothing for our bodies,
and food for our growth. They have given us all these things,
but what have we given to them? Even how hard we try, we
will never be able to thank them enough for all the important
things that they have given us.

This essay was written by a fifth-grader who hit on the main
point: *"Our possessions take up too much time ... in life."*
That's exactly right. Our acts of love, honor, reverence, and respect take that time back ... that is the true lengthening of time.

Honoring Parents in Sickness, Not Just in Health

In this society, we don't much believe or feel that our lives
should be "shortened" by having to sacrifice for the ill or
dying. Having to give up our precious time to visit or minister
to our elderly, ill, or dying parents is seen as an imposition
rather than as a potential, albeit difficult, blessing. The proliferation of homes for the aged and dying is a sad commentary
on the selfishness of our young people, who see life only as a
tree to pluck, not a tree to groom. Fortunately, there are those
who see things differently. Here are a few of their stories.

First is a letter from a woman who signed herself "forty-
four-year-old daughter in Tucson." *"I was out at my mother*
and father's house, a seventy mile round-trip from my own, be-
cause my mother needed a little help. She needed a little help be-
cause my father, who has full-blown Alzheimer's, had taped duct
tape all over the three long windows in the bathroom so that the
'little people' who haunt his days and nights wouldn't be able to
look in. She needed a little help because her mother (my grand-
mother) who lives with them and who will be one hundred and
two in December, likes to snack in bed and bugs were starting to
show up in her room, which was generally a mess anyway. This
is to say nothing of my mother's normal daily routine of cooking,

cleaning, shopping, banking, medicating, driving, washing, ironing, not sleeping more than five or six hours a night due to dad's 'little people pounding on the windows,' and other mortally tiring duties and distractions that would fell any lesser human being. My mother is seventy-five and has had a hip replaced.

There were certainly other things I'd rather have been doing that day, but I love them dearly, so there I was, 'helping.' I emptied and washed my grandmother's reeking chamber pot, scrubbed the bathroom floor where she regularly misses the toilet, took Daddy shopping for a bathroom curtain, pulled off all the tape, hung the curtain, washed and hung out several loads of really stinky laundry, scrubbed and swept, changed bedding and tablecloths, loaded the dishwasher, etc.

Then, weary and depressed, I sat down to dinner with my three darlings and a peculiar thing happened: I was overcome with a feeling of immense gratitude. It occurred to me that it was my honor to give them that measly gift of a single day's servitude out of so many thousands of such days my mother puts in singlehandedly without a word of complaint. It was my privilege to empty their chamber pots and wash their dirty clothes. I felt an overwhelming sense of existing, for a brief moment, in a glow of divine grace.

I am decidedly not religious, but that day I realized that to serve others selflessly to the point of bone-tired, without expectation of reward or recognition, is the ultimate spiritual high. In a world where 'looking out for number one' is a cultural icon, where a whole generation (to its shame) is dubbed, 'The Me Generation,' where millions can't decide whether dear old Dad is worth the extra fifty bucks a day in this nursing home, or if the other worse but cheaper one is enough, it is not surprising that so many were baffled by Mother Teresa's life in the sewers and leper colonies of the hell that is Calcutta.

I'm just glad I got the tiniest glimpse into the paradise where she must really have lived."

Perhaps the "lengthening of days" may also refer to a more divine or spiritual time clock, with a more infinite quality to measuring time.

The second letter is from Beth, who wrote after listening to a call concerning the true elements of sacrifice: "*I was listening to your program three months ago. You talked briefly about the true meaning of 'sacrifice.' You said that we often take on responsibility that requires sacrifice only when it gives us warm fuzzies—You told your caller to stick it out because sacrifice is only sacrifice when it is uncomfortable and inconvenient—or else nothing is being given up—there is no sacrifice—there is no nobility.*

At the time of this call, I was struggling with whether or not to continue caring for my grandma. She suffered a stroke two-and-a-half years ago and became mildly disabled. I assumed about 50 percent of the responsibility for caring for her. Hospital visits, medicine and groceries became my responsibility. A lot to take on at twenty-four on top of a full-time job. I had gotten very tired of the responsibility when you offered that advice to your caller. I was ready to put the burden back onto my parents. At twenty-four, I didn't want to be on a first-name basis with a pharmacist anymore. 'I'm too young for that,' I thought. Needless to say, your advice inspired me to 'stick this out.' Grandma died January first. Standing at the coffin, I found the inconvenience of spending Saturdays at the hospital didn't matter. The inconvenience of not sleeping in on weekends, of not travelling as much as I would have liked and the rest of the burdens didn't matter anymore. I looked around the room at the mourners and knew that I was one of the few people there with enough character to sacrifice my own plans, time and goals to provide for Grandma's needs.

I realize that what I did got my eyes off of me-me-me, and taught me a valuable lesson about love, sacrifice, responsibility, and selfishness. I was one of the only people to show Grandma love and compassion at the end of her life. That far outweighs any inconvenience I endured over the last two and one-half years."

Perhaps yet another way of looking at "lengthened days" is by the depth brought to your life through the meaning you put into it by honor, nobility and sacrifice.

Before It's Too Late

Both of us are asked about being there at/before the death of a parent with whom the individual did not feel close or loving. There is often a profound unwillingness to give anything to a parent perceived as being unloving or undeserving. Sometimes a determination exists to punish that parent by denying him or her any opportunity for repair or repentance. Also present may be a fear of facing death as well as the death of the dream of being well parented. Avoidance is one all-too-human way to avoid difficult situations and emotions. So many folks stay away, thinking they're actually doing something better for themselves. That avoidance is part of the mentality that says, "If it doesn't obviously serve me, I won't do it and I shouldn't have to!"

There are some reasons for saying good-bye. Joyce's experience with her alcoholic father is an example. "*We never had a close relationship because he was an alcoholic when I was growing up. In his later years he quit drinking and then developed serious health problems. At this visitation, my brother came up and said quietly to his wife and myself that dad was a mean, ornery, bullheaded s.o.b., while we were growing up— but that after he quit drinking we finally got a chance to start to know him. This last year he was in a wheelchair and on oxygen one hundred percent of the time. He was no longer that mean, loud dad we had known but someone who needed our help and I only hope that in some way we were able to help his last days go better. A few months before he died he*

*was in the hospital recovering from a surgery, and as I left his
room alone after a visit with him, he looked at me and said
that he loved me. I was so shocked that I just looked at him
and left. I do not know why I responded that way, but I did.
My message is that if there is someone in your life whom you
want to tell that you love—just do it, and do not sit and wonder later why you could not do it. I treated him as if I loved
him, but could not say the words to him. Now it is too late.
Now my way to also show dad that love is to make sure we
take care of mom. If you are a parent and have never told your
child that you love them, do it until you get a response, so they
know it is not just a one-time fluke that you managed to say
while sedated. Just keep telling them until they believe it. It
will be the greatest legacy that you can leave them. Forget leaving them a big inheritance and leave them knowing that you
loved them. Then there will be a chance for better closure and
not so many unanswered what ifs."*

Joyce cannot be expected to feel a loving, close bond when
her father's demeanor and behavior made such a response impossible. In spite of the lack of closeness, the commandment
to honor kept her in close enough proximity to receive her father's deathbed blessing and to learn the lesson of speaking
love to one's children.

Bridget's experience of her father's dying was also an important lesson: *"During my father's final few days, my mother,
brother and I were with him almost constantly. He died of pneumonia. As I sat with him on that last day, I realized how proud
I was of him. Through the years, my dad and I had enough misunderstandings. He wasn't an easy man to know. Yet I realized
then that much of what he'd done through his life he faced the
same way he faced his final battle, quietly determined to do
what had to be done. If dad had taken a less painful way out, I
would not have had the chance to recognize his courage, his dignity. I would have been robbed of the opportunity to give back
to him some of what he had given me all my life—his care.*

I'm proud of my dad, not just for the way he faced his death but also for the things he lived for, like fighting in the war and always providing for his family. I'm glad he died with dignity and pray I would have at least some of the same courage when confronted with difficult circumstances."

The current fashion is to consider valuable only our parents' constant verbalization of our wonderfulness and correctness. If they do not agree with or support everything we do, if they don't shower us with a constant flow of affection and approval, they are bad and to be shunned, according to pop-psych philosophy. I have been concerned for decades about the ultimately destructive impact of so-called therapeutic "confrontations" and the trend toward blaming one's parents for all one's current ills and problems.

Bridget learned valuable lessons at her father's death, not only from the courageous way he died but from her awareness, in spite of his faults, of his many contributions to her development and welfare she hadn't even considered.

Honoring Parents After Death

Can you honor parents after they are dead? While funerals and mourning are for the support of the living, the loving survivors, in the Jewish tradition, one of the most significant ways of honoring a parent is through bereavement and memorial rituals, which include: the obligation to attend the funeral and to participate in the intensive mourning rituals of Shiva, the seven-day period during which all mourners stay at home together to recover from their grief and accept condolence calls of the community and recite the Mourner's Kaddish (memorial prayer) daily for a full eleven months. In addition, the Mourner's Kaddish is recited in synagogue and a memorial candle lit at home annually on the anniversary of the death and on the major holidays. Furthermore, Jewish law requires a mourner for a parent to demonstrate acts of mourning far in excess of those required when mourning the loss of a spouse or child. Some people find this shocking, considering that adults recognize the normalcy of parents dying before themselves or their children. Although there are many philosophical arguments that attempt to explain this, one interpretation is that one's relationship with a parent is unique and irreplaceable. Though each child or spouse is unique, it is clear that people can be consoled by their other children or by an eventual new love. There is no way to make up for the loss of a parent (*How Does Jewish Law Work?* by Rabbi J. Simcha Cohen, Aronson Press, 1993). That children don't easily replace a parent is a lesson I try to teach divorced, custodial parents who have found a new romance, only to discover that their children may not be equally enthralled.

Some years ago, a well-known Jewish comedian, who was not particularly observant of Jewish law, made sure that he recited the Mourner's Kaddish every day when his father passed away. Rabbi Vogel remembered him coming to the synagogue service every evening when he was in town. Even more impressive, no matter what city he was touring in, he made sure to find a synagogue where he could recite this prayer as part of the Jewish community. Show times and schedules were adjusted to allow him to fulfill the ritual. His dedication to reciting the Mourner's Kaddish was his way of honoring his father and keeping his memory alive. Through the honoring of his father he was brought closer to his faith community. A parent cannot offer his or her child a more beautiful legacy.

Individuals who have lost a parent never get over the loss of that parent. Rabbi Vogel once went to the house of a congregant whose mother had just passed away. As he walked in the house a large man, fifty-five years of age, put his arms around him and cried, barely able to utter the words "I am an orphan." Parents, by the very nature of their existence, even with all the conflict, provide a sense of generational comfort, like the comfort of the womb when we begin life.

Posthumous rituals in memory of parents not only emphasize the importance of honoring parents, but bring individuals back to their faith community and preserve a relationship between parent and child even beyond this world.

Why Does It Not Say "Love Thy Parents"?

The Bible does not specifically command us to love our parents. We are commanded to love God, the stranger, and our neighbor, but nowhere are we told that we must love our parents. The interpersonal dynamics between parent and child are filled with conflicts. Sometimes the parent and child come out of the adolescent and early adult years with a strong bond of attachment and love. Other times they barely escape with a relationship intact. Sometimes too much has transpired for the child to love the parent. God, strangers, and neighbors do not place the same ego demands upon us that parents do. Just ask any sixty-year-old who always feels like a child when in the presence of his parent.

As former children now grown, we've all had the experience of realizing our parents weren't so stupid after all. Children of any age almost always think they know more than their parents. Parents want to share their hard-earned wisdom with the next generation. These contradictory forces are more pronounced when most children know more about computers and how to access global information than their parents. It is harder to answer the question "What can I learn from my parents?" The commandment to honor parents was given to ensure that the elderly, although they may not feel wanted by family or society, are still given their appropriate reward.

We are commanded to honor parents because it is the best way to compensate for the tension-filled parent-child relationship. It can serve as the thin thread that keeps the parent and child attached.

This issue also brings up the question of "doing good deeds" because "it feels good," you are ensured of "getting good stuff back," or because you "want to." Human nature being what it is, if we relied on feelings, emotions, or guaranteed reciprocity, doing good would be the exception and not the rule. Especially in the often perpetually emotionally charged relationship between a growing child and a parent, responsibility to a higher value than one's feeling keeps both the parent and the child connected. It is actually of greater moment for one to do things because they are right to do, rather than simply because you may feel like doing it at that moment (but maybe not the next). To rise above your mood, circumstance, desires, or whims and do an objective good deed describes a person of honor, a person of holiness.

What Happens When a Parent Needs to Be Sent to His/Her Room Without Supper?

We both get questioned about the appropriate technique of reprimanding a parent who is doing the wrong thing. This includes inquiries from a ten-year-old boy who wants to know how to get his father to stop stealing with a pirated TV cable box, to an adult whose parent is driving drunk or is dangerous on the road due to neurological losses of aging. This letter from William brings up such an instance: *"My son-in-law was telling us about his father who is so unstable with his feet that he shuffles along and sometimes falls backwards. After Christmas one night, he and his wife got into their car. He started the car and then backed out. While backing out, he scraped my son-in-law's car and kept on backing up across the street. After that he knocked down two small trees and hit a corner of a house. He continued backing until he got stuck in a snow bank.*

I asked him if his family had taken away his keys and had forbidden him to drive anymore. The father is seventy-six. My son-in-law said they would mention the episode to him and suggest that he might not drive anymore. Then they would let him make that decision.

My question is: is it the responsibility of a child to mention that the father is wrong in his actions and what age should the child do this? Should the child forcibly stop the father from doing an action that is dangerous to some other human being or even go so far as to notify the police and have him arrested? This has always bothered me when I thought about it."

One should try not to embarrass or humiliate a parent in public. This might include not retaliating if your parent behaves inappropriately toward you. Always let a parent save face or give them the benefit of the doubt. It is the responsibility of any child, adult or otherwise, to remind the parent, respectfully and privately, of any duty for which the parent is responsible. The idea is to correct the parent without shaming him, even in private.

When parents refuse to be responsible, when they break civil and moral laws or jeopardize life and limb of innocent "neighbors," you are required to stand between your parents and those laws or innocents. This may indeed mean that authorities must be notified. The chaplain of the Glenburn Evangelical Covenant Church of Glenburn, Maine, wrote in this regard: *"Since honor does not mean unquestioned obedience, we truly honor our parents when we hold them accountable to God's law. If my parents abandon me, I will honor them by seeking, though not forcing, reconciliation. If my parents abuse me, I will honor them by praying for them, so that they might see their error—and by escaping, if possible, so that they cannot continue to sin upon me. If my parents are unfaithful, I will honor them by calling for righteousness and by being willing to forgive them when they repent. If they are breaking the law, and refuse to heed my warnings, I will honor them by calling the police. Making them accountable to the highest moral order is honoring them in that I esteem them capable of responsible action."*

Ultimately, children of immoral or weak parents can greatly

honor their roots by being adults who add to the greater good of the world through their own actions. In this instance, we are honoring what our parents *should* be living, teaching, and standing for.

But My Parents Don't Deserve It!

Some people say, "My parents don't deserve to be honored." The commandment does not say to honor parents *only* if they are good parents. Even bad parents deserve to be honored if only at a minimal level. We often only see the weaknesses of our parents and swear that we will be better than they. We will deserve respect when we get old like them. But alas, as time goes by, we find ourselves more and more like our parents—imperfect beings. Some people pray that their children will not treat them as they treated their own parents.

The command to honor parents cannot be absolute. If a parent tells his or her child to violate a civil or moral law, the child has no obligation to honor the request. Judaism and Christianity place ultimate value on the adherence to God's law as well as the idea that civil law is part of God's desire for an ordered society. Our relationship to God always has precedence over our relationship to our parents. If doing the right thing alienates us from our parents, we are not culpable for dishonoring our parents.

One vivid biblical example of a son not following through on an evil parental command comes from I Samuel (19:1–7). Saul let his son, Jonathan, and all his servants know of his intention to have David killed. Jonathan warns David, **"My father Saul is trying to kill you, so now be cautious tomorrow morning and stay in the secret place, and hide yourself."** Saul expects his son, Jonathan, to follow through on his command. After reiterating the good that David has done for King Saul, Jonathan asks his father, **". . . so why should you sin with innocent blood, to kill David for no reason?"** Ultimately, Saul relents.

The point of that story is well stated in a letter from Nick on the issue of honor versus obedience: *"Honoring your mother and father does not include doing something immoral or illegal just because your parents say so. We have a Father in heaven we must obey first and then we are also subject to the law of the land."*

Some religious authorities hold that a child is not bound to honor a wicked parent as long as that parent does not repent. Still, that child is forbidden to *cause* that parent grief. Dealing with evil or awful parents is probably the singular most difficult issue of this commandment. One of the problems is in formulating just what is evil or awful enough. When speaking with adult children angry with their parents, I ask the question, "Were they profoundly or frankly evil, or more typically just annoying or irritating?" The latter is something you need to accept as a reality of the parental challenge you were given, while the former creates the necessity quite often for escape and/or self-defense. Parents who are violent, sexually aggressive, or emotionally destructive with their persistent and devious manipulations, gossip, and interference surely justify the distance their children make in order to survive. Somewhere between annoying and blatantly evil is where most of the confusion derives for adult children, who struggle with personal survival measured against their guilt for not staying involved with the parent.

Since the pop-psych revolution, the notions that all problems are externally created and personal feeling and behavior can be blamed on someone else have reigned. Parents have taken the brunt of that blame. As Aleta, a listener, wrote, *"When we get hung up with thinking that we are victims of our parents' doing . . . rather than understanding that we are the products of family and parents who were not perfect . . . we hang ourselves up. Rather than staying in the past and blaming and becoming permanent self-created victims of our past experiences and contact, it is adult and responsible that we understand where we have come from but decide where we are going . . . and whether we have the strength to make it different than they did. To stay in the blaming of the past only sentences and limits us to living in the past rather than growing and going forward and becoming responsible, able-to-live-with-the-consequences adults of stature and honor. We will find all too soon (if we become parents) that we are neither perfect nor perpetually honorable either!"*

One of the questions we generally ask of individuals or groups who speak of their current lives in terms of the failures of their parents is, "Did each and every one of your siblings turn out the same way?" The answer, of course, is never yes. Each individual reacts to stresses and challenges in a unique way, based upon his own personal characteristics of temperament, determination, resilience, courage, intelligence, and so forth. Our personal style of reacting determines our quality of life, not just the particular challenges. To blame one's parents for one's lot in life is simplistic, unfair, and untrue. Ultimately, in spite of all, we remain the final architects of our lives.

This point is driven home in a letter from Michelle: *"This letter is in response to the comments about the 'sad life' that Karla Tucker, the pickaxe murderess who was put to death in Texas (1998), must have had which led her down the wrong path. Maybe her life was like mine . . . at age five I was molested by my brother-in-law; at age eleven I was molested by an uncle, and for all the years in between I was molested by my cousin. My father died when I was seven and my mother married seven more times to abusive, alcoholic men. By age sixteen I was a drunk and a drug addict. At seventeen I was raped outside the bar I had been drinking in. By graduation from high school I had attended ten schools in twelve years. Yes, I actually did graduate. I then spent one year in college and moved in with the man of my dreams to get away from my mother. He beat me and spent all of my money on gambling, drugs and other women.*

Two weeks before our wedding, I called it off. My mother was

*very upset with me. She couldn't understand what I was going to
do without a man in my life. I decided to get away from all of
them. I moved one thousand miles away; enter the ADULT me. I
am now twenty-eight years old, have been married for two years
to my best friend (we dated for four years before marrying and
there was no shacking up!). We have a beautiful home, filled with
love, and happy children. My mother does things with them I
only dreamt of her doing with me as a child . . . and I thank God.
Though I also know God as the provider of my blessings and I
have never been in jail (because I was never caught), but I know
that he kept me alive for a reason . . . I am discovering those reasons every day."*

History, even parental history, is not destiny. We each have to
take the credit or the criticism for what we've made of our lives,
even in spite of nasty circumstances like Michelle's. In so doing,
she found out that sometimes, you can go back home . . . but it's
for the direct benefit of a later generation, her own child.

It is difficult to imagine wanting to "try again" with a seemingly terrible parent after a disappointing childhood, but some
people successfully accomplish just that. Cindy explained how:
*"There were times when I was growing up that I actually
hated my mother. It seemed she was never there for me. She
was a musician and worked nights, so she would be asleep in
the morning when I was getting ready for school and when I
got home, she would either be busy working with roses or just
push us out of the house to go play. I married young, had my
first child, and then my marriage broke up. Mom didn't offer
any help or support. She has a cranky personality at times and
can be downright rude. I honor my mother by forgiving her,
overlooking her faults as much as I can, and seeing the goodness in her. I honor her by sharing my life with her. I honor her
by listening to her advice, although I may not always take it. I
honor my mom by taking the time to call and visit regularly,
even though it may be a sacrifice at times. I honor my mom by
trying to correct the mistakes she made with me by not making*

the same ones with my children. No mention of dad? They were divorced when I was three. He only picked me up at Christmas each year—no phone calls in between. He passed away in 1971. I honor him with my loving prayers and remember the times we did have together. He was my one and only dad and the little time we did have, I cherish."

The impulse to just blow these kinds of parents right out of the water, erase them from your memory banks, and get on with life may seem hard to resist. As you constantly confront and challenge them with the intent of punishment or the determination to have them change, you carry that ugly fire inside your belly. In order to cope with the ongoing loss or the guilt you experience as a result of your rejection of such parents, you often resort to perpetual rationalizations, which only serve to keep the anger simmering. This state is not generally constructive or conducive to a good life, a life of peace, a life of joy.

We are saddened by the folks who come to us still as angry as though yesterday were today. These people are usually the folks living with an attitude and lifestyle that perpetuates ancient realities. They can become adults who can't form relationships; who bury their feelings in drugs, alcohol, or sex; people who treat all humanity as though they were still defending against their parents. They most often are helped by giving up the rage and/or hurt without denying the truth of their mistreatment. This is not an issue of pretending there was no ugly past, nor of forgiving where there is no admission of responsibility or repentance. When that parent is more pathetic than dangerously evil, it is healing to find safe and reasonable means of showing honor—a call, a card, or a visit. Perhaps those efforts might even result in an opportunity for a parent to express remorse and make attempts to repair their damage. Certainly, there is a better chance of that happening in a nonconfrontational arena.

It takes great courage and great spirituality to follow this commandment under difficult conditions. Bernardin Lochmueller, pastor in the United Church of God, offered his struggle for instruction: "*There are tragic circumstances, when a child necessarily cuts off from his parents, such as in cases of abuse or drunkenness, etc. where the parent is a clear and present danger to that child. Even so, under all circumstances we are to honor that parent to the extent that circumstances allow. A personal example will illustrate this.*

My mother died when I was six years of age. My father was an alcoholic who abandoned me and the two younger siblings. I had no contact with my father between the age of seven and nineteen, and frankly did not know whether he was dead or alive. When I was nineteen, a relative informed me that my father was seriously ill in the hospital, and might not survive. I went to see him in the hospital, and re-established something of a relationship with him from that time on.

It was very distressing to me that he never attempted to make amends for his abandonment. He simply reappeared in the lives of my siblings and me. These circumstances continued for about another eighteen years, until his death in 1990. During this time, I maintained contact, and would see him regularly, particularly during the time when we lived in the same city. There always was a hurt and a desire that he would at least apologize for his behavior—but that never occurred. I felt compelled to go the extra mile to show him some respect as my father—while at the same time recognizing that there were barriers which only he could remove."

It is possible to maintain cordial contact, assist a bad parent with such basic needs as food or housing and medicine, and not spend a lot of time marinating in negativity in front of them or behind their backs. It may not be ideal, and it may not salve your feelings, but that small something you do ennobles your soul anyway.

Mom, Dad . . . Don't Bug Me!

Parents should not place unnecessary or unreasonable demands on their adult children, especially married children with families of their own. Parents should not treat their adult, married children as valets or handymen, expecting them to be on call for their every need or whim. Although it is understandable that aged parents might sometimes feel lonely or helpless, they should not take their children's goodwill for granted.

Parents should not display outbursts of rage or ill temper, be constantly nitpicking or nagging. It is sad to hear the pained calls to my radio program of married children and their spouses, not wanting to reprimand or exclude a parent, but not knowing how to balance the welfare of their family and themselves with the obligation to visit that difficult parent.

It is certainly wrong for parents to force immoral or inappropriate behaviors upon their children's home, something I've lately been hearing more of. Parents, starting their second love life, often choose the road of casual shacking up. That behavior is difficult enough to explain to the children. Expecting the married children to put up that parent and their honey for the night, under the same roof as impressionable children, is often the last straw.

Substance abuse, chain smoking, and bad language are all complaints we've heard. The annoying aspect of getting along with such a parent is feeling as though one is parenting the parent—and failing. Parents should refrain from all of those things, since they would be provoking their adult children to misbehaviors out of retaliatory frustration—thus sharing responsibility for the response.

I Remember When You Kissed My Boo-Boo, Now We've Kissed Each Other Off.

Fault for a troubled or difficult relationship is usually not so black and white. It is a combination of behavior and interpre-

tations of that behavior, or the attitude about it, which ultimately ends in hurt and anger. Sometimes the absence of a
parent-child relationship seems to be the fault of the parent. If
a parent does not want to be involved in the life of his or her
child, there is not much that can be done. If a parent places
too many demands on the child, using ultimatums or guilt, the
child may be forced to retreat to superficial boundaries of
honoring parents, without the depth of a meaningful relationship. Just as the role of parent is to make sure that the child
knows the door is always open for communication, it is the
obligation of an adult child to let his parent know that the
door is always open for him.

Sometimes the fault more fully lies with the child. He or
she may not want the obligation of dealing with a parent or
simply can't cope with feeling like a child. One of the more
common themes we observe is the rejection of parents who
sacrificed a great deal to provide a good and loving home for
their children. That love is not wasted. According to a Jewish tradition, "The love of parents goes to their children, but
the love of these children goes to their children." The love
given from parents to children should be returned with the
deserved honor, and the love itself is passed on to the next
generation.

Most often both sides contribute to the breakdown in the
relationship. Coming from opposite ends of the parent-child
spectrum, each cannot respect the needs of the other. Since the
struggle is so painful, the ties are cut to avoid the pain. This
short-term benefit of conflict avoidance is usually insignificant
compared to the long-term price of a nonexistent relationship
between parent and child. Rabbi Vogel has seen too many
cases of parents dying before they can reconcile with their
children. The parent passes away, feeling a profound sadness
over the lost relationship, and the child usually feels some
sense of guilt that things should have been different.

The commandment of honoring parents ensures that there will be some type of civil interaction that can lay the foundation for a future stronger relationship.

Ask Not What Your Parents Can Do for You . . .

We honor parents by addressing them with respect even if we do not respect them. It is especially important not to talk to them condescendingly or to raise your voice unnecessarily. Most of us have seen adult children dishonor their parents by speaking sarcastically toward them or even yelling at them in public. There can be no worse model of parenting than to raise your voice to a parent in front of their grandchildren. We dishonor parents when we treat them like errant children.

We honor parents when we are appreciative for whatever they give us; we dishonor them when we expect too much. Incredibly, many children feel that parents owe them perpetual financial assistance or are obligated to serve as baby-sitters and helpers. We have seen too many cases in which parents help their adult children with the down payment on a house, or cosign on a car or some luxury item, and their generosity was considered obligatory, rather than an exemplary act, by their children.

We honor parents today by making sure they are taken care of when they can no longer care for themselves. Whether it is allowing a parent to move in, arranging for home care by a professional caregiver, or helping them to move into a care facility for seniors, we fulfill the commandment of honoring parents. Just as parents cared for us in the early years, the act is reciprocated in their later years. According to Jewish tradition, children are not obligated to pay for this care if parents can afford it. When needed, we are financially obligated to extend ourselves.

We honor parents by not constantly resenting what they are

not and what they did not do and then throwing it in their faces. There are times we simply have to accept their quirks, idiosyncrasies, bad habits, unfortunate personalities, and communication styles. We do that by passing by that which does not have to be confronted. For the duration of a visit or a phone call, surely not every objectionable moment needs commentary. Such deference often leads to a greater number of shared good moments.

We honor parents by keeping them connected to family. This form of honor is more complicated because it may depend on the attitudes and actions of the parents. Relationships are a two-way street. At a certain level, parents do have to give more in order to receive more. If parents create a negative family dynamic, then these occasions will be limited. In general, to deprive parents of family relationships is to dishonor them. For elderly parents, connection to family gives meaning to life. It is sometimes all they have. We do not believe there is any greater honor than giving elderly parents a connection to the generations that provide a sense of immortality for them.

What most parents desire from their children is contact, plain and simple: letters, calls, visits. After that, most parents desire that you lead a life of integrity, that you achieve success in your ventures and happiness from your personal life, and that you ultimately find your life to be meaningful.

It is not a surprise that issues of what children owe parents have made it into the courtroom. The results were alarming. According to Cleveland's *Plain Dealer* (May 21, 1998), a woman's conviction on charges of nonsupport and involuntary manslaughter in the death of her seventy-nine-year-old mother had been overturned by an appellate court. The woman had been convicted in her mother's death because, according to court records, she "died of pneumonia, attributed to gangrene and what prosecutors characterized as months of gross neglect. Photographs of her body shown during her daughter's trial showed oozing skin ulcers and a gangrenous wound on her buttocks. The elderly woman had cataracts in both eyes, a dislocated shoulder, bruises, a broken pelvis and open sores on her foot." She was released from jail by the court of appeals, which said she was not guilty because she provided financial support to her mother. The Ohio Supreme Court, upholding the reversal, said, "The only legal responsibility adult children have in caring for aging parents is to provide adequate financial support." Supreme Court Justice Douglas, who wrote the opinion said, "We do not believe that the General Assembly intended to place adult children in such untenable situations and create fertile grounds for unreasonable and excessive prosecutions. An adult child's duty in these types of cases rests upon a moral obligation, not an obligation enforceable by law."

We are horrified that such a case of neglect, which would likely be successfully prosecuted if the caretaker were not the elderly person's child but a hired caretaker, should be considered outside legal remedy. It does seem to follow a trend of disavowing responsibility for our elderly.

I'm Only Old . . . Not Finished

The commandment to honor parents influences the honor we show others. According to the Bible, we are commanded, "**In the presence of an old person shall you rise and you shall honor the presence of a sage and you shall revere your God— I am the Lord**" (Leviticus 19:32). The Jewish tradition respects experience and the wisdom that comes with age. Unfortunately, we live in a society that worships youth, looks, power, and health. We have lost the sense that the elderly have anything to offer us. By denying their worth, we cheapen the worth of society and find ourselves having to reinvent the wheel with each generation—cutting down the time we can actually benefit from those things that their wisdom could afford us.

Japan, where people have always venerated age, has been able to retain respect for the elderly. Annually they celebrate a holiday know as *Keiro No Hi* (pronounced, "Kay-row-no-hi"), or "Respect for the Aged Day." This holiday was established in the early sixties, probably at the time when traditional family structures were undergoing dramatic transformation. On this day in Japan, the elderly are invited to public ceremonies where they receive gifts. A number of senior citizen artists are designated as "Living National Treasures." Special recognition is given to those who are over one hundred.

During the two years Rabbi Vogel lived in Israel, he was constantly amazed at the consideration given the elderly. Whether it is giving up a seat on the bus or offering assistance, Israeli culture knows how to treat its national treasures.

We must re-endow our elderly with the respect they deserve, to see them as national treasures rather than national relics. "It is true that youth is bursting with strength and vigor, but a person's worth is not to be measured by physical endowments. The body is but an accessory of the soul" (Rabbi Naftali Reich, *Legacy,* 1997).

Teachers Are Not Pets

It is a shame that teachers, who were once held in great respect, have lost their elevated status in America. According to Jewish tradition, anyone who teaches a child is considered to be like a parent and accorded the same respect: **"You shall place these words of Mine upon your heart and upon your soul; . . . You shall teach them to your children to discuss them. . . . In order to prolong your days and the days of your children . . ."** (Deuteronomy 11:18–21).

Today, parents demand that the teachers fulfill parental responsibilities, in addition to the three Rs. The failure of a child to succeed, to be good, or to be happy in a classroom has become the full responsibility of the teacher—with little respect or backup from parents. These parents, too busy to follow through on homework assignments or teacher's meetings, become enraged when their child's work or behavior at school gives them "something more to deal with." We have seen parents insult teachers in front of children. By doing so they undermine the status of the teacher and diminish the important role model the teacher can be in the life of the child. Anybody who dedicates himself to the education of children deserves respect.

What Goes Around . . .

The Hebrew word *kavod*, "honor," comes from the word *kavad*, "heavy." Honoring parents is not easy. It is a heavy responsibility. The Fifth Commandment sets a minimum standard of parental honor. The command to honor parents concludes the first five commandments, tying the commandments dealing with God to those establishing our responsibilities to other people. Honoring parents not only helps us to honor God, it also helps us to honor other people. The last five commandments would be much more meaningful and easier to obey if we honored people and wanted to avoid hurting them. Struggling with this commandment, dealing with decency and kindness in the midst of the powerfully wrenching emotions that can be engendered in the parent-child tug-of-war, should make it easier to deal decently with folks who are at a more comfortable distance.

A final story: Once upon a time, when families lived in extended units, with children and grandparents living together, there was a home in which a man lived with his son, daughter-in-law, and grandchildren. The meals they ate together were always a wonderful time of sharing. As the years went by, the man's health began to decline. He couldn't help as much around the house, and his hands began to shake. He some-times would spill his food on the table or even on the rug.

One day when he was shaking particularly badly the spoon he was holding in his bowl broke, spilling the food all over. The son said to his father in anger and frustration, "Dad, I can't take this any longer. Can't you control yourself? You will just have to eat by yourself in your room." And so the son gave his father a wooden bowl that could not break, and for every meal would bring food to the father's room.

Time went by and the meals at the dining-room table were much quieter and neater. The old man was very lonely eating his meals in his room, but he didn't say anything because he didn't want to make his son even more upset.

Several weeks later the son came home and found one of his children making something out of wood.

"What are you making?" he asked.

"I am making a wooden bowl," answered the young boy.

"It is very nice, but what will you use it for?"

"Oh, it is not for me, Dad, it is for you."

"For me? Gee, maybe we can keep fruit in it," said the dad.

The son answered, "It is not for you yet, Dad. I am saving it for when you get older and your hands begin to shake. When I see it is too hard for you to eat with us, then I will give it to you so you can eat in your room."

The father silently walked into the house and went to his own father's room. "Dad, I'm so sorry for what I have done. How many years did you take care of me, assuring me that I would grow out of my clumsiness? Never once did you make me eat a meal in my room; and look at what I have done to you. Can you ever forgive me for not giving you the respect you deserve?"

That night the old man returned to the dining-room table. Though the table was a little less quiet and a little less neat, the family was whole.

Through the command of honoring parents, we can save

our families and help bring respect back into a society sorely in need of it.

Finally, Jewish tradition envisions the ultimate homecoming for Messianic redemption. It is when "The hearts of the parents will be returned to their children, and the hearts of the children returned to their parents. . . ."

6

The Sixth Commandment

"You shall not murder."

This is probably the first commandment you think has little real relevance to your life. After all, how many times have you actually plotted someone's demise other than in vengeful, wishful fantasies? Your lack of follow-through might be explained by the fear of being caught and punished, fear of people's negative judgment, fear of living with guilt, fear of the actual act of terminating someone else's life, or an ambiguous fear of God's retribution.

These restraints that prevent people from acting upon homicidal thoughts are not foolproof. "Road rage," the expression of anger against those who lack driving etiquette or by those with a low frustration level for traffic, has led to increased incidents of highway shootings and unsafe driving maneuvers that result in many deaths. Perhaps, encased in a steel cocoon, we tend to forget about the humanity contained in each car.

Not identifying and regarding others as humans as important as ourselves is a major issue in the occurrence of murders. Liberal abortion laws and attitudes have contributed, in my opinion, to the horror of newborn murders and abandonment. Once we depersonalize pregnancies as "fetal tissue," subject to our whim and convenience, it is not a great leap in attitude to feel similar immediately after childbirth. The proliferation of violent entertainment for children, supported by the ready availability of weapons, has led to children perpetrating massacres in schoolyards. The lack of cohesive families and communities due to more liberal attitudes toward single motherhood, shacking up, and divorce has resulted in fatherless, unstable homes—the spawning ground for violent, gang youth. The permissiveness and inappropriate compassion for alcohol- and drug-addicted and/or violent or neglectful parents has resulted in a mentality of reunification of vulnerable children with dangerous parents, leading to child abuse and murder.

Nowhere in the world is immune from such inhumanity, for passions of nationalism, tribalism, religion, economics, power, revenge, competition, or just hatred provide a constant bloody flow of deaths throughout the world. We are a species that eats our own.

The First Murder

"Abel became a shepherd, and Cain became a tiller of the ground. After a period of time, Cain brought an offering to the Lord of the fruit of the ground; and as for Abel, he also brought of the firstlings of his flock and from their choicests. The Lord turned to Abel and to his offering, but to Cain and to his offering He did not turn. This annoyed Cain exceedingly, and his countenance fell" (Genesis 4:2–5).

Sibling rivalry for God's attention, approval, and affection was the cause of humanity's "first murder." God addresses

Cain's emotional pain (**"Why are you annoyed . . . ?"**) and its association to the acceptance of an evil response (**"Sin rests at the door . . ."**) and clarifies further that the final choice of behavior is his (**"Yet, you can conquer it"**). In spite of God's attempts to help Cain face what is difficult in life, Cain slays Abel.

God then gives Cain the opportunity to confess and repent, but Cain chooses to lie about his knowledge of Abel's whereabouts: **"I do not know** [where Abel is]. **Am I my brother's keeper?"** (Genesis 4:9).

The cosmic answer to that question is, "Yes!" According to the Bible, human life is sacred; its wanton destruction is seen as a crime against God.

Isn't All Killing Murder?

A confusion exists in the translation of what is forbidden by this commandment. The New King James Version's translation of the commandment, **"You shall not** *murder,"* is correct. The many other translations in which the commandment reads **"You shall not** *kill"* do not convey the true meaning of the Hebrew word *tirtzach*. This Hebrew word reflects wrongful killing, which is different from the killing that occurs in capital punishment, war, and self-defense that are permitted in the Bible.

The difference between killing and murder is not a simple matter of semantics; we view the act of taking a life, which may be permitted at times, with varying degrees of severity. Some forms of killing are considered worse than others. Our judicial system makes distinctions between murder and manslaughter based on the degree of premeditation, negligence, or intent. Given these distinctions, someone can go free for accidentally killing someone, when there is no negligence; be imprisoned for a short time for killing someone out of negligence; receive a sentence of life in prison for murder, or a death sentence for murder with special circumstances. We respond differently when we hear about an accidental shooting than when we hear about the torturous, wanton, gleeful acts of murder committed by the followers of Charles Manson. One saddens us, and the other shocks, sickens, and frightens us. We intuitively understand the differences between the various acts that cause death. The simple wording of this commandment acknowledges that all killing is not equal.

"Every Murder Is an Attack on God"

If you believe that the prohibition of murder is related to the verse "Love your fellow as yourself" (Leviticus 19:18), or as Jesus taught, "Do unto others whatever you would have them do to you" (Matthew 7:12), or its rabbinic twist, "What is hateful to you do not do to your neighbor," then murder is wrong because we do not want to be killed. It is a rule of social order. If you consider young gang members who kill because they do not value life, you realize there are people who do not care about being killed and see nothing wrong with killing.

If you believe that the laws established by society must be adhered to by all citizens, and that murder is wrong because society says so, then you have to respect that in Nazi Germany, and much of eastern Europe, it was acceptable to kill Jews, gypsies, homosexuals, the severely retarded, and any other group deemed inferior. Hitler came to power through a democratic process, and the support of the people kept him in power. If German society said it was acceptable to kill these people, then that was the social order. There are societies today where it is acceptable to murder certain ethnic groups. Look at the "ethnic cleansing" that took place in Bosnia or the tribal feuding in Africa. Who is to say that their age-old way of dealing with conflict is wrong? The fact that something is approved of by society does not make it objectively right. If murder is objectively wrong, then there must be a reason that makes it so. That objective reason, superseding all emotions and tyrants, is that God said murder is wrong.

Murder is wrong because life is a gift from God. Not only is life a gift, but also our very existence is tied to God; **"So God created man in His own image; in the image of God. He created him; male and female He created them"** (Genesis 1:27). We are not merely well-developed protoplasm; humans are unique in their essence because God **"blew into his nostrils the soul of life; and man became a living being"** (Genesis 2:7). Therefore, **"Whoever sheds the blood of man, by man shall his blood be shed; for in the image of God He made man"** (Genesis 9:6). Since the human gift of life is endowed with the spark of divinity that makes us different from all other life, to take another life wrongfully can be likened to stealing from God and even viewed as the murdering of something divine.

Did God Murder Humanity?

When Adam and Eve were evicted from the Garden of Eden into the world at large, they did so without instructions, without laws. By the time of Noah, a humanity without laws produced a humanity without order and without a sense of sanctity. The result: **"Now the earth had become corrupt before God"** (Genesis 6:11). In a remarkable passage, God, like a parent whose heart is broken by an errant child, **". . . saw that the wickedness of Man was great upon the earth, and that every product of the thoughts of his heart was but evil always. And the Lord reconsidered having made Man on earth, and He had heartfelt sadness"** (Genesis 6:5–6).

In His regret, God designs to blot out the men whom He created, along with beasts, creeping things, and birds of the sky; every living thing but Noah, who **"walked with God"** (Genesis 6:9). There are many ancient stories from various pagan cultures that tell of great floods that exterminated various peoples for motivations peculiar to their particular god's emotional personality. This commonality has been used either to dismiss the Noah story as simply a rewrite of preexisting mythology or as proof of a real geological cataclysm. What is historically and spiritually unique about this story is that it is a story with a moral, whose themes include sin, righteousness, an opportunity for turning over a new leaf, and growing personal responsibility (albeit with God's blueprints, Noah himself builds the ark—a leap from God having to make clothes for Adam and Eve). This isn't just a story about God's disappointment and vengeance, it is a story about redemption and the opportunity to become righteous by means of laws that govern our behaviors and an awareness that behaviors bring sanctity and godliness to humanity.

When God created the flood, did He murder humanity? By definition, murder suggests wrongful death. God's actions follow man's private corruption and the loss of public shame, which led to generally accepted immoral behavior. Evil mankind received the divine death penalty—but not the righteous Noah. And this was not the end of humanity. Through Noah, the new "father" of future humanity, God provided laws to assist and direct people, in spite of "human nature," toward righteousness. These first laws included the prohibition against murder: **"However, your blood which belongs to your souls I will demand, of every beast will I demand it; but of man, of every man for that of his brother I will demand the soul of a man. Whoever sheds the blood of man, by man shall his blood be shed; for in the image of God He made man"** (Genesis 9: 5–6). These laws given to Noah and his descendants, according to Jewish tradition, are called the Seven Noachide Commandments. The laws are as follows:

➤The establishment of law courts

➤The prohibition against blasphemy

➤The prohibition against idolatry

➤The prohibition against sexual immorality

➤The prohibition against murder

➤The prohibition against theft

➤The prohibition against eating a limb torn from a living animal (compassion for animals)

Jewish tradition holds that these are universal divine expectations of God and that all non-Jews who observe the Noachide laws will participate in salvation and in the rewards of the world to come.

The First Covenant

What is special about these laws is that they are rooted in a covenant. Before Noah, there was no covenant. God made a "legal relationship" with Noah, through which He made ethical demands through laws.

God placed a rainbow in the sky as a token of the covenant that **"waters shall never again become a flood to destroy all flesh"** (Genesis 9:15). We have no way of knowing if God regretted what He had done, or if the sight of the death of his creatures weighed heavily on his heart. God did what God decided had to be done. If there was divine regret, perhaps it was that the situation had gone so far.

The next time God decided to punish humanity this severely, He first consulted with Abraham. In the ensuing discussion (Genesis 18:23–33), Abraham convinces God that even the presence of ten righteous people demands the saving of all the inhabitants of Sodom and Gomorrah. In the end, not even ten righteous people were found to save the inhabitants

of these cities. Once again, this God of justice could not punish the righteous with the wicked—Lot and the righteous
members of his family were saved. Human life is so sacred
that even God must have good cause to take it.

Murder Punishable by Death

Although the accidental taking of a life is not punishable by
death, according to the Bible, murder is. The Bible suggests a
number of reasons for capital punishment as the consequence
for murder. As retribution and deterrence, capital punishment
reflects God's desire: **"you shall destroy the evil from among Israel"** (Deuteronomy 17:12).

Even stronger is the image that **"blood defiles the land"**
(Numbers 35:33). Just as Abel's blood called out from the
ground (**"The voice of your brother's blood cries out to Me
from the ground!"**, Genesis 4:10), murder is so abhorrent that
the call of the blood can only be silenced by removing from
the world that person who stole the life. While Cain is spared
from the ultimate punishment, later the Bible is very explicit
that **"Whoever sheds the blood of man, by man shall his
blood be shed"** (Genesis 9:6).

This position applies to the issue of capital punishment. Although the biblical tradition is quite clear on the acceptance of
capital punishment, subsequent Jewish and Christian teachings are cautious in its application. For example, Jewish law
and tradition maintain that the death sentence in a capital
case is prohibited if the conviction is on the basis of a strong
presumption or circumstantial evidence, even though it appears conclusive. In fact, it is also necessary that there be at
least two eye witnesses (**"A single witness shall not stand up
against any man for any iniquity or for any error, regarding
any sin that he may commit; according to two witnesses or according to three witness shall a matter be confirmed,"**

Deuteronomy 19:15), and that the death penalty cannot be in-flicted if the judges found in favor of the death sentence by only one vote ("... and do not respond to a grievance by yielding to the majority to pervert the law," Exodus 23:2). The intention of these limitations is that no capital punish-ment is to be inflicted unless there are witnesses who testify that they know for certain what happened, without any doubt whatever, and that there is no other possible explanation. These precautions are necessary so that authorities "... do not execute the innocent or the righteous ..." (Exodus 23:7). In other words, be extremely careful not to put a person to death when it is possible that he did not do the capital crime.

It is typical of rabbinic law and thought that the written text of the Bible is not followed slavishly but is interpreted and reinterpreted by Jewish scholars and teachers in order to preserve its dynamic qualities and respect for the balance be-tween compassion and justice. Although the state of Israel has virtually banished capital punishment, it is permitted for the offenses of treason and genocide.

Some religious groups are particularly strong in their oppo-sition to capital punishment because they believe that it is not the place of humans to terminate sacred life except for self-defense or moral wars. Others who oppose capital punish-ment do so based on its irreversible nature, considering the possibility that the individual might be innocent.

C. M. Adams, who describes himself as a Christian interested in the subject of capital punishment, wrote us: *"Man did not in-vent capital punishment, God did! But, being merciful and just, He established a protocol for the implementation of the penalty. Though not a student of Hebrew, I agree that 'Thou shall not kill' has been misinterpreted. Murder deserves justice. There is no 'moral dilemma' when it comes to capital punishment. God Him-self determined that. Capital punishment is not about deterrence, nor is it about closure, nor is it cruel. It is Scriptural and it is Just."*

As for the argument that society degrades itself when it extracts the ultimate in punishment, Richard G. Durant eloquently expressed his response, which showed this argument to be fallacious, in a syndicated column published June 23, 1997: "What a society does to one who murders an innocent person proclaims quite clearly to one and all how much it values the life of that innocent person. A truly civilized society has no other choice than to demand the ultimate punishment. Anything less demeans the society—and life."

As for the notion that "only God can take a life," note that capital punishment for murder of an innocent is mandated in each of the (Torah) Five Books of Moses (Genesis 9:6, Exodus 21:21, Leviticus 24:17, Numbers 35:31, Deuteronomy 19:20). In fact, it's the only law in the Torah repeated in each and every one of the Five Books! Obviously, this was an important divine consideration!

I find it morally abhorrent that some equate capital punishment with murder. The murder of an innocent is clearly different from the societal determination to eliminate an evildoer. A murderer and one seeking justice cannot be considered morally equivalent. *The Midrash,* a compilation of ancient rabbinic reflections, summed up the problem very concisely: "Those who are merciful when they must be cruel, will, in the end, be cruel to those who deserve mercy." I am often stunned and saddened at the crowds who hold vigils at the prisons in support of a cold-blooded murderer of a child. On my radio program, I have often challenged those same people to carry candles in front of the homes of the victims—and, more importantly, to volunteer to help and support the surviving relatives and friends in their grief and loss. That they don't is a clear example of how their compassion is misdirected and distorted in a knee-jerk, easy way to feel holy.

Even if one is in favor of capital punishment, the act of retribution should not be done with celebration. Though the Bible describes public executions and even the subsequent display of the corpse (Deuteronomy 21:22) so that people could see justice, public executions should not be accompanied by applause, jubilation, cheers, and jeers, which demean the integrity of life. This is inhumane and barbaric. It is one thing to permit a family member the satisfaction of seeing the murderer of a loved one put to death, but it is another to make it a form of grandstanding celebration.

According to one Jewish tradition, after the Israelites had passed safely through the Red Sea and water crashed down upon the Egyptian army, annihilating every last soldier, the angels began to sing the praises of God. But God silenced them, saying "my creatures are drowning and you are praising me?!?" Not even the angels are able to rejoice in divine retribution. It is possible to feel a sense of justice and yet retain respect for the sanctity of life.

A Time to Kill?

Human beings can rationalize anything as okay if it's something they desire to possess or to do without consequences. This is precisely why divine law is so crucial. In a recent movie, *Nick of Time,* a regular guy is set up to murder a female presidential candidate or his young daughter would be murdered. It would be easy to rationalize that a child is more important than an adult, or that family is more important than a stranger, or that what is being done is under duress, so that responsibility is shifted outside. If any one of us were in that situation, we would be tempted. The "hero" chose not to murder. Instead, he tried to protect the candidate as well as save his daughter.

The same plotline is recorded from fourth-century Babylon, when a man came to an important rabbi and said that the governor of his town ordered him to murder an innocent or he would be killed. The rabbi responded by asking, "Who says your blood is redder?" In other words, on what basis can someone argue that his life is more important than another's? Killing the innocent victim would not be self-defense. Since that governor aimed to murder him unjustly, he is justified in eliminating the governor if there is no other way to survive.

Jewish law justifies the taking of the life to protect another from certain death: "... **you shall not stand aside while your fellow's blood is shed** ..." (Leviticus 19:16). However, whenever possible, you must warn the attacker first. If you can save him by any means short of killing him without endangering yourself, you should.

Self-defense is also justifiable. In II Samuel (2:22–23), Asahel would not stop pursuing Abner, who begged him to: "**Why should I strike you to the ground? How will I be able to show my face to your brother Joab?**" When he refused to desist, Abner struck him in the belly with a backward thrust of his spear, "**... and he fell there and died in his place.**"

Although many people believe that the Christian notion of "turning the other cheek" prohibits self-defense, the Catechism of the Catholic Church holds that it is legitimate to insist on respect for one's own right to life. Someone who defends his life is not guilty of murder, even if he is forced to terminate the life of the aggressor. Furthermore, mortal defense is not only considered a right, but a grave duty for someone responsible for another's life, or the common good of the family or of your country.

Jewish tradition would say that not to prevent someone from murdering you is suicide, and suicide is always forbidden.

And then there is the question of war. Though there are too many religious factions declaring so-called "holy wars" to justify their barbarous, immoral actions, there is such a thing as a moral, obligatory war. We must acknowledge that, in the words of Ecclesiastes (3:8), "There is a time for peace and a time for war." Although war is sometimes a necessary evil, the worst thing that might happen to us is that we become arrogant, insensitive, without compassion or pity. That is why civilized countries have rules of war and demand justice for war crimes. God is divinely compassionate and, as we have seen earlier in this chapter, is concerned with justice and law.

This kind of compassion was best expressed by the words of Prime Minister Golda Meir, the first female head of a Jewish state since the time of the Bible, who, upon reflecting on the wars with Egypt for Israel's survival, said, "We can forgive the Arabs almost everything. We can even forgive them for killing our children. We cannot forgive them, however, for turning our children into killers."

Each of Us *Is* a World

Is it any worse a crime to murder ten people than to murder one? Ask the parent, child, or spouse of the one murdered, and they will tell you the only thing that matters is the person they have lost. It is as if the whole world has perished. For this reason, Jewish tradition teaches that "if a person saves one life, it is as if a whole world had been saved. And, if a person destroys one life, it is as if a whole world had been destroyed." Look at your family tree and go back to your great-great-great-grandparents. Take note of the number of offspring. Dozens, perhaps even hundreds of people are alive because of them. Imagine if they had been murdered before they were able to have children. The murder of a single person has profound implications for the future.

If a single life is like a whole world, the magnitude of six million Jews who were murdered by the Nazis is overwhelming. Imagine what it would be like during a season of sold-out Dodgers home games if the fans were marched off after each game to a crematorium, never to be seen again. Even then it would not equal the number of Jews murdered by the Nazis. Six million is too hard to imagine. In this staggering number, the significance of the individual is lost. Perhaps if you think of six million *and one,* you can gain an understanding. "One" we can relate to, because it reminds us of ourselves.

Just as we can feel unrecognized or anonymous in a large group, the sense of horror for the loss of life can actually be diminished when considering large numbers of victims. Capturing the magnitude of the number of those who died was the motivation for the design of the Vietnam Memorial in Washington, D.C. The starkness of the stone with thousands of names speaks for itself. People can come and find the name of a friend or loved one. Each name represents a tragedy. Six million *and one* is an attempt to emphasize the uniqueness of each life that was taken. The death of so many worlds is too difficult to imagine.

The Murder of Yourself

Judaism and Christianity reject the idea that our bodies are ours to do with as we wish. Mormons prohibit ingesting certain unhealthy products into the body like caffeine, alcohol, and nicotine. Some rabbis have prohibited smoking as an unacceptable risk. Judaism and Catholicism forbid any kind of mutilation of the body. Judaism even prohibits any permanent changes to the body like tattooing. All these religious prohibitions are related to the fact that God has placed our souls within an earthly vessel that must be cared for accordingly. Both the spiritual essence of the soul and the physical nature of the body are gifts from God. For some religious traditions, it is possible to "sin in the heart." Though the pleasure of the flesh can lead us to sin, we can perform the righteous acts that God desires almost exclusively through the physical nature of our bodies. We can look at our bodies as a kind of lease program in which we must return it with only "reasonable wear and tear." The biblical idea that "... **from dust of the earth we were created and back to the earth shall we return**" (Genesis 3:19) is the image for the return of our leased vessel to God.

Since our bodies are not ours, not only is the taking of another life forbidden, but so is the taking of our own life. If we believe that life is a gift from God, we forfeit certain rights with the acceptance of that gift. Namely, we cannot terminate the lease prematurely. Though the individual contemplating suicide may feel that life is unfair or God is punishing him or her, taking one's own life potentially undermines the cosmic order of the universe. Our lives are endowed with purpose, and the challenge is to find that meaning. That is why people who recover the best from the loss of a loved one or personal tragedy are the ones who find meaning in the experience. One need only think about Elizabeth Glaser, the wife of actor Paul Michael Glaser, who suffered the loss of a child to AIDS and was diagnosed herself with the disease. She spent the remainder of her life raising awareness of the disease, fund-raising for AIDS research, and serving as an inspiration to many people to make the most of life. Christopher Reeve is another example of someone who could have given up after his accident. Using his fame, he has brought new attention to the needs of the disabled. In addition, he has served as an inspiration to the severely disabled that physical limitations are unrelated to finding meaning.

The rejection of suicide is an attempt to force a person to find meaning rather than taking the easy way out. The physical and emotional condition of terminally ill people, like those suffering from the advanced stages of AIDS, challenges the compassion of a no-suicide policy, but the theological difficulties of establishing acceptable criteria for suicide are too problematic. The Jewish perspective on suicide is that the individual has sinned only if he has killed him or herself "with one's full wits." Most people who kill themselves are at wit's end. In this situation, the suicide most usually occurs in the midst of depression. Unless it can be proven that the individual killed him or herself as a decided, informed act, it is not considered deliberate. The despondent suicide would be given burial rights and respect. The Catholic Church's doctrine is similar. Grave psychological disturbances, anguish, suffering, or torture can diminish the responsibility of the one committing suicide. The eternal salvation of people who have taken their own lives is, of course, God's venue. By ways known to Him alone, God can provide the opportunity for salutary repentance.

Some of our most difficult moments as a rabbi and a therapist have been with suicidal individuals on the phone. Most people would say these individuals must have something to live for, but, in such instances as being without a spouse or children, disabled and unemployed, without friends or socialization, there does seem little reason to live. When speaking with such people, theological issues tend to be less compelling because of the emotional pain. They question why God is doing this or that to them. Rabbi Vogel often quotes a favorite Jewish teaching: "There is no person that has not his or her hour." Everyone has a purpose. This purpose is not always easy to discern, especially when one is in despair. Pain can be overcome, if there is a sense of purpose. Unfortunately, a prescription for purpose is often harder to come by than a medical prescription for a physical symptom.

Suicide is a crime against the self and against God. Many people, isolated and depressed, often forget that they have the duty to become a blessing unto the world, each in special ways. Each suicide is a profound loss for all humanity and history, since that person's contribution and the subtle or dramatic impact that might have been lost.

Suicidal behaviors are also contained in this prohibition: not taking care of the body and health, as well as putting oneself intentionally in risky, life-threatening situations without noble cause. Promiscuous sex in the era of AIDS, drunk driving, drug abuse, overeating, and so forth fall in this category.

Abortion

The "pro-life" and "pro-choice" activists do not agree on whether abortion is murder. There have been attempts at medical and legal definitions of "beginning of life" and when the developing embryo or fetus can be considered a human being.

The biblical source for understanding the morality or legality of abortion is not specific and is generally misinterpreted and misunderstood. The grammatical ambiguity of Exodus 21:23 allows for two possible readings. Jewish tradition translates the verse from the Hebrew as follows: **"If men shall fight and they collide with a pregnant woman and she miscarries, but there will be no fatality** [to the woman], **he shall surely be punished as the husband of the woman shall cause to be assessed against him, and he shall pay it by order of judges. But if there shall be a fatality** [to the woman], **then you shall award a life for a life; an eye for an eye . . ."** The long list of equalities between "act" and "retribution" (eye, tooth, and so forth) was to ensure that the punishment not exceed the crime—a concept not commonly held in prior pagan cultures, where a person might lose his life for a stolen loaf of bread.

The Christian interpretation of Exodus 21:23, on the other hand, is reflected in the New King James Version translation: **"If men fight, and hurt a woman with child, so that she gives birth prematurely, yet no harm follows** [to the fetus], **he shall surely be punished accordingly as the woman's husband imposes on him; and he shall pay as the judges determine. But if any harm follows** [to the fetus] **then you shall give life for life. . . ."** In the Jewish reading, a miscarriage resulting in the death of a fetus is not considered murder (that is punishable by death), while in the Christian reading it is.

The Christian reading creates a very clear prohibition and punitive attitude toward abortion as murder. The translation of the original Hebrew does not establish a biblical prohibition of abortion; however, traditional rabbinic interpretation forbids abortions for birth control. The abortions that are permitted according to the Jewish approach are not done so on the theory that "our bodies are ours," but are mostly related to the threat to the mother's life or sanity. Motivations of economics or convenience are considered unacceptable. Although the fetus is not considered a full life for the purpose of defining murder, it is considered a potential life—not to be terminated without sufficient cause.

In point of fact, sometimes abortion is required in Jewish law; for example, to save the life of the mother. The Oral Tradition, said to also be given to Moses along with the Torah at Sinai, states, "If a woman is having difficulty in giving birth, the embryo within her must be dismembered limb by limb and taken out, because the mother's life takes precedence. However, if the greater part of the child comes out (the head), it must not be touched because one life must not be taken to save another." Therefore, partial-birth abortions are prohibited. In Jewish tradition, the status of the fetus as independent life does not occur until after the birth of some part of the fetus.

This does not indicate any lack of seriousness with which Jewish tradition holds the creation of life. Each newborn infant is considered a precious gift from God, which enables them to participate in the process of creation: **"Behold! The heritage of the Lord is children; a reward is the fruit of the womb"** (Psalms 127:3). Additionally, Psalms (139:13–14) emphasizes how the act of creation of new life is a special partnership between God and humans: **"For You have created my mind; You have covered me in my mother's womb. I acknowledge You, for I am awesomely, wondrously fashioned. . . ."**

Sadly there is an ever-increasing volume of calls attempting to justify abortions mostly on the basis of "bad timing" and "wrong guy." These reasons for abortion trivialize the blessing and miracle of life.

Although I have spoken to a number of women over the

years on my radio program who have raised children conceived in incest and rape, these are two categories of conception considered by some to be reasonable exceptions to the prohibition on abortion. In fact, the *Los Angeles Times* (April 13, 1998) reported that a panel of Muslim clerics in Algeria has "decided to allow women raped by Islamic militants to undergo abortions. An estimated 1,600 women have been raped since an insurgency began in 1992, prompting government officials to appeal to religious authorities for an exception to the country's abortion ban." According to *Al Khabar,* a major Algerian newspaper, the term *abortion* was avoided to "ensure that the ruling was not used as a general authority to end pregnancies." Clearly, it is the intention of the terrorists to demoralize and demean the population through these rapes. A similar conspiracy of such depravity was also reported in Bosnia, with the Serbs attacking Muslim women. Permitting abortions under such situations is probably intended to protect the women from further extreme emotional anguish.

Euthanasia

On the issue of euthanasia, Judaism, Catholicism, and some other Christian denominations are in agreement that active euthanasia is forbidden because it is murder. Active euthanasia, however noble the motive, can never be condoned, even if intended solely for the purpose of ending the suffering of a patient. Even if the individual asks for assistance in terminating his or her life, it is forbidden because of the issues we have discussed earlier in the chapter, including that we are made in the image of God and suicide is expressly prohibited. Therefore, Dr. Kevorkian and the physician-assisted suicide bills that have been approved in some states lately are contrary to the Jewish and Christian teachings. The simple fact is that it is not for us to play God by deciding when someone's time is up.

While active euthanasia is clearly considered murder in Judaism and Christianity, the status of passive euthanasia is less clear. Many religious disciplines believe that, whatever its motives and means, direct euthanasia is morally unacceptable. These same traditions generally consider discontinuing medical procedures that are burdensome, dangerous, extraordinary, or disproportionate to the expected outcome to be legitimate. In this so-called passive mode, one does not will to cause death—one is accepting the inevitable. Ordinary care should not be withheld.

We have both been involved with many families who have had to deal with a dying relative. Many times a decision will have to be made whether to permit heroic measures. Even when families have made this decision in advance, second thoughts and even changed decisions occur at the moment a parent goes into cardiac arrest. We have witnessed patients who wither away, losing a sense of dignity in their death, and the families who have to suffer through the deterioration of a loved one.

Compassion and horror naturally cause us all to struggle with the wisdom of religious teachings, which prohibit active euthanasia. We see the discomfort of loving family members in making the decision of immediate life or death or suffering. We worry about the inherent inaccuracy of human beings trying to guess the future of the course of a disease, or having inappropriate motivations for their decisions. But reason does not remove the pain. Conflict between personal pain and a value that has greater good for humanity is understandable. We know that the role of this commandment is to prioritize values and to help us countermand the overwhelming temporary emotions that can be contrary to what we accept as right.

Oregon's first-in-the-nation Death With Dignity statute permits physicians to knowingly prescribe medicines to people who plan to take their own lives. The Oregon law basically allows a patient who has been diagnosed by two physicians as having less than six months to live to seek a doctor's prescription for a lethal dose of barbiturates. According to a report in the *Los Angeles Times* (June 6, 1998), "The law then requires that doctors determine that the patient is not suffering from depression or other mental illness and to impose a 15-day waiting period before completing the prescription for the drugs." Since the physician is not permitted to inject or administer these drugs, whether the physician's actions qualify as active euthanasia may be debated. Since the patient committing suicide is deemed to be of "right mind," this is certainly a sober, determined act of suicide—morally prohibited by Jewish and Catholic law.

Medical advances will continue to challenge the distinction between what we *can* do and what is *appropriate* to do. At this point, guidelines of medical ethics lag behind medical advances. For example, there is currently a national debate over the question of whether to ban experiments in human cloning. Imagine having stored clones for the ideal DNA match in organ transplants. As part of one of my middle school science projects almost forty years ago, I projected this possibility for the future of medicine. As a child, I saw this as a blessing. As an adult, I now see this as a threat to the integrity of that clone's humanity.

God gave us imagination, creativity, and ingenuity to be able to imagine such things, and then make them happen. With this gift comes awesome responsibility. Regrettably, we have the ability to bypass considerations of ethics and morality, where power, money, and ego are invested in their place.

We Are Our Brother's Keeper

It does not take an active form of murder to be culpable for someone's suffering or death. In the book of Leviticus (19:16) we are told "... you shall not stand aside while your fellow's blood is shed, . . ." implying that we must come to the aid of someone who is in trouble. This condemns those who stand by, not wanting to get involved, or to be inconvenienced. The infamous New York City case of Kitty Genovese is a horrible example of ignoring this commandment. She was attacked several times, and finally murdered, on the steps of an apartment building, where no one came to her aid or even called the police. Windows and shades were quietly shut—and a young woman died alone.

When the prophets chastised the people and warned them of impending divine punishment, the warning was directed toward nations as a whole and not individuals. In the biblical world, there was communal responsibility. People were responsible for the deeds of their neighbors. What a different world we live in today, when people don't care what others do wrong as long as it doesn't affect them, and when they will not speak out against immorality if it would in any way jeopardize their position or possessions.

According to the Bible, we are not to be pedestrians in the great journey of life. We should not stand back and watch people suffer while doing nothing. In our own time, this means speaking out on issues like global warming, pollution, sweatshops, and human rights abuses and doing something to stop them. The products that we purchase, the companies we invest in, and the services we provide have vast implications. Our financial support of any inappropriate industry, such as tobacco, or government, strategic but corrupt or cruel, not only implies acceptance of their policies, but also helps to support them. It is not acceptable to say, "Someone else will sell them guns if I don't." Life takes on additional meaning when we stand for something; unfortunately, today many people don't stand for anything other than personal comfort and acquisition.

Though very few civilians actually killed Jews in Nazi Germany, many civilians of other countries, such as Poland, helped the Nazis in their plans against the Jews. Many Lithuanian civilians managed to help the Nazi regime score the biggest "kill rate" in all of Europe. Nevertheless, very few of the people in any of those European countries admitted to knowing anything about the atrocities. Those who knew and did nothing were guilty accessories to mass murder. It was only the very few, those known as Righteous Gentiles (generally Christians), who had the courage and moral imperative to do the right thing. Most analyses of these Righteous Gentiles conclude that they were brought up by caring parents, in religious homes, which lived and taught profound values. Having been taught to "honor their parents," they honored God and saved human lives.

Moses serves as a biblical model for acting out against injustice. He was very comfortable in the house of Pharaoh and could have stayed in the palace, choosing royalty over slavery. He was pushed over the edge when he saw an Israelite being beaten by an Egyptian (Exodus 2:12) and felt compelled to intervene. He killed the Egyptian, saving the life of the Israelite. He was forced to flee from Egypt because of this incident. Having been brought up as royalty, with life-and-death power over the multitude, it is difficult to imagine what moved Moses to intervene. He had witnessed the multitude being mistreated as slaves every day of his life. Perhaps the humanizing effect of seeing one Israelite being mistreated made him realize the tragedy of what was happening. Moses could have done nothing. Moses had so much to lose, yet he could not stand idly by the blood of his neighbor.

In the end, a society in which individuals do not feel an obligation toward one another is a society in which each will feel alone and unsafe. In the words of the Jewish sage Hillel, "If I am not for myself who will be, *but if I am only for myself what am I?*" The German Protestant minister Martin Niemoeller wrote the oft-quoted, "They came for the Communists, but I wasn't a Communist so I didn't object. They came for Socialists, but I wasn't a Socialist so I didn't object. They came for trade union leaders, but I wasn't a union leader so I didn't object. They came for the Jews, but I wasn't a Jew, so I didn't object. Then they came for me, and there was no one left to object."

Give Me That Ole-Time Gossip

By rabbinical interpretation, the Sixth Commandment includes not just the literal taking of life. According to rabbinical sages, publicly humiliating someone is figuratively akin to murder. Whereas the Third Commandment warns us about how words can harm our relationship with God, this commandment warns of the danger of words against people. Words have the power to hurt or heal, depending on how we use them. If one removed negativity, gossip, slander, hostility, cruel sarcasm, anger, divisiveness, derision, ugly threats, and insults from one's vocabulary, one automatically and dramatically improves his own life and that of others. Words have a tremendous potential impact upon situations and people—they can convey compassion and encouragement, blessings and love. Or, they can kill spirits and relationships.

The Bible tells us, **"You shall not be a gossipmonger among your people . . ."** (Leviticus 19:16). A gossiper is someone who goes around telling stories, unnecessarily sharing insights into the lives of people who would rather remain private. Gossip has the potential to destroy people's lives. Gossip is therefore like murder. Even listening to gossip is like standing idly by while your neighbor is murdered.

In spite of the biblical condemnation of gossip, it is a social epidemic. We know it is wrong, and yet everyone does it to one extent or another. Even the great Miriam of the Bible, called a prophetess, is punished with leprosy for gossiping with Aaron about Moses (Numbers 12:1–13).

There are at least three reasons why people gossip:

➤To feel or seem more important:

"... *I was a real gossip monger. . . . I loved to hear gossip and I totally enjoyed repeating it. I felt important. I've elevated myself to a better place and even though it's a struggle sometimes, I plan to stay elevated. I never really knew the damage gossip did. I take that back—I knew but I didn't care. Now I care. I must thank you because you told the story recently about the man, the rabbi and the feather pillow. I'd never heard it before and it made a big impression on me."* (Donna)

The story Donna relates is an old rabbinical story about a man who spread gossip about his rabbi. After getting out his frustrations with the rabbi, he realizes the wrong he's committed and admits his guilt to the rabbi. The rabbi agrees to forgive him, but first assigns him a task of taking a feather pillow to the top of a windy hill and releasing all the feathers. The man is relieved that his forgiveness will come with such a simple act of retribution and fulfills the tasks. When he returns to the rabbi anxious for his forgiveness, the rabbi assigns him just one more task. Somewhat annoyed, but anxious for absolution, the man agrees. The rabbi tells him to go back up the hill and retrieve all the feathers. The man is aghast, proclaiming the impossibility of the task. The rabbi explains that each feather represents someone who has heard of the false gossip and has formed an opinion of the victim of the gossip. How can one repair all that damage?

➤To raise their status through the lowering of someone else's:

"*Well, you got me! I am ashamed of myself! On your show, Dr. Laura, which I heard last night, you were discussing the way the media was gossiping and snickering about the recent problems of an unnamed TV host who is well-known for continuously talking about her children, husband, and religion. I was in full agreement with you when you said how unfair and shamefully this person was being treated, as if she deserved to have this happen to her be-cause she had talked happily about her personal life. And then—EUREKA—a revelation! I suddenly flashed back to a little while ago when I heard about this issue and my initial reaction had been 'HA—serves her right!' I felt myself go bright red from embar-rassment as I seem to have forgotten how basically stupid and petty thoughts such as those were. Then I sat down and spent the rest of the night reflecting on why I even had the gall to think them! Well, guess what—I had no justifiable reason—just maybe a combination of envy about someone who seemed to have it all, and sloppy thinking on my part." (Linda)*

➤Just for the entertainment value:

"I have the best story in regards to gossip. My brother, age fifty-two now, started telling a story about my dad years ago. This story is about something that supposedly happened before my dad was even twenty-three years old. He has repeated to all that would listen and received enjoyment destroying my dad. As a result of all of this and more gossip, my brothers and sisters are not part of my life. I am a middle sibling and have been the target of gossip also. I have yet to hear the latest gossip about me. All I know is this gossip in regards to all in my family has destroyed our family. Never will I have a relationship with my brothers and sisters. It was never my choice. But when I saw the enjoyment from not just my brother, but the rest of my siblings when deal-ing with gossip, I had to remove myself. I could not be a part of it. Gossip seems to be the tie that binds them together. I just don't understand it." (Ginny)

Sometimes gossipers try to pass on the responsibility of the gossip to the listener. Some people begin a juicy tidbit of infor-mation with the statement "I know this is gossip, but. . . ." The disclaimer of the content of the message is intended to transfer responsibility for the gossip if the listener accepts it. Clarifying what he is sharing is gossip should not ease the mind of the gossiper. This is an example of the classic misperception that admitting something makes it better. Yet, Jewish law considers the listener to be much worse than the one who spreads the gossip—it is on the listener's account that the gossip can be spread! **"An evil-doer pays heed to malicious talk, a liar listens to a slanderous tongue"** (Proverbs 17:4).

American law only forbids slander; that is, knowingly publishing or stating false and harmful information with the intent of malice. But try fighting this in a court of law! The lawyer's fees, emotional battering, and further public humiliation are often worse than the original insult.

Stories of false accusations constantly fill the headlines, and not only tabloid newspapers and magazines. Some are done knowingly, others with incorrect information, and still more for the sake of sensationalism. You rarely see an apology or retraction in equally large print. The media does not care about destroying people's reputations, or the impact that the shame and embarrassment have on the individuals and their families, as much as they care about ratings and revenue. They mostly care about selling magazines, newspapers, or commercial time, and lawsuits are seen as the price of doing business.

In an article by Chuck Moss in the *Detroit News* (May 21, 1998) entitled "Journalism Is the First Casualty of Gossip," he mentions three downside issues of today's climate of gossip: "The first casualty is the credibility of journalism. If gossip, slander, rumor, and innuendo are part of the process, whom do you turn to for the facts? . . . The second casualty is the human being subjected to gossip . . . no one smeared in the rumor mill emerges unscathed. The experience sears the soul and coarsens the spirit. . . . Finally, the ultimate casualty of institutionalized gossip is truth itself."

It disgusts me that many contemporary sociologists are contemptuous of privacy, compassion, and values, and have proclaimed positive qualities of gossip. In the *Los Angeles Times* (May 19, 1998) several of these researchers were quoted as saying that despite prevailing social disapproval, the importance of gossiping to a social species has been profoundly underestimated. "Gossiping," they say, "is an essential bonding ritual for dynamic and diverse social groups. It forges common ground, allows us to gauge opinions without disclosing ours, provides a navigating map of social relationships and lays out power structures." Prayer in churches and synagogues, and communal efforts, such as Habitat For Humanity, do it better.

Debra Tannen (*The Argument Culture,* Random House, 1998) explains that the focus of journalism has shifted from the domain of public policy to the "vaguer notion of character in the form of personal foibles and inconsistencies. And rather than exposing specific acts of wrongdoing, the aggression often surfaces as a sneering and contemptuous tone . . . a kind of weird, free-form nastiness—spleen without a purpose."

In addition to outright slander, Jewish law forbids the sharing of true but harmful information. Accordingly, all those tabloid magazines you see at the supermarket checkout are not kosher. Imagine how you would feel if your life were portrayed in unflatteringly graphic details in one of those publications. Job (30:9–10) lamented, **"And these are the ones who now make up songs about me and use me as a byword! Filled with disgust, they keep their distance, on seeing me, they spit without restraint."**

Even when the information has a basis in truth, it may be out of context, magnified in significance because of the emotional aspect of the attention, and distorted by attempts to describe complexities simplistically. Widely broadcast negative gossip can leave the individual little leeway for remorse and change, when those around them are fixated deliciously on that historical information.

Gossip affects how we look at people we may not even know at the moment. When we are predisposed to view someone negatively, that impression negatively affects our behavior toward them. That attitude may be justifiable when the person has a history of being frankly dangerous, but that is the exception and not the rule for slander and gossip.

Our reputation is one of our most precious possessions. We work hard to achieve a good one. Character assassination through gossip or other means kills the good name that someone has worked for. When people have lost their good reputation, they are often as good as dead. Every time we gossip, we send out lethal words that have the potential to kill innocent people, yet we fail to realize the danger of what we say. None of us likes to be gossiped about, and yet we gossip about others. As Shakespeare so wisely wrote: "Who steals my purse, steals trash. But he that fetches from me my good name, robs me of that which enriches him not, and makes me poor indeed."

Though not engaging in any gossip is ideal, here are some ways to manage gossip in our own lives:

➤ We should try to share only firsthand information. Just as hearsay is not accepted in a court of law, we don't pass on secondhand gossip. Even this firsthand information should have some important purpose; for example, when warning a person about potential harm from a business or potential marital partner.

➤ When somebody begins a statement with "I know this is gossip, but . . ." we should say something like, "In that case, please don't tell me." In our experience, the gossiper becomes sufficiently embarrassed to make him think twice before doing it again. Admittedly, this is difficult to do. Such a response will likely be met with annoyance, insult, or anger. Additionally, giving up "dishing the dirt" is tough to do, as Tanya, one of my listeners, admitted in her letter: *"Yesterday, Ash Wednesday, I pondered what I would give up for the Lenten Season. I decided rather than give up something superficial like sweets, I would do something for my character. While at work I decided to give up gossip.*

When a co-worker of mine called me into the office, we discussed what we were giving up. I told him I was digging deep and giving up gossiping. He thought it was a fantastic idea. In the very next sentence, he teased, 'Hey, did you hear what happened to Mary?' My immediate response, 'No, What?!' We both laughed and laughed. This is going to take more self-control and reconditioning than I originally expected."

➤When we are speaking of someone, we can assume that what we say will get back to him or her. There's no point blaming the person to whom you gossiped because they're only showing the same respect for you that you demonstrated when you gossiped. The best rule to follow is never to say unto others what you don't have the guts to say directly to the subject of the gossip.

➤When leaving a party or get-together, don't gossip. It is common for couples and friends to gossip about the hosts on the way home. Those who have extended themselves in hospitality don't deserve such treatment.

➤We refrain from gossip on the Sabbath with the hope that associating gossip with a lack of spirituality will inspire you to refrain from it during the rest of the week.

➤We always give people the benefit of the doubt. If someone has done something good, don't speculate on the possible disingenuous motivations—instead, take it on face value. If someone appears to have done something wrong, he still deserves the benefit of the doubt. It is better to assume that someone has done something unwillfully, out of ignorance, or rightly (perhaps we don't understand the situation) rather than to assume that he or she is malicious.

➤The easiest and most immediate way to stop harming people and to help create a society that cares about people is to stop gossiping and fill that conversational time with discussion of things of beauty, such as art, books, and the theater, or with philosophy and so forth.

Someone sent the following poem to me anonymously:

My name is Gossip. I have no respect for justice.
I maim without killing. I break hearts and ruin lives.
I am cunning and malicious and gather strength with age.
The more I am quoted, the more I am believed.
I flourish at every level of society.
My victims are helpless. They cannot protect themselves
    against me because I have no face.
To track me down is impossible. The harder you try, the
    more elusive I become.
I am nobody's friend.
Once I tarnish a reputation, it is never the same.
I topple governments, wreck marriages, and ruin careers—
    cause sleepless nights, heartaches, and indigestion.
I spawn suspicion and generate grief.
I make innocent people cry in their pillows.
Even my name hisses. . . .
I make headlines and headaches.
Before you repeat a story, ask yourself, Is it true? Is it fair?
    Is it necessary? If not—shut up!

Unfair Business Practices

The aphorism "All's fair in love and war" is a terrible philosophy. Getting the girl does not entitle someone to do whatever it takes. Unfortunately, this philosophy is often also applied to business to become more successful or rationalized as necessary for survival. No matter the motivation, using methods like starting rumors about someone or even intentionally making someone look bad at work, thereby diminishing their professional worth, is unethical. Intentionally undermining the work of a colleague can result in that person's failure to receive a promotion or worse, even termination of employment. To take away someone's livelihood is comparable to murder.

The United States government is concerned about monopolies and unfair business practices because capitalism requires competition for a thriving economy. In reality, to undermine someone's business, to use unethical methods to achieve professional advantage is a personal attack on the owners, employees, and even stockholders of the company. We would argue that nonfactual negative advertising—criticizing a competitor based on negative imagery or innuendo—can be considered a form of murder. We do not feel the personal nature of the attacks when large companies are involved, but large companies are composed of individual workers and investors, all of whom can be seriously hurt financially. Although there are laws concerned with truth in advertising, clever marketers and advertising geniuses know how to manipulate laws and the perception of reality. They can get real close to that line. Negative publicity for business as well as for political campaigning is often not used, because people know that diminishing the worth of a competitor does not reflect the actual value of a product or candidate, but it would be foolish to deny that negative perceptions don't give at least a subliminal impression.

One can elevate oneself in whatever way one wishes, but it is unethical to do so by diminishing the worth of another. When the Israelites were about to enter Canaan, after forty years of wandering in the desert, God clarifies twelve curses (Deuteronomy 27: 11–26). Among these is, **"Accursed is one who strikes his fellow stealthily. And the entire people shall say, 'Amen.'"** Jewish tradition applied this to killing someone's reputation. Though it may be possible to escape human law, due to stealth, he will not escape God's.

Embarrassing People

The Jewish tradition teaches that embarrassing someone in public is one of the greatest sins. When people get a little embarrassed, they turn red. When their embarrassment turns to shame, they turn white. Jewish tradition looked at this phenomenon and commented that the whitening of the face is a result of the blood leaving it and is comparable to the shedding of blood. One could argue that unlike gossip, which is done behind someone's back, publicly embarrassing someone is acceptable because the person can defend himself. If gossip can be compared to burglary (when no one is at home), then public embarrassment is like armed robbery. The words used are like bullets aimed at the heart. Many of us been in positions in which having the earth swallowing us whole seemed a welcome option to the shame and humiliation felt at the hands of another.

Jewish law forbids insulting anyone either by word or deed in public. In fact, the sages say, "He who insults his fellowman in public will have no share in the world to come." Also, we must refrain from calling anyone by an offensive name, or from telling stories in his presence about which he feels ashamed. If anyone has sinned against us and we need to rebuke him for it, we must not insult him in public.

When we humiliate somebody publicly, we give him less motivation, opportunity, and public support for repentance. Once the reputation is destroyed, the road back is made more difficult by the lingering negative impressions we've left with the observers of the public disgrace. Consider, and even identify with, the pitiful cries of Job (19:1–2)—**"Until when will you sadden my spirit and crush me with words? These ten times you have humiliated me"**—before we cause another such hurt.

In conclusion, live the kind of life that can be described in the prayer of King David in Psalms (17:3–5), and all the world will be able to rejoice in your existence:

"You probe my heart, examine me at night,
you test me by fire and find no evil.
I have not sinned with my mouth—as most people
do.
I have treasured the word from your lips,
My steps never stray from the paths you lay
down. . . ."

And let us say, "Amen."

7

The Seventh Commandment

"You shall not commit adultery."

A mother, writing to me, offered her small daughter's definition of adultery: *"While making school lunches, my six-year-old daughter and I were having a conversation about her Religious Education Class she would be starting the following night. We were having quite a question/answer session, she being the one asking, and I answering. Then, to change things around, I starting asking her questions about things she knew while throwing in a couple of things to teach her. A question to her was, 'Do you know about the Ten Commandments?' 'Hmmmm,' she said, thinking a minute, 'No, I don't think I do. What are they?' I explained they were God's rules we must all live by. She asked, 'What are the Ten?' 'Arggghhh!', I thought to myself, now I have to delve into my memory I was sure I lost during both my pregnancies and recall what I learned all those years in school. I began to recite them. She listened, and didn't say too much because I explained them a little as I went along. I got to 'THOU*

SHALT NOT COMMIT ADULTERY' and as quick as I said it, she asked, 'What does that one mean, Mom?' I chewed my lip a bit and thought about how I was going to tackle this one. But I got my thoughts together and began to try to explain when she stopped me abruptly grinning ear to ear, extremely proud to come up with the answer herself. 'Oh wait, I know! It means you can't cut down an adult tree.' I thought I was going to die. It was so cute and innocent—and of course I tactfully told her what it meant."

I remember when, at about the same age as this little girl, my father was annoyed with me for doing something naughty. I don't recall what I had done, but I remember my dad was fairly fed up. In a fit of frustration, he said something about leaving me in an orphanage if I didn't straighten up. I told him that he couldn't do that.

"And why not?" he retorted indignantly.

"Because," I said triumphantly, "it is against the law!"

"And what law is that?"

"When parents leave kids somewhere it's called adultery!" I said.

I remember my father cracking up. Although I didn't know what was so funny about what I had said, I was relieved to have the tension broken and to get off the hook for my transgression.

Lately, with all the presidential sex-scandal media frenzy, parents across the nation have been forced to confront this behavior with their children at incredibly early ages. Children have been exposed to "debate" on the issues of whether oral sex constitutes adultery, whether adultery is such a bad thing if a person is doing his job well and his spouse doesn't seem to be complaining. Certainly, no one can believe that children are unaffected by the apparent intellectual and spiritual malaise that seems to have swept the land. Children learn by everything they see and experience. A lack of societal consensus about character, fidelity, responsibility, and consequences teaches them a lot about the growing "gray area" in which they can experiment without judgment and seemingly with impunity.

Jason wrote to us about a class on leadership at his local university: *"One of the discussions focused on downsizing, and the instructor asked the class if they had to downsize the Ten Commandments, which commandments would they remove. I was horrified, but not surprised that the majority, not including myself, felt that the commandment not to commit adultery should be removed. When the instructor asked why the majority felt this way, the responses were typically that this commandment was outdated and that nobody obeyed it anyway—so why even have it?*

It deeply saddened me that something as basic as not committing adultery would seem so insignificant to the majority of students in the class. I was brought up believing that this principle concerning the sacred nature of the covenants made at marriage. What scares me to death is that these students will probably become very influential leaders and teachers of future generations."

Clergymen of all denominations recognize that their congregations are probably not going to be more observant or religious than the standard and role model they set. Perhaps we need to recognize that the behavior and character of our leaders and public figures also set a standard of expectation to which our culture, especially our children, will aspire to—or drop to. The pressure to relax the judgment against all sorts of behaviors, including adultery, has deeply troubled and challenged the clergy. Although it is prohibited in both Catholic and Jewish law for clergy to perform the wedding ceremony for known, unrepentant adulterers, because adulterers are not allowed to marry, the ubiquitousness of the behavior and the apparent general societal acceptance of this aspect of "human nature" (except when it's their own spouse's actions) make it an extremely difficult and sensitive issue to pursue.

The Reverend William A. Thompson from All Saints' Episcopal Church in California described such a situation: *"It seems to me that there are far too many people in the Episcopal Church that think judging anybody's actions as wrong is the worse sin! I personally, however, have taken a firm stand. There was a couple, who were parishioners, who separated due to the wife having an affair. Before any divorce, the wife moved in with her lover. Unfortunately, there were three children involved. The wife made an appointment to talk with me about officiating at her wedding to this new stud. Besides being just flabbergasted, I, of course, said I would not. Then, on Father's Day, the children were at church with their father. The wife (still just separated, not yet divorced) came to church that day, sat with the kids and brought her boyfriend/shackup with her. This I could not take. The following week I called on the woman and her lover and told them how inappropriate and awful this was. Neither of them got it. They said I was being nasty and judgmental. I then wrote her a letter saying that if she comes to church, it would not be spiritually healthy or appropriate to receive communion given the circumstances. They got mad and went to another Episcopal Church. At that church, the priest married them within six months without even calling me to find out the circumstances. So much for collegiality."*

Our society is constantly redefining morality, and generally, it's in a downward, permissive, nonjudgmental, self-focused, and self-centered direction. According to a story published in the *New York Times* (February 3, 1998), there are those who see an erosion of American moral standards. In this article, the Reverend Anthony Brankin, a Roman Catholic priest from Chicago, stated that he was already worried by the loss of guilt and shame in American culture, the loss of clear distinctions between right and wrong, the drift toward "moral relativism," even in the Catholic Church. Reverend Bracken is quoted as saying, "Have we as a nation become so corrupted that as long as we get what we want, as long as times are good and the money rolls in, that we don't care what the hell goes on?" In the same article, Dr. Steven Klein, an anthropologist, suggested that the Clinton scandal not only reflects the trend away from strict morality but accelerates it. "We're really relinquishing the fundamental Judeo-Christian values ... how far down the public is willing to ratchet their standard of acceptability—is there a floor?"

To those who would say that private sexual behavior is not relevant to the public, it is increasingly difficult to keep the private from becoming public. When the promiscuous private lives of our leaders become public, "It makes a mockery of leadership," says Rabbi Daniel Lapin, a popular radio talk-show host on Seattle's KVI. "What is the most serious threat confronting teenagers today? It's promiscuity and pregnancy. Can anyone imagine Clinton getting up and telling our young people to be chaste, to be restrained? That's why he pretends that tobacco is the biggest threat to young people today. His position as a leader of the country is compromised" (*Insight*, March 2, 1998).

Today, there clearly is an unwillingness to condemn adultery. "We have become a society that is increasingly reluctant to make any judgments about sexual behavior," says David Blankenhorn, president of the Institute for American Values in *Citizen's Issues Alert* (January 27, 1998). In this same publication, Richard Land, president of the Southern Baptist Convention's Ethics and Religious Liberty Commission, says society's attitude toward sex is a direct result of the 1960s sexual revolution. "The revolution so lobotomized our morality on the sexual front that people are blinded to infidelity. People refuse to judge sexual impropriety because so many of them have been guilty of similar actions."

The statistics from polls and surveys about what percentage of folks have committed adultery are not very reliable, because people lie about it. In the *New York Times* (June 9, 1997), a sociologist is quoted as saying, "The data indicate that the vast majority of Americans think adultery is wrong, pure and simple—maybe eighty percent of them. But the interesting thing is that more people think adultery is wrong than have been faithful. People think adultery is wrong the way people think it's good to be thin, yet lack the will to keep off the weight." Perhaps the explanation for the discrepancy is that too many people don't want to admit to condoning what is basically seen as sinful or immoral behavior, nor do they wish to be betrayed, but they want to leave the door open for their own desires to be actualized.

Sadly, according to a 1994 University of Michigan study, "infidelity is indeed the primary cause of divorce." In support of that conclusion, Dr. Frank Pittman, an internationally renowned expert on sexuality and marriage and an author of a book on infidelity, reports in the same *New York Times* article that in thirty-seven years of practice as a therapist, he has encountered only two cases of first marriages ending in divorce in which adultery was not involved.

The Adultery Culture

There is no question that our culture glamorizes, defends, and even promotes adultery. As Katie Roiphe described in an illuminating article in the *New York Times Magazine* (October 12, 1997), ". . . we've grown much more tolerant of adultery, at least when it comes to women. Women's magazines practically recommend it to their readers as a fun and healthy activity, like buying a new shade of lipstick, or vacationing in the Caribbean. In *Elle* we read that 'an affair can be a sexual recharging, an escape from a worn-out relationship, a way into something better.' *Harper's Bazaar* breathlessly tells us about women whose 'marriages are improved by their affairs. Because they get their fill of rapture elsewhere, these wives are not apt to complain or nag or find fault with their husband.' If a woman has an adulterous affair, she is, according to *Harper's Bazaar,* 'asserting her femininity.'"

Ms. Roiphe went on to discuss the double standard of affairs. Kelly Flinn, the twenty-year-old fighter pilot who had sex with an enlisted woman's husband, and Princess Diana, with her numerous affairs, were seen as "victims" of love and emotional need and desire, while the men were seen as manipulative, opportunistic pigs. Raoul Felder, a prominent divorce lawyer with four decades of watching people who have committed adultery, says in Ms. Roiphe's article that "Women are motivated by the same forces as men—loneliness, hostility, boredom, the need to feel younger and attractive, the need to be worshiped."

In *Women's Day* magazine (November 1, 1997), Barbara Bartocci laments the number of Hollywood contributions to making adultery a source of slapstick humor (Bette Midler's *That Old Feeling*) or romantic hilarity (*Four Weddings and a Funeral*), or a heart tug (*The English Patient*). "When we romanticize adultery or use it as a slapstick tool to provoke laughter—as if the hurt and betrayal are inconsequential— what kind of values are we teaching? People arrive at values through exposure to what their society accepts, and sociologists tell us that what people laugh at or yearn for will spark imitation and acceptance."

The *Vancouver Sun* (September 19–25, 1997) published a *TV Times* cover picture for a new TV series called *Riverdale*. The picture shows a married man and woman facing each other, while she is secretly holding hands with another guy standing behind her. The "other guy" has a caption under him that says, "He loves her, . . ." while underneath the married couple's picture is the caption, "But she's married to him." There is a heart drawn around the illicit handholding and the caption at the bottom of the whole scene says, ". . . and that's only part of the fun on *Riverdale*."

So what's a person to do with all that positive endorsement for a negative activity? One of my listeners wrote, *"It's too easy when you are married to look for comfort elsewhere when trouble is occurring at home. Steps I personally took: didn't read romance novels for an 'unreal' image of life and love. I didn't watch soap operas for the same reason. I avoided programs, movies, or videos that condoned or glamorized adultery. Through my married life I've been attractive enough to get serious looks. I've been careful of how I dress. The words of my dad to his four daughters come back to me, 'Don't advertise unless you have something to sell.' That scared me."*

Of all the impulses and human drives of man, sex is probably the most powerful and difficult to manage. Since sex is "natural," why should the human animal attempt to control its expression? Of what benefit is it to the individual and those close to him/her, to society, to humanity, to God? This chapter will explore these questions.

To Know You Is to Love You

We often use the phrase "he *knew* her in the biblical sense" to refer to a couple who has engaged in sexual relations. We first find this expression when **"Adam knew his wife"** (Genesis 4:1), and later when Rebecca who was described as **"fair to look on, a virgin, and no man had known her"** (Genesis 24:16). Sex can only occur as a sacred act, when two people really know each other. It implies a mutual understanding between the two people that their sexual union is part of a sacred relationship. When the two people do not share this understanding, they estrange themselves spiritually from one another and from God. One-night stands and couples who profess a purely physical relationship deny the sanctity of sex and diminish their relationship through such activity. Likewise, teenagers who engage in sexual relations by the nature of their age are not able to understand the meaning of their act and, therefore, sex can hardly be sacred. In times when teenage marriage was common, the special relationship between sex and marriage was clear. Today, with the definitions of commitment and fidelity growing ever flexible, sex is rarely perceived as meaningful or sacred by teens.

When animals engage in sexual relationships, the act is instinctive. Courtship has less to do with romance and shared values, and all to do with selecting the healthiest, most powerful mates to ensure the continuation of the species. Animals are not usually loyal to their mates. Those that are loyal don't make a conscious choice; they are driven by instinct because of such biological imperatives as protecting offspring or ensuring a partner for repetitive matings.

When we accuse humans of sexual impropriety, we often compare them to animals, and indeed, Dr. Helen Fisher's book, *Anatomy of Love: The Mysteries of Mating, Marriage, and Why We Stray* (Fawcett, 1992), presents a sociobiological approach to explaining the animal contribution to our adulterous behavior: the males are interested in sexual variety to ensure a widespread dissemination of their genetic material, and the females' motivation for philandering is an alternative strategy for the acquisition of resources to support herself and her young ones. I am sure that this is exactly what male or female adulterers have in mind when they're in the midst of cheating. This sociobiological reasoning has been well exploited by those who want to justify adultery and prove it "natural."

When two humans, made in the image of God, share sexual intimacy, it should have meaning, not simply to fulfill the animal urges. Animals do not have sexual relations, they engage in instinctual procreation. Humans, on the other hand, can feel satisfaction or shame from the same act, depending on its context and their partner.

"And I shall betroth you to Me forever; And I shall betroth you to Me in righteousness, and in justice and in love and loving

compassion: And I shall betroth you to Me in faithfulness and you shall *know* the Lord" (Hosea 2:21–22). With these words, the prophet Hosea uses the metaphor of marriage to describe our ideal relationship with God, the coming together of two partners who understand each other because they know each other. God is a mystery to us. In this case, the attempt to know leads to the relationship of love. The idea of knowing God and a spouse lies in the ability to understand the nature of the commitment and the energy that is required to sustain the relationship. We say, "to know him is to love him"—this type of knowledge reflects the building blocks of appreciation, realistic expectations, and acceptance. The knowing of sacred sexual relations and the knowing of God are one and the same—a prerequisite for a meaningful relationship.

Hosea's story encompasses the pain of adultery, and the suffering caused by betrayal. God actually orders Hosea to marry a promiscuous woman, Gomer. They have three children together. The book of Hosea is a parallel telling of the suffering of God caused by the infidelity of the people to Him—as demonstrated by their dishonesty, murder, false swearing, theft, and adultery. The book concludes with compassionate hopes for both relationships—that of Hosea and Gomer, and the Israelites with God. The significant point in Hosea is the parallel between our fidelity to each other to our fidelity to God. What we do against our spouse has greater relevance.

Holy and Unholy Sex

The Bible distinguishes between holy and unholy sex. Holy sex is that which takes place between a husband and wife in fulfillment of their marital relationship. Unholy sex is everything else. The Bible presents the sexual relations of a man and woman, married to each other, as the ideal. On the other end of the spectrum are sexual relations deemed inappropriate, like adultery and incest, which are forbidden by law and carry a punishment.

"There shall not be a promiscuous woman among the daughters of Israel, and there shall not be a promiscuous man among the sons of Israel" (Deuteronomy 23:18). According to some biblical scholars, this passage includes all forms of premarital intercourse. Others interpret this as referring only to prostitution. The daughter of any priest who engages in prostitution is to be put to death (Leviticus 21:9), but no such punishment is stipulated for other harlots. It would seem, therefore, that these sexual behaviors, while displeasing to God, are tolerated, or at least, unpunished.

If You Break It, It's Yours

"If a man will find a virgin maiden who was not betrothed, and takes hold of her and lies with her, and they are discovered, then the man who lay with her shall give the father of the girl fifty silver shekels, and she shall become his wife, because he had afflicted her; he cannot divorce her all his life" (Deuteronomy 22: 28–29). This verse makes it clear that sexual relations obligate the man to marry the woman. In the Bible, sexuality and obligation are intimately connected and commanded.

In some Jewish traditions, all nonmarital sexual relations are defined as "prostitution." In its technical sense, the Bible looks at prostitution as "sexual intercourse from which ensues no binding or enduring relationship. It is usually indiscriminate in nature" (*The Interpreter's Dictionary of the Bible,* 1986, vol. 3).

Marriage Sanctifies Sex

Marriage is usually referred to as holy matrimony, acknowledging that the relationship of these two people is sacred. In the Catholic tradition, marriage reflects a sacred covenant that cannot be broken, except through a specific religious annulment, while Judaism and other Christian traditions allow for divorce with some serious motivation such as infidelity, physical abuse, child molestation, addictions, fraud, and sexual refusal. Just because divorce is permissible does not mean that marriage is not taken seriously. In Hebrew the word for "betrothed" is *kiddushin;* it is related to the word *kadosh*—commonly translated as "holy," which is also defined as "set aside for a special godly purpose." The use of the word *kiddushin* reflects the idea that a marriage partner is set aside for a special godly purpose. Marriage is not just a contract between two people, but rather it is a sacred covenant, much like the relationship between God and people. Marriage is stage two, after betrothal, and is called *nisuin,* which means "uplifting"—being raised together into the sacred sphere.

Through the institution of marriage, we sanctify the need for human companionship: "**... For it is not good that man be alone ... therefore a man leaves his father and his mother and clings to his wife so that they become one flesh**" (Genesis 2:18, 24). Marriage is also the institution through which we fulfill the biblical commandment to procreate humanity: "**... and you shall be fruitful and multiply**" (Genesis 1:28).

What Is Adultery?

Today adultery is defined as the voluntary sexual intercourse between a married person and someone other than the lawful spouse. In the polygamous society of the Bible, adultery is defined as sexual intercourse between a man (whether married or unmarried) and a woman married to someone else. In biblical times, most societies allowed men to marry more than one woman. Just think of Jacob, who married sisters Leah and Rachel and even had legitimate children through Bilhah and Zilpah, their handmaidens (the Bible later forbids marrying an

ex-wife's sister while the ex-wife is still alive; Leviticus 18:18).
Even after the giving of the Ten Commandments, the Bible
tells us that Israelite kings must not have too many wives
(Deuteronomy 17:17)!

In the postbiblical world, the rabbis interpreted, "**You shall
come to the Kohanim, the Levites, and to the judge who will
be in those days; you shall inquire and they will tell you the
word of judgment. . . . You shall do according to the word
that they will tell you. According to the teaching they will
teach you and according to the judgment that they will say to
you, shall you do; you shall not deviate from the word that
they will tell you, right or left**" (Deuteronomy 17:9–11) as a
mandate to interpret Scripture for their generation according
to the developing social conditions, utilizing the principles set
forth in the Bible. Although the Bible limits the definition of
adultery to the married status of a woman, the rabbis subsequently prohibited polygamy and criticized strongly the sexual relations between anyone other than a husband and wife.
The gradual process within Judaism of discouraging
polygamy and eventually prohibiting it was motivated by the
desire to create a stable and healthy home environment. By establishing that all wives had to be treated equally in everything, including food, clothing, furnishings, presents, and
sexual relations, the early rabbis made it financially and emotionally difficult to marry more than one woman. No wonder
that Jewish tradition states, "The more wives one has the
more troubles." Nonetheless, one still sees polygamous Jewish
communities within such cultures, which are polygamous, as
Morocco.

In the New Testament period, it appears that the definition of
adultery was extended in its scope in several ways. "**But I say
unto you, That whosoever shall put away his wife, saving for
the cause of fornication, causeth her to commit adultery: and
whosoever shall marry her that is divorced committeth adultery**" (Matthew 5:32) extends the definition by including "new

marriages" following divorce as adultery (save for the reason of infidelity); and second, "**And he saith unto them, Whosoever shall put away his wife, and marry another, committeth adultery against her. And if a woman shall put away her husband, and be married to another, she committeth adultery** (Mark 10:11–12), suggests that putting aside your spouse for a new model is adulterous for both men and women.

"**But I say unto you, That whosoever looketh on a woman to lust after her hath committed adultery with her already in his heart**" (Matthew 5:28) is another development that umbrellas thoughts and actions as equivalent, most likely because thoughts might precede the action. While Jewish law and tradition urge modesty and the avoidance of focusing excessively on such natural feelings, it does not prescribe any punishment for sinful thoughts.

In biblical times, adultery was such a serious offense that what every violated person wished to do to his or her adulterous spouse was done—he or she was put to death, along with the other adulterer (Deuteronomy 22:22). As we discussed in the previous chapter, postbiblical Jewish legal tradition was cautious in its application of the death penalty. Therefore, as in all capital punishment cases, a warning must have been given the accused adulterer before the crime was committed, and two witnesses actually had to see it committed in order for the adulterers to be put to death. Since inviting people to an adulterous party would be fairly uncommon, such convictions were almost nonexistent. However, the adulterers could be forced to divorce their spouse (the adulterous woman forfeited any financial compensation stipulated in their premarital contract—the *ketubah)* and were forbidden to marry their adulterous partner. With this ruling, the rabbis forced individuals who lusted after someone else to think twice about consummating the act.

Today, people also resort to legal redress. According to a report in the *Washington Post* (April 2, 1998), a betrayed husband successfully sued his best friend and neighbor for $60,000 for having sex with his wife. "It was the sheer evilness of a man coming into my home, having sex with my wife while I was asleep upstairs and my children were asleep. I filed the lawsuit for some accountability. I never once heard an apology."

Most states have eliminated alienation of affection as grounds for recovering damages, on the theory that courts should not in effect be judging a person's morals. This case was in one of the states that eliminated alienation as grounds for a suit, but permitted this case on the basis of "intentional and negligent infliction of emotional distress." In 1997, a North Carolina jury ordered a woman to pay one million dollars to the wife of a man she had an affair with while in his employ. The jury agreed that the woman, by seducing the wife's husband away from her, destroyed a seventeen-year marriage. While courts may not be in the business of legislating or judging morality, they are responding to the obvious damage done to individuals and families, and, as it spreads through society, undermines the foundation of society.

Why Is Adultery Wrong?

With parents, *honor* is divinely mandated (the Fifth Commandment) through specific actions. No such commandment is directed toward a spouse. With the Seventh Commandment, a specific rule is set up to honor the institution of marriage. Adultery comes from the term *adulterate,* which means to contaminate or make impure. We make ourselves impure (spiritually, not like the ritual impurity of the Bible) when we violate the promises of marriage: **"You shall not lie carnally with your neighbor's wife, to contaminate yourself with her"** (Leviticus 18:20).

There are a number of biblical concerns with adultery, which still apply today. One is a practical issue relating to the ability of a child to honor parents. If a woman has a child while she is involved in an adulterous relationship, whom does the child have the obligation to honor? There is also the problem of potential incest. If the paternal status is uncertain, the child could end up marrying a relative forbidden by the rules of incest. Though this may seem far-fetched, there are documented cases of couples falling in love and even marrying who were conceived through artificial insemination with semen from the same donor.

Adultery is also a form of theft. The outside adulterer, who trespasses into a marriage, steals the affection of one spouse from the other. Sometimes the outside adulterer will state that he or she is meeting the sexual and emotional needs that the actual spouse is not able to. In the end, the outside relationship is only a distraction, depriving spouse and family of the attention and love they deserve.

One of my listeners wrote of the rationalizations of the other woman: "*I work in a sales office. One married rep is handsome and has a great personality. I observed my female co-worker coming on to him and he was flattered. He couldn't resist the easy sex in his hotel room far away from home and his wife. His wife discovered his adultery and has asked him for a divorce, even though she is pregnant with his/her first child. I was disturbed by my co-worker's lack of compassion for the wife. I told her that she was partially responsible for this family's destruction. Her reaction was that since she just had a few 'one night stands' with him, and he didn't leave his wife for her, she wasn't at all responsible for ruining this marriage. I guess some people can rationalize anything they do to avoid admitting they did something immoral.*"

Most importantly, adultery affects the stability of the family, undermining the trust of husband and wife and threatening the integrity of the family unit. By succumbing to the temporary urges of the flesh, the future of the family is jeopardized. As one of my listeners wrote: "*After thirteen years of marriage, my husband's lunches with a woman he had met ended him up in a hotel room. Only by the grace of God did he come to his senses and not go 'all the way.' I found a card, and after questioning him he admitted what had been going on over the past couple of months. He ended the affair immediately and we entered counseling. It has been two years later and I have to tell all the would-be-innocent-lunchers out there: NOT A DAY has gone by without my paying the price for my husband's selfishness. His ego needed the gratification and our marriage will NEVER be the same. It saddens me to think I may never trust the man that I, under the Covenant of marriage, have nonetheless decided to work this out with for the sake of the children. I hope I will trust him again someday. Our lives will never be the same due to that first (so-called) innocent little lunch."*

Affairs often produce illegitimate children. I have had innumerable calls to my radio program from each point in the triangle between spouses and a lover where a child is the result. The mess that produces because of divided resources of money, time, and love are agonizing to hear. Normal sibling rivalry under one roof becomes stretched absurdly to children under other unseen roofs. It is not unusual for these children to be sexual earlier and to produce offspring while they are still minors, in part due to the role models of their parents, and in part due to the need to make a stable attachment which is, of course, missing with the two-family parent. Additionally, these children in single-mother homes have increased risk for poverty, academic and social failure, criminality, violence, and death (*City Journal,* Winter, 1998).

Finally, Proverbs 6:22 clearly warns that adulterous behavior ". . . destroyeth his own soul."

The Aftermath of Adultery

According to Dr. Lana Staneli, author of a book on marital triangles, "Of those who break up their marriage to marry someone else, eighty percent are sorry later. Of those who do marry their lover, which is only about ten percent, about seventy percent of them get another divorce. Of that twenty-five to thirty percent that stay married, only half of them are happy. Having an affair is an invitation to an awful lot of pain and tragedy" (*NET News Now,* Washington, D.C., January 22, 1997).

In the *Washington Post* (April 16, 1996), there was an article about a support group for the "other women" who were grieving the death of their married lovers. The premise of the article was that these women, because they were banned from the hospitals and funerals by the wives, didn't have the opportunity to grieve their loss. As Gina, one of my listeners, wrote of this article: "*We are encouraged to feel sorry for them when they were engaging in behavior that is clearly WRONG. Throughout the article, the women justified their relationships as legitimate, not destructive to the man's marriage nor the family. The only bright spot of the article, was that the to-be leader of the group was having trouble finding members to participate!*" After the outrage had subsided on reading about this, we were struck by the sadness and isolation of people who sneak pieces of the lives of others.

Other Sexual Prohibitions

The Bible is clear that extramarital sex (adultery) is the most unholy type of sexual relation between a man and a woman, but premarital (before getting married) and nonmarital (no intention of getting married) are also unholy types of sex. In these cases, there is no biblical violation of forbidden sexual relations, but traditional Judaism does not condone sexual relations outside the institution of marriage. It is disappointing that to conform to the behaviors of modern society in an attempt not to alienate unmarried Jews from Torah, synagogue, and community, some Conservative and Reform rabbis are willing to create new definitions of commitment, with guidelines for so-called ethical, unmarried sexual relationships. I believe that religious leaders should set standards, not conform them to common desires.

The sexual relationships that were forbidden throughout history were defined by close blood or matrimonial relationships. Incest was considered a way to preserve superior bloodlines among ancient Egyptians and certain royal families of Europe. Incest was later avoided because of genetic implications. Definitions of incest have varied greatly throughout history. In most cases, the prohibition extends to mother and son, father and daughter, and all offspring of the same parents. In many societies, taboos are broadened to include marriages between uncles and nieces, aunts and nephews, first cousins, and, occasionally, second cousins. Today, many states prohibit marriage between first cousins. The biblical prohibitions of incest are quite extensive. Contrary to popular thought, the prohibitions are more concerned with family integrity than genetic abnormalities.

In Leviticus (20:10–21) there is a long list of forbidden sexual unions, specifying siblings, grandchildren, half-siblings, aunts, in-laws, male relatives, animals, etc. These laws of incest go far beyond the simple bloodlines of parent-child and sibling relationships. The prohibited relationships of a man and his daughter-in-law or stepmother are not forbidden because of a fear of genetic defects. In fact, most of the relationships forbidden are not blood relationships (like an aunt by marriage or an ex-daughter-in-law). The most interesting prohibited relationship is perhaps that of marrying a woman, divorcing, and then marrying the woman's sister. I have had a handful of calls from men who have dated one sister, only to tell me they've fallen in love with her sister. I always advised them to take a hike from both their lives, before damaging the women's sibling relationship. The criterion that a marital relationship should be forbidden is if it creates multiple relationships, especially for children.

The biblical punishments for incest are not as clear as adul-

tery. While the Bible prescribed death for incest with one's
mother-in-law (Leviticus 20:14), it then states, **"A man who
shall take his sister, the daughter of his father or the daughter of
his mother, and he shall see her nakedness and she shall see his
nakedness, it is a disgrace and they shall be cut off in the sight of
the members of their people ..."** (Leviticus 20:17), implying
some kind of excommunication or divine punishment. The Bible
distinguishes between the more serious (children) and less serious forms (more distant relative) of incest, applying a range of
punishments from death by stoning to flogging.

Rationalizing Behavior

God's intentions for us are clear: that we lead holy lives, sanctifying our human desires and appetites in ways which elevate
their meaning above that of animals and the mundane. In the
vernacular, "easier said than done." So many of the standard
jokes about Moses being sent back to renegotiate the Ten Commandments with God have to do with eliminating the commandment on adultery. Our sexual passions are probably the
most difficult to tame. If we let ourselves calm down a moment,
the urge to murder the person who just flipped us off subsides.
There is little we can get from that same calming down when we
feel intensely sexually turned on to someone with whom we frequently have to interact. The pains of unrequited sexual passion
infest our psyches worse than the flesh-eating bacteria. We
search for ways to make the adultery something beautiful and
special instead of a sin.

We can look at the Bible for some examples of how people
tried to rationalize extramarital relations. The beginnings of
humanity are unclear. Adam and Eve had two sons, Cain and
Abel. There is a question of with whom did they engage in
sexual relations to propagate humanity. Eve, their mother,
was the only woman. The rabbis were uncomfortable with the
idea of mother-son incest, although there were no command-

ments at this time (except for the fruit of "that" tree), and suggested that there may have been other unrecorded siblings with whom Cain and Abel produced offspring.

The early family accounts of Genesis offer no other sexual relations of such questionable status until Lot and his daughters. Following the destruction of Sodom, Lot, Abraham's nephew, escapes with his two daughters to a cave. Fearing that all the world was destroyed with Sodom and Gomorrah, Lot's daughters devise a plan to perpetuate the human race with their father. Although this takes place prior to Leviticus and the laws of forbidden incestual relations, it is clear that there must be some type of taboo of such relations because the daughters must resort to getting their father drunk for their plan to work. The readers of the text know that this is wrong, because the daughters must conspire to seduce their father. They consider their behavior acceptable based on their perception of the world. Their concern for the future of humanity sets aside the moral implications of the incest. If, after a nuclear disaster, only a brother and sister remain, they would be obliged to "be fruitful" to propagate the world. This unlikely case of allowable incest is an issue because there are no alternatives for the survival of humankind.

Many people attempt to validate adultery with the belief that it is permissible for a higher cause. People have countless rationales for setting aside the moral implications of their act; for example:

➤ "I love my wife and children and do not want a divorce, so it is better that I have an affair for the sake of my family."

➤ "My husband is not fulfilling me sexually, so it is okay to find sexual satisfaction instead of divorcing my husband."

➤ "I think my husband is being unfaithful, so there is nothing wrong with me having an affair."

➤ "I wasn't looking for an affair—it just happened."

➤ "We are soul mates."

➤ "I have needs my spouse can't fulfill."

➤ "I thought I was in love when I married—but this is really the real thing."

➤ "I've been under a lot of stress."

➤ "She/he really understands me."

All these rationalizations are attempts to transform an immoral act into an acceptable behavior. Several centuries ago, a rabbinic commentator anticipated one particular rationalization for adultery: "Some misguided patriots or politicians might try to persuade the public that it is the duty of each male to impregnate as many females as possible to increase the population of the country, and that for him to do so is not a sin, but a patriotic act."

Adultery: Just Say No

The *Los Angeles Times* (March 1, 1998) published some interesting definitions of adultery submitted by readers. One definition: "Adultery is when you participate in the type of close behavior with someone who is not your spouse—and you would not want your spouse to behave likewise with someone else." Most people are hurt by their partner's sharing of emotional closeness as well as their bodies. I have been shocked by the rampant cyber-adultery on the Internet. There are folks who will spend hours on the computer, sharing and teasing with complete strangers, whose motivations, identity, and even gender are ultimately unknown. The pain that this alienation of attention and affection causes in the spouse is considerable. No one knows how to compete with a fantasy. This is disturbed, self-absorbed, and destructive behavior.

Another form of adultery is the obsession with pornography, whether in print or video. Some folks, generally men, will spend an inordinate amount of time masturbating over photos and videos. This form of sexuality is devoid of sanctity, true feeling, and a relationship to another person or anything divine.

Most people fantasize about certain relationships from time to time. These may include incestuous, premarital, extramarital, and nonmarital relationships. Although it is almost impossible to stop fantasies, one can avoid engaging in these relationships. The easiest way to avoid adultery is not to put ourselves in positions that could lead to the fulfillment of these fantasies.

The potential for adultery is magnified when a person places himself in a situation that allows for the indiscretion. Rick, one of my listeners, wrote about this very issue: *"I also wanted to comment on the way people should handle temptation. As a Christian, I have been taught to do like Jesus did when he fasted for forty days and then Satan came and tempted him. I am taught that when that happens, just do as he did and quote the appropriate scripture to the devil. The New Testament says 'resist the devil and he will flee from you.' That works well for almost all temptations except one, sexual temptation. Proverbs is just full of advice about this for both Jews and Christians ... condense it down to one sentence and it would say something like this: 'When you are tempted sexually, run like hell, don't look back, just run!'"*

The wonderful thing about sex is that it is also a relief, a release, and an oasis from pain and worry. The bad news is that there are certain times when this means of "escape" should not be used. David, one of my listeners, wrote about that: *"When our second child was born, there were severe complications with the pregnancy and childbirth that left my wife unable to have sex and/or without sexual desire for two years. During that time, I thanked God for the safe birth of our sec-*

ond daughter and prayed for my wife's good health to return. There was stress and temptation, but the thought of cheating was overwhelmed by my thoughts of what my wife had gone through, and the beauty of our daughter's life. Dr. Laura, it burns me up when I hear people complain about the lack of good sex they are getting in their marriage. As a healthy, sexually vigorous man of 30, I wanted sex! I could tell you titillating stories of how I was tempted, too. I could also tell you the horrid details of my wife's physical pain, but that is beside the point. Even today, six years later, our sex life is not as active as before but there is a lot of love, dedication, and most importantly, a new child whose life was brought forth with love. I believe that we grow based on the challenges we face in life. I look forward to each one knowing God has honored me with a good life. My wife is a beautiful woman whom I honor, respect, and love. I cherish our relationship. Together we faced the burning fires and returned a little older, but with more heart, more spirit, and more true love."

Kerry, a woman in her thirties, had just broken up after a year and a half. She wrote me about her "solution to that pain" and how she kept herself on the right track: "*In my customary stupid fashion, I sought to circumvent my grief with a dangerous and stupid flirtation. This time with a married man—ugh. A wonderful distraction for how much I was hurting. Here's the unusual part—I nipped it in the bud before it was too late! I am so proud of myself I can't stand it. He was quite wonderful about my communiqué. Here it is: You make me feel special, attractive, sexy and feminine. Over the course of our conversation these past weeks, I have grown quite fond of you; perhaps even dangerously so. I've been thinking a lot about this and here's the deal. The way I see it, there's no good way for me to emerge from a tryst with you. You're surrounded by wife and family. I'm still alone, only now with a big black mark on the karmic record. Our integrity is worth more than orgasm. Of course, how it turns out circumstan-*

tially for me is far from our biggest problem. Of infinitely greater magnitude is a fundamental issue of conscience and character (Yes, Dr. Laura—I read your book, How Could You Do That?!*). I don't mean to sound pompous. Marcus Aurelius said to esteem nothing that, despite its apparent advantage, would require that your world is compromised. That declaration is as valid today as it was a couple thousand years ago. Honor me by honoring your family and the covenant you have with them. Carl Jung said that there is magic that emanates from a woman of high principles who still expresses her passions. I shall aspire to that brand of magic rather than the more immediate brand I've been indulging in of late. No longer can my need for gratification come at the ultimate expense of my dignity. The rationalizations fail me utterly."*

I get many calls from anxious spouses, doubting themselves because of the pressure put on them by their partners to tolerate inappropriate behaviors with an opposite sex "friend" or co-worker, such as:

➤Frequent lunches or dinners.

➤Private telephone conversations.

➤Solo car-pooling.

➤E-mail interludes.

➤Intimate, frequent gifts.

➤Trips out of town.

➤Discussions of marital problems or intimacies.

➤Socializing alone with introductions to the children.

These are only some of the outrageous demands made by spouses who declare that their wives or husbands are insecure, insensitive, or suffocating if they do anything but acquiesce.

My bottom line, in these calls, is this: When you love someone you do not behave in ways that bring pain, fear, doubt, or insecurity to their lives, minds, and hearts.

Bastards—Implications for Our Children

The term *bastard* is generally applied to a child born out of wedlock, but in the Jewish tradition it is defined as the offspring of the two forbidden relationships we have discussed—adultery and incest. This makes sense if we remember that a bastard is also called an illegitimate (illegal) child, meaning the offspring of a relationship forbidden by law. The bastard, referred to as a *mamzer* in the Bible, is, with rare exception, forbidden from marrying into the community. While it seems unfair that a child is punished for the sin of his parents, the status of the *mamzer* is a reminder of the tremendous implications of incest and adultery on the life of the child. Consider this a divine attempt at deterrence. This is not just an issue of snobbery. Clearly, the *mamzer* suffers from the unhealthy family environment that inevitably results from these relationships. This worries families whose children fall in love with *mamzers*. Will such a child be able to commit himself to a relationship or have good parental models to draw upon when he becomes a parent? When adults engage in these selfish acts they would do well to remind themselves of the long-lasting effects their actions can have on their children.

I have been struck by the increasing numbers of calls I have received from people who have had children out of wedlock and how complicated so many lives become because of this indiscretion. These children, when they have the opportunity to meet and visit with their fathers, often come to intact homes with new children. They tell me how sad they are to be visitors in their own dad's home. They express jealousy for his new children with his new wife. They feel less important, less connected, less wanted, and less loved.

There have been many wives calling, after just finding out that their husband made a child with another woman either before they met, while they were engaged, or sometime during the marriage. These women feel torn between compassion for the child, who desires a connection with their father, and a sense of defensiveness for the family that they have established. They don't want their own children to be neglected by his divided attention and resources. And, they worry about the moral implications for their children—what knowing their father has committed adultery will do for their own values and behaviors.

The men call, frustrated that a single act or brief affair has resulted in embarrassment, financial obligation, and moral questions. It is amazing how many conversations I've had with men who imagined that passion devoid of real emotion was a valid contraception.

So far, I've given the impression that only men commit adultery. Of course, that isn't so. I've taken difficult calls from women who have discovered their pregnancy after they came back to their husbands. Sometimes the situation is that they were intimate with the boyfriend and the husband at the same time, making paternity dependent upon a DNA test. There are times when I have recommended, either to the woman or the husband who called me, not to bother finding out—just to get on with their lives together and raise the baby as their own. I believe it is in the best interest for the child to have an intact, stable home—without other parent-types visiting. I have told many of these husbands to consider this birth the product of artificial insemination, or a form of adoption. Many of these husbands, anxious to keep their families, and who still love their wives, have expressed willingness to accept the challenge.

A simple, natural, pleasurable act like sexual intercourse, when not done within the covenant of marriage, can be a sharp pebble, rippling painfully through so many lives. Respecting and maintaining the sacredness of covenantal sex not only elevates the experience, it avoids generations of hurt.

Marital Vows of Fidelity Are for Better and for Worse

In his address to the 1997 graduation class at East Stroudsburg University, U.S. Senator Rick Santorum told a story seemingly unrelated to the usual commencement speeches about success and happiness. This is the story: A Baptist preacher in South Carolina wanted nothing more out of life than to run a Bible college. All his life, he worked for the position and eventually attained it. As he fulfilled his life's dream and vocation, Alzheimer's disease struck his wife. Her health degenerated to the point where he could not possibly take care of her and work his full-time job. The preacher came to a decision—to give up his position as president of the Bible college. His peers were incredulous. "What are you doing?" they asked. "Your wife doesn't even know who you are!" The man answered, "She might not know who I am, but I know who she is. She's the woman I made a promise to until death do us part."

Sex not only unites a man and woman in a spiritual relationship, it brings them closer to God as they engage in a creative act. Therefore, when the sanctity of marriage or family is violated, not only are the husband and wife estranged, and often from other members of the family, but all the violators are estranged from God. It is not accidental that throughout the Bible, the notions of adultery between people are paralleled with an estrangement of a people from God. It is the sin of adultery that comes to symbolize the broken faith between God and people. "How shall I pardon you for this? Your children have forsaken Me and sworn by those that are not gods. When I had fed them to the full, then they committed adultery" (Jeremiah 5:7).

The keeping of our faith with each other and with God is what separates us from the rest of the animal world.

8

The Eighth Commandment

"You shall not steal."

People spend a lot of time redefining stealing in order to increase their comfort zone as they assert themselves in a world of needs, wants, possessions, power struggles, fame, fortune, desire, envy, loss, hurt, greed, and antisocial personalities. Such questions arise as, "Is it stealing when it's from a company or the government, instead of from people?" or, "Is it stealing if they wouldn't really notice it's gone, because they have so much?" or, "Is it stealing if it's just not fair that I don't have what so many other people have?" or, "Is it stealing if I mean to give it back eventually—before they notice or need it?" The answers to these questions are not dependent upon normal circumstances.

Debby, one of my listeners, agrees: *"It's funny how in America everything is negotiable. I am an elementary school teacher. Recently a student and I were having a discussion about certain Jewish laws. I asked him why we were not permitted to steal. He had a whole host of reasons—because someone will steal from you, because it will upset everyone, because then no one will be able to trust each other. I told him that he missed the essential point. The reason I don't steal is simply one: BE-CAUSE GOD SAID NOT TO. End of reason."*

While some people may perceive that those who follow the commandments are somehow burdened and enslaved by an external force, consider that accepting a commandment sets you free from the struggle with your internal, more primitive drives toward selfishness. If you accept the divine value system as yours, the guilt-ridden agonizing required to make something you know to be wrong appear right is eliminated from your life. Strife is readily replaced with peace in your psyche.

Does that make you a mere robot? Of course not. Free will goes into choosing any lifestyle. If you need or want something, it is your constructive and creative effort that is required in order to find a just way to obtain those things.

What's the Big Deal About "Things"?

The commandments so far have dealt with issues of divine authority, life and death, honoring family, sacred time, etc. Suddenly the gears are shifted from holy spirits and holy relationships to the issue of things. God considered the possession of things of sufficient importance to include respecting ownership as one of the Big Ten.

When we spoke of not murdering (chapter 6), the focal point was that human beings are all God's children, that human beings are made in the image of God, and that within each human being is a God-given spirit, and that the human body is to be respected for the spirit within it. Just as God gave humans life, body, and spirit, He gave humans the earth and all that is on it. As soon as a human being has legitimately acquired some "thing," by gift, inheritance, earning, purchase, trade, or personal creation, it becomes an inanimate part of himself, much as his body is part of himself. In this commandment, God expects us to respect a person's property because of the human spirit who owns it. Stealing becomes an offense against the human spirit who owns the property, as well as against God, because of the command not to steal.

Most of the justification for stealing comes from the notion that other people exist only as an opportunity for exploitation and gain—to serve you. Our religious traditions remind us that we must love our neighbor as ourselves, that we are to serve each other through God's laws.

Paying the Price

The Bible is not interested in abuse excuses or Twinkie defenses. When it comes to dealing with criminals, the Bible maintains social order through the mandate, **"Righteousness, righteousness, shall you pursue"** (Deuteronomy 16:20). In the book of Exodus (22:3) we are told that if **"the theft be found in his possession . . . he shall pay double."** What a fitting punishment. Justice in its purest sense. Steal twenty dollars from me, you must pay me back the twenty, plus another twenty. That which you wished to take from me is taken from you.

Anybody who has had his house broken into, or been robbed at gunpoint, knows the painful feelings of violation, vulnerability, and loss. The Bible tries to compensate the victim for the emotional violation that took place and make the thief feel the exact loss he wanted to perpetrate. Could you imagine if every convicted pickpocket, car thief, and burglar were required to give full (or double) restitution to their victims? Unfortunately, the criminal justice system as it exists generally punishes the perpetrator for his/her actions against the state, while not often demanding reparation.

Owning Up to It

If you steal something and then feel guilty about the crime, is the punishment the same? In this case the Bible tells us, **"A man or**

woman who commits any of man's sins, by committing treachery toward the Lord, and that person shall become guilty—they
shall confess their sin that they committed; he shall make restitution for his guilt in its principal amount and add its fifth to it,
and give it to the one to whom he indebted" (Numbers 5:5–7).
So, if the thief turns himself in, he is only fined a 20 percent
penalty in addition to the return of the principal, instead of the
100 percent penalty demanded if he doesn't own up to it.

With his confession, he has saved the community and the
victim a legal battle and cleared up the matter in a way that
everyone feels settled and not aimlessly distrustful of neighbor
and stranger. Additionally, the admission of guilt may be the
first step of genuine repentance. In making amends and seeking forgiveness, the thief begins his journey back to God and
back to the community. With this diminished penalty for own-
ing up, the Bible provides incentive and opportunity for the
thief to change his life.

Crime Doesn't Pay but the Criminal Does

Should the penalty for spontaneously picking up a five-dollar
bill you notice someone dropped be the same as someone
who planned an armed bank robbery? The Bible differenti-
ates between different kinds of stealing based on the degree
of effort and planning. For example, "If a man shall steal an
ox, or a sheep or goat, and slaughter it or sell it, he shall pay
five oxen in place of the ox and four sheep in place of the
sheep" (Exodus 21:37). One could argue that animals from
the herd were essential for survival in the ancient world, like
the horse thief who was hanged in the Wild West because
horses were essential to life. Whether as sources of food, bar-
tering, gifts for treaties, or sacrifices to God, these types of
animals were the measure of wealth. The act of theft is made
worse when the thief sells or kills the animal, because by
adding the killing to the stealing, he is continuing his act of

evil and creating an irreversible situation. For each move in the wrong direction, he is punished.

Why is there a difference between stealing a sheep and a cow? One Jewish tradition explains that the more a thief conspired and premeditated, the more he is fined. For a thief to walk off and hide a sheep is one thing, but to do the same to a big ole' cow requires even more planning and deceit. The bottom line is that biblical justice appears to acknowledge the degree of intentional behavior and react proportionally.

Greg, one of my listeners, wrote about how he had his son follow directly in these biblical footsteps: *"My son Daniel, the oldest, now a freshman in high school, while in eighth grade, saw a small bag of cookies on his teacher's desk. I know that it wasn't due to starvation that he took those cookies because he eats breakfast—but anyway, he decided to have a mid-morning snack. I received a phone call from the principal who was trying to play this act of theft as 'I know that it's just a bag of cookies,' and he started to chuckle. I told the principal not to make light of this and throw the book at Daniel. Call it what it is: stealing.*

Daniel was suspended for one day. I took off from work the next day in order to supervise his day of freedom from education. My wife had the idea to have a work day for Daniel. He weeded the vegetable garden, cleaned the yard, shoveled dirt, washed cars, etc. until his five siblings came home from school.

Daniel thought his day was over. Now for the restitution. I told him to get his allowance from his room and hop in the van. We went to the nearest Stop 'n Shop and purchased flour, sugar, butter, pecans, and chocolate chips. Daniel made five dozen cookies. I took an early lunch the next day and went to meet him at the school, found the class, and called Daniel and his teacher out into the hall. Daniel apologized to his teacher and he was instructed by me that he also owed the class an apology, and if he needed persuasion I would accompany him into the class and introduce him. Daniel quickly grabbed the cookies and walked into the classroom and said, 'I just want to apologize to the class because I'm the one who stole the cookies off Mrs. XXX's desk. I made a bunch of cookies for us to all share.'

The class erupted with applause. I walked down the hallway and didn't touch the floor until I reached the parking lot. Later that day Daniel told me that more than one of his friends told him that it was cool that he told the truth and shared with the class. Dr. L., sometimes I feel like a real jerk when doing things like this. But how can we tell our kids to be responsible and make restitution for our actions if we don't show them how. Pay back what you owe plus. . . ."

Compensation Not Based on Ability to Pay

Not even the impoverished status of the thief provided an excuse for stealing or not compensating the victim. If a thief could not pay for what he stole, he was sold into slavery to repay the victim (Exodus 2:22). However, the Bible presents a fair approach in the case of such punishment. While demanding justice, the Bible is also compassionate. According to ancient Jewish tradition, the thief could only be sold to pay for the property and not for any fines. Regardless of the magnitude of the theft, he could not be required to work it off for more than six years. It was hoped that in those six years, he learned to know his intended victim, not as a "fat cat" who was responsible for his poverty, but as a caring employer, who contributed to his spiritual rejuvenation.

In today's judicial environment, we rarely hear of judges demanding perpetrators to make restitution with repayment through money, goods, or services. Although public-service time may serve the community at large and give the perpetrator an opportunity to seek goodness, it does not reflect specific justice for the victims' losses. Facing jail time is a form of justice for the community and the victim, but early releases, paroles, and time off for good behavior do not require restitution as a condition of release.

Stealing a Life

Some rabbinic commentaries interpret this commandment as a prohibition against kidnapping, because there is another command prohibiting theft, **"You shall not cheat your fellow and you shall not rob"** (Leviticus 19:13), which is clearly dealing with property. Whether by slave traders engaging in human commerce, soldiers for sexual pleasure, or gangs who would kidnap prominent leaders and then exact a ransom, kidnapping was very common in the ancient world. **"He who kidnaps a man—whether he has sold him or is still holding him—shall be put to death"** (Exodus 21:15). This mandatory death sentence points out the Bible's fundamental opposition to slavery. Biblical and rabbinic law recognized the reality of slavery as an institution, while clearly functioning to limit it and demand that slaves be treated humanely: **"You shall not turn over to his master a slave who is rescued from his master to you. He shall dwell with you in your midst, in whatever place he will choose in one of your cities, which is beneficial to him; you shall not taunt him"** (Deuteronomy 23:16–17); **"If a man shall strike the eye of his slave or the eye of his maidservant and destroy it, he shall set him free in return for his eye. And if he knocks out the tooth of his slave or the tooth of his maidservant, he shall set him free in return for his tooth"** (Exodus, 21:26–27).

Judaism is a religion that teaches that every person is created in God's image. It is a religion with freedom from bondage (the Exodus) as its central theme. It is also a religion that, stressing compassion and justice as God's demands on all people, has always been on the forefront of freedom as civil rights. The abolition of any type of oppression resonates with the whole of Jewish thinking. Indeed, Jewish history is pitted with millennia of attacks on its existence, through aggressive campaigns of war, pogroms, anti-Semitism, and the Holocaust. The Jewish people understand philosophically, as well as personally, the blessing of freedom.

That the issue of stealing people for pleasure and profit is still alive in this modern world is evidenced by innumerable horror stories, including one 1997 *60 Minutes* television exposé on the virtual slave trade of young girls from the Philippines to be used as house servants and prostitutes in the Middle Eastern countries. The April 2, 1998, *Los Angeles Times* featured a story of a female companion of a high-ranking Thai diplomat who was indicted for holding two illegal immigrants from Thailand as indentured servants for more than six years at her home. She was said to have "forced the immigrants, both women, to work eighteen hours a day at her home and restaurant while withholding their wages, denying them urgent medical and dental care, censoring their mail, and threatening harm to their families back home if they tried to escape."

These actions are not just an affront to national and international laws. These actions are an affront to God, who expects us to value our fellow as ourselves and not to steal the divine gift of freedom.

One of the most heinous crimes of kidnapping, and still pervasive, is that of parents stealing their children from the other parent after a separation or divorce. This is usually done out of spite. The children are often brainwashed into thinking that the other parent died or didn't love them. Sometimes, the angry parent, feeling unfairly treated and resentful, will actually kill the children to keep them from the other parent.

In my opinion, one modern, legalized form of child stealing is the growing tendency for courts to honor the custodial parent's desire to move away with the children from the noncustodial parent. This severely limits contact between the father and his children, since the custodial parent is generally the mother. Should she desire to get married to someone who wants to move away, or take a new job elsewhere, or move for her "spirits," many courts are justifying this, in spite of the obvious fact that it is not in the best interest of the child. I have spoken to many of these women and told them that, unless the father was dangerous or destructive, it was immoral to separate the children from him. Most of these women argue that they have the right to a new life. What these women and the courts that support them seem to ignore is the right their children have to both parents.

Making Excuses

The first biblical excuse attempt was when Adam tried to get out of trouble in the Garden of Eden. Not only did Adam blame Eve for his decision to eat from the Tree of Knowledge, he blamed God for making Eve—insinuating that if God had never made Eve, he would not have sinned: "... the woman whom You gave to be with me—she gave me of the tree, and I ate" (Genesis 3:12). When God confronts Eve, she too tries to pass the buck: "... The serpent deceived me, and I ate" (Genesis 3:13). God doesn't even bother to ask the serpent for his excuse; he moves on to the business of "curses" and changing the ground rules for all their lives; he presents the consequences of their actions, in spite of their attempts to make someone else responsible.

The human capacity to rationalize behavior allows people to ease their conscience by attempting to diminish the apparent seriousness of the act. Rationalizing eventually has people deluding themselves into believing that their actions are not wrong. When it comes to stealing, people find many rationales to make their behavior tolerable if not acceptable:

➤**I didn't know it was "hot."**

"But your honor, I didn't know it was stolen! When I bought the brand-new, in-the-box, thousand-dollar stereo for one hundred dollars I thought it was a legitimate close-out sale. No, your honor, I didn't think it strange that he worked out of a van."

Such defenses occur every day in our judicial system by people who claim ignorance in receiving stolen property. Courts must decide whether the individual knowingly received stolen property. In the case described, it is obvious that something was fishy. While the American judicial system may have the burden of proof to demonstrate that you knew the object was stolen, the Jewish tradition places more of an onus on the purchaser.

When buying something we must do our best to ascertain that it is not stolen. Even suspicion should be enough to make the purchase unthinkable. But how can we pass up the deal? One rabbinic example is the prohibition of buying a goat from a shepherd who is in someone else's employ, because he might be making the sale without the knowledge of his employer and will keep the money. A Jewish law states that it is forbidden to buy something from a known thief even if he assures you it is not stolen. This law is designed not only to avoid buying stolen property but also to put thieves out of business. When you buy stolen property, you are an accessory to a theft, which is as great a crime as the theft itself. If the thief could not find a buyer for his stolen goods, he would ultimately no longer steal. By buying anything that you have reason to suppose is stolen, you further the cause of evil and ensure a repetition of the act.

To make this situation right, if you realize you have or may have bought stolen objects, return them to the victim, when you can. When you can't, deliver them to the proper authorities.

Mike, one of my listeners, still suffers from having retained stolen property: *"When I was about eleven years old, I was in a toy store with my thirteen-year-old brother. I was admiring this extra special toy Matchbox car. I really wanted that car. My brother came up and said, 'Why don't you buy it?'*

I told him I had no money. My brother continued, 'I will get it for you.'

I thought, 'wow!', what a nice brother to buy me a toy. I just about died when he looked around to see no one was watching, opened the display case on the counter, removed the toy car and put it in his pocket.

I was shocked beyond belief. I can still feel how terrible my heart felt at that moment. We went outside, he pulled the car from his pocket and gave it to me. I still hurt over being involved with that theft. I never played with the car. I still have it. I regret I never returned it to the store before it went out of business."

➤ "Finders keepers . . ."

"You shall not see your brother's ox or his sheep driven away, and hide yourself from them; you shall surely bring them back to your brother" (Deuteronomy 22:1). Thus far, we have talked about active forms of stealing, cases in which an individual takes something. This biblical verse requires us to return any lost object to its rightful owner. The rule "Finders keepers, losers weepers" is not representative of biblical values. And lest you think that word "brother" limits this requirement to someone you like, the Bible further tells us, **"If you encounter an ox of your enemy or his donkey wandering, you shall return it to him repeatedly"** (Exodus 23:4). We must return lost objects even of people for whom we don't feel a fondness, even people whom we think are despicable. We are not permitted to distinguish between worthy and unworthy people, because, given the potential financial benefit, we will be tempted to classify almost everyone as being unworthy.

Every day people take and keep things that do not belong to them. If the object is truly lost and there is no way to ascertain the identity of the owner, then in fact it is permissible to keep the object. In our society, most of what is taken or kept is validated by rationales in which people *feel* they deserve the object. The human capacity for rationalizing is at its greatest in the reasons people come up with to declare their rightful ownership.

Mike, one of my listeners, wrote of his brush with "finders-keepers": "*When I was fourteen years old, I was in a department store with my dad. We were walking along and he whispers to me, 'Mike, see that money over there on the floor, go get it.' This seemed simple enough. I walked over, bent down and picked up two $20 bills folded small. We made our purchases in the store and went outside.*

'Dad, shouldn't we leave this money with the store in case someone comes back to get it?'

'Mike,' my dad responded, 'finders keepers. I saw the girl who dropped it and when we were making our purchases she was back looking for it. We got out just in time.'

He took $20 and gave me $20. I felt horrible."

Fortunately, not all dads are like Mike's. This extraordinary story is from Harvey: "*After filling up my truck with gas, I went and paid for it in cash. The clerk gave me my change which I counted on the way out. I realized he'd given me $5 too much, so I returned and asked him to check for his error. He was very surprised when he realized what he had done, and my response.*

He thanked me and noted that this had happened only once before. That customer, the clerk remembered, was a little older. But his vehicle was a van and had the same signs on the side as my utility truck. It was my father. This was almost twenty years ago.

I was very fortunate to be able to work side by side with my father for many years. This is but one of the lessons I learned from him by example."

➤ **"I didn't steal it—it's their stupid mistake!"**

Frankly, it's amazing how many people believe they simply have the right to possess something that they rightfully do not own simply because it's in their possession. For many people, this thinking validates keeping the extra ten dollars given by a cashier, not paying for the pasta that the waitress forgot to include on the bill, or not paying for the piano lessons because the accounting department doesn't send a bill.

One of Rabbi Vogel's favorite stories is about the woman who bought some lamps on sale at one large department store and returned them to the same chain at a different location only to be given a refund for the regular price, a 20 percent profit. Instead of correcting the error, she wanted to go back to the first store, purchase more lamps on sale, and return them again to the second store! She could have made a nice living doing this, but it was wrong. She was stealing.

Sadly, Donna, one of my listeners, represents a large group of people whose personal frustrations, ego-centered sense of entitlement, and lack of compassion lead them to justify stealing on the basis of others' inadequacies: *"Is it stealing if a clerk doesn't know the difference between cucumbers and zucchini and charges you the zucchini price, which is cheaper? You know this, but keep your mouth shut. Is it stealing? No. It's stupidity. It is her job to know the difference and if she is not qualified then she should not be hired. I've gotten many laughs when I see that I saved a couple bucks due to someone's stupidity. Would I go back? Hell no. I didn't steal it, she gave it to me. I didn't do anything illegal, and in fact, neither did she. She's just ignorant and stupid."*

While it may not be illegal, it certainly is immoral knowingly not to pay fair price for your purchases, regardless of the IQ level of the clerk.

➤ **"It's only fair, considering all my past bad luck and problems!"**

This rationale is used by people who believe that the error in their favor is designed to even out all the other times mistakes in billing are made against them. These people tend to believe that it is okay to take advantage of other people, because they have been taken advantage of before. Included in this category are people who falsify information on their income tax returns. For some, it is simply the desire to keep as much money as possible, but many others who cheat the government proclaim "The government wastes too much money" or "I give more than I should." These people believe that the amount they are willing to pay the government is fair and anything more is unfair. They are the defenders of righteousness in their own minds. Don't try this defense with the IRS.

Molly, one of my listeners, didn't want to try this defense with her insurance company either. Many folks feel put-upon by the requirement to pay premiums for insurance on their health, homes, and property. This mentality often erupts into a desire to get something back. Not so with Molly: *"A month ago I lost my wedding ring and have since turned it [a claim] into our insurance company. The ring was worth between five and six thousand dollars and was covered under our home insurance. After I turned in the claim, I found the ring. And, Dr. Laura, I considered not telling the insurance company and profiting from this. I could have bought a big-screen TV, went on a trip or bought more jewelry. But because of you nagging at me every day on the radio, I didn't. I called the insurance company and told them I found my ring and wanted to cancel my claim. I decided that if I were to buy a TV, go on a trip, etc. . . . I WANT TO EARN IT, NOT STEAL IT. It feels good to have done the right thing, but the temptation was there and it was strong."*

Certainly the temptations are strong. If you really believe

the ultimate holiness of the value system, the inner debate doesn't wage long.

Jamini, one of my listeners, realized that the issue is not simply one of "not getting caught," the issue is character and conscience: "*I work an extra part-time job in the evening on occasion at a large engineering firm. I keep quite close tabs on what my pay is because I work a varied number of hours. My last paycheck was around $100 too much. I knew right away that I had been credited twice for one day's work. I also knew there really was no way anyone would know except me, because it is such a large company.*

I toyed with the idea of keeping the money, but knew that I couldn't as my previously untapped 'Dr. Laura Conscience' kicked into gear. So I called my supervisor and she let payroll know of the mistake, and the money will come out of my next paycheck.

My supervisor said, 'You know, if you hadn't said anything, no one would have known.' But I would have known."

➤ **"I deserve it because I don't have it!"**

Not too long ago an armored car crashed off a freeway overpass and fell onto a street in a low socioeconomic area. The door of the armored car opened from the impact of the crash. The money flew through the streets. Adults and children ran everywhere for the crisp paper bills. When the police arrived, the money that had fallen onto the streets was gone. Nobody returned any to the policemen who were there. When interviewed by the local newspaper, several residents replied that this was "a gift from God." Since they had lived difficult lives, many of these people felt that they deserved the money that had been given them. This is despicable behavior, and it is stealing, legally as well as morally wrong.

I remember a young male caller from twenty years ago. The

topic of my then late-night radio program was, "What illegal or bad things would you do if you knew you wouldn't get caught?" This young man called and informed me that he was stealing motorcycle parts from a local store. When I asked why he was stealing, he responded that he didn't have the money to buy the parts and wanted to build his own motorcycle. I complimented him on his ability to build a motorcycle from scratch, and suggested that he return the parts to the store and ask for a job by demonstrating for the store owner his superior mechanical abilities. Even over the phone, I could tell that he lit up with enthusiasm, never having considered that there was a right and fair way to get what he needed and wanted.

There are those who would make God's laws contingent upon circumstances that could and should be met in honorable ways. Melanie wrote, "*Stealing is never right. I lived overseas in a very desolate third world community where people felt justified to steal from whomever had more than they did. The nun that lived in the community always said she didn't know what she would do if she were that poor—and didn't judge them for stealing. As I could see one side of her argument (it's always easy to be self-righteous when you have enough to eat and clothes to wear), I would hope that my values would stand through such trials and tribulations.*"

In truth, under despotic or corrupt regimes, where resources simply aren't available, stealing of food may become necessary when there aren't alternatives. We must be reminded that everyone's life is equally important. Stealing food, shelter, or medicines from others also in need is never acceptable.

We inquired of clergy, "Are there any conditions under which your tradition condones stealing?" Pastor Dennis Gundersen of the Grace Community Church of Tulsa, Oklahoma, wrote: "*None whatever. The poorest people I have ever known have always been able to find help getting the necessities when they really sought it, either at the mercy and charity of others, or by offering to do whatever work they could do.*"

Ronald Chapman, a forty-year scholar of the Bible and a Baptist himself, wrote to us, "*The Biblical approach is to give the poor an opportunity to supply their own needs and not to just give them what they want. In the Old Testament, the farmer was not to harvest all of the crop, but was to leave the edges and the corners of the field for the poor to harvest. The poor still had to go out and work to supply his need (work-fare). In this way, the poor would still have the dignity of work. Sustenance to the poor on a short-term basis (welfare) is also a Biblical concept.*"

Mr. Chapman refers in part to Deuteronomy 24:19–21: "**When you reap your harvest in your field, and you forget a bundle in the field, you shall not turn back to take it; it shall be for the proselyte, the orphan, and the widow, so that God will bless you in all your handiwork. When you beat your olive tree, do not remove all the splendor behind you; it shall be for the proselyte, the orphan, and the widow. When you harvest your vineyard, you shall not glean behind you, it shall be for the proselyte, the orphan, and the widow. . . .**" More than ordinary charity, this commandment recognizes that it is your property, with your pride of ownership from your efforts, but it is also a gift from God to share with those in need.

This appropriate mentality has filtered down the ages. The United Nations educational programs talk about not giving a person a fish, but by teaching him how to fish so that he can experience the dignity of being able to care for himself.

Some people find it unfathomable that people would choose to do something wrong or illegal. Since they wish to maintain their fantasy that "people are inherently good unless something outside them makes them do it," they search for economic and psychological motives rather than accept the fact that people choose to do evil.

Poverty does not create evil. The preface to Marvin Olasky's important book, *The Tragedy of American Compassion* (Regnery, 1992), points out that ". . . the problems of the under-class are not caused by poverty. Some of them are exacerbated by poverty, but we know that they need not be caused by poverty, for poverty has been the condition of the vast major-ity of human communities since the dawn of history, and they have for the most part been communities of stable families, nurtured children, and low crime."

Certainly, there are enough stories about so-called "poor people with character" that the issue is clearly one of values, not economics. For example, in August 21, 1997, a newspa-per in Gainesville, Florida, published a story about Betty Mann and her three children. They were homeless and living in a shelter. The article said, "But that didn't keep her 8-year-old son from turning in the wallet he found at a local super-market.

"'I've always told them that if you find something and it doesn't belong to you, you turn it in,' Mrs. Mann said when reached at St. Francis House in downtown Gainesville.

"Even though her family is in dire financial straits, Mann said she never considered keeping the wallet. That's not the way she was raised and not the way she is raising her chil-dren."

In another story published September 14, 1997, in the *Courier-Islander* in Canada, a woman went to the bank to cash a child benefit tax check and withdrew $200 in cash from the bank machine. The woman accidentally walked away from the bank machine, leaving the cash on the narrow shelf. Another woman, unemployed, happened by, noticed the money, and searched through the nearby trash can, looking for some document that would shed light on the money. She found the stub of the check, then waited for about ten minutes for someone to return for it. When no one did, she first asked the bank executives if anyone had called. When the bank ex-ecutives said, "No," she delivered the money to the police. The next day, the bank phoned her to say the owner had been reunited with her money and that a reward was offered.

The woman, Betty Craig, turned down the reward. The bank manager removed all service charges from her account "forever" as a sign of respect for Ms. Craig's character.

"I never thought about keeping the money," said Craig, unemployed and looking for work. "I knew I'd be physically sick if it was me. I'm glad I made her happy."

And finally, this testimony from another of my listeners: "*Last Sunday night, I found myself without a place to stay. So needless to say my financial position is a little tight right now. Last night I went through a drive-thru restaurant. When paying for the order I handed the woman a five-dollar bill. She gave me change for a twenty-dollar bill. I pulled forward to get my food and then putting the money away realized I had over fifteen dollars. At this point I was faced with a little dilemma. I sure could have used the extra money, and after all, it wasn't my mistake right? Wrong. I pulled out of the parking lot—I want you to know I could hear you, Dr. Laura, in my head—nagging. Then I saw the cashier in my head. She was not real young. Probably had kids and making probably half my meager wages. A till that was short fifteen dollars could be a real problem to her. I turned around and went back—parked my car and walked up to her window. She looked nervous—probably thinking I was there to complain. When I handed her fifteen dollars and said, 'I think you gave me too much change,' she didn't know what to do. Once the look of disbelief left, then came the look of great relief, and finally she was able to mutter, 'Thank you.' I want you to know that the look on her face was worth fifteen thousand to me. I felt better about everything in my life after that. I cannot describe the sensation it gave me.*"

In that case, the woman with immediate problems discovered that an act of goodness may not have changed her predicament, but it sure changed her attitude about her predicament, and probably opened the door to creative ways to solve her problems. Goodness opens inner doors.

Ultimately, God teaches us that the haves and the have-nots have the same moral responsibility to the law: **"You shall not commit a perversion of justice; you shall not favor the poor and you shall not honor the great; with righteousness shall you judge your fellow"** (Leviticus 19:15).

➤ "It's not hurting anyone!"

This is the preferred rationale given by people who steal from large department stores, large corporations like the phone company, and banks. It is one thing, they think, to steal from the small-time owner of the corner drugstore, but for businesses that make multimillion-dollar profits, the loss is insignificant. "They lose more money than this every hour because of accounting mistakes," "If it is a big store I'm not taking away money from anyone," or "It's just the cost of doing business."

The same attitude holds true for people who file frivolous insurance claims, medical malpractice, and other lawsuits. They feel that it is not the individual they are suing but rather it is the insurance company, who makes lots of money. They would never think of hurting "the little guy." These cases are often settled out of court because it is cheaper than paying legal fees and the negative publicity can affect business.

The only problem with this rationale is that it is wrong! This kind of stealing impacts the insurance and HMO rates that we all pay. It also forces up prices we pay for merchandise in stores. No department-store CEO is going to say, "I guess we will just subtract the cost of merchandise stolen from our annual profits." Insurance companies, HMOs, large retailers, and even small companies who must turn over delinquent payments to a collection service build these costs into their operating budgets. All of us pay higher prices for everything because of the people who claim they are not hurting anyone.

➤ **"I was only borrowing it!"**

Many people believe that they can designate something as a long-term loan, like an art piece that is on loan to a museum. The only problem is the lack of permission from the owner. When we talk to children about the meaning of this commandment, it is very easy to make it relevant by telling them that borrowing anything without the permission of the owner is stealing. Whether it is "borrowing" ten dollars from mommy's purse or borrowing big brother's shirt to wear to school, these are not just matters of courtesy—until the owner is notified, it is stealing.

"Never take it for granted that just because you live in the same house with someone you are at liberty to take or use their personal things. This behavior usually leads to taking liberties with other people who do not live in the house." This recommendation came from Joseph, one of my listeners.

➤ **"He deserves it!"**

Borrowing implies the personal use of an object with the owner's knowledge and consent. But what if a sister took her brother's favorite sweater because she was mad at him? The goal in taking the sweater was not to keep it or wear it. Jewish tradition is clear in this case, that taking something even just to upset someone is considered stealing.

Tasha, one of my listeners, wrote about stealing as revenge: *"I used to steal from my mom because I thought it served her right. Then my sister began to steal from me. I guess that served me right. I am now a little wiser at 23."*

➤ **"I haven't really taken any*thing*!"**

This is one of the more popular rationales. In this category are people who lie about the ages of their children to get child discounts for movies, theme parks, and all forms of entertainment. It also includes people who lie about their own ages to get similar discounts. "So what does it matter if I fudge a bit about my age?" These people believe that they have used legitimate means to save money. The only problem is that they have lied, and in doing so, they have taken money away from a business that rightfully deserves it.

Also included in this category are people who use bootleg cable television descramblers, borrow copyrighted computer software from a friend and download it into their computer, make long-distance calls from a pay phone without paying. In each case a company is defrauded of rightful revenue. Whether we like big companies or not, we enter into illegal activity.

Students will often argue that it is okay to cheat on exams because no one else is being hurt. But cheating on an exam is stealing a grade.

On April 14, 1997, *Sports Illustrated* published a special report that researched the following question: "You are offered a banned performance-enhancing substance, with two guarantees: (1) You will not be caught. (2) You will win. Question: Would you take the substance? This question was asked of almost two hundred U.S. Olympians and aspiring Olympians. More than half the athletes said "yes."

These results clearly demonstrate that to many, winning has become more important than sportsmanship, character, and godliness. Contrast that to the Christian runner in the movie *Chariots of Fire,* who wouldn't run on the Sabbath to compete for a gold medal. Contrast that to this story conveyed to us by Rob: *"I am a huge tennis fan and competitive player; so naturally I watch Wimbledon. In the quarter finals, Mal Washington of the U.S. was playing Romanian-born German player Alex Radulescu. At 4–4 in the deciding and tense fifth set of their match, Mr. Washington hit a very impressive backhand overhead which he felt, and the TV replay seemed to verify, landed on the sideline. The linesman called the ball out, and Mr. Washington protested. His appeal to the chair umpire fell on deaf ears as he said he could not overrule the call. Mr. Radulescu, who was the closest to the ball as it hit the ground, did a marvelous thing. He approached the umpire and saying that he was sure the ball was good, conceded the point to his opponent. Remember—it was 4–4 deuce in the final set!*

I was impressed that this player would put character ahead of personal gain, and I felt the commentators would praise him.

Here is, though, what John McEnroe, NBC analyst, said of the incident: 'Radulescu was obviously showing his inexperience on the professional circuit by giving up a point he didn't have to, one that cost him most likely the match.'

His opponent, Washington, said, 'That was probably the biggest show of sportsmanship by any athlete I've ever seen. I think only one guy on the tour would have done that, and it was him.'"

➤ **"I did it for a good reason!"**

One of our favorites. This rationale does more than just make stealing acceptable—it elevates it to a higher purpose. The ends justify the means. Unless it is the plans for Iraqi biological warfare, illegal drugs, or a gun to be used in a murder, all things that are illegal or will result in innocent deaths, stealing cannot be elevated to a higher purpose.

Jewish tradition rejects the idea that stealing can serve a higher purpose by legislating that a *mitzvah* (divine commandment) cannot be fulfilled with a stolen item. For example, the commandment to light Hanukkah candles cannot be fulfilled with a stolen Hanukkah menorah (eight-branched candelabrum used for the holiday).

➤ **"Everyone else does it."**

And finally, the winner for the most childish rationale. Adults who use this rationale find it difficult to state this one publicly because it sounds as ridiculous as it is. These sins are unspoken ones because people are usually too embarrassed to admit to them and certainly wouldn't want "everyone else" to be in their home without their supervision!

The more frightening version of this excuse is gang and mob mentality. It is true that larger groups of people are capable of greater evil than most of the individuals would commit independently. The mob gives each individual permission and acceptance for baser behavior than the individual would feel conscience-free to do. Emotions, passions, and impulsiveness often have freer range with a mob.

➤ **"All's fair in love, war, and in business."**

If you cannot trust the owner of the corner store to be honest with you, who can you trust? The Bible does not subscribe to the idea that "all is fair in business." Since commerce is the backbone of society, laws are needed that ensure trust between buyers and sellers. **"When you make a sale to your fellow or make a purchase from the hand of your fellow, do not aggrieve one another"** (Leviticus 25:14). Based on this verse, the rabbis established a rule that a seller cannot charge more than one-sixth above market value, nor can the buyer pay less than one-sixth below the market value, unless the other party is aware that they are overpaying or underselling the object. What is unusual about this law is the protection given the merchant for not being swindled. The Bible is concerned that buyers get a fair deal and sellers make a fair profit. In establishing guidelines of fair behavior, issues of mistrust are removed and honest business can flourish.

In this spirit we applaud Chris Webber, pro basketball player. According to the *Detroit News* (November 10, 1996), Webber severed ties with Nike because they refused to lower the price of its basketball shoe named after Webber. "How can I charge that price for my shoe when I speak to all those inner-city kids and preach to them?" The shoes, priced at $140, actually cost Nike $5 to make in foreign manufacturing markets. Webber "didn't like Nike's idea to target inner-city youths in an attempt to initiate buying trends that could spread to the suburbs." The welfare of the children was above profit.

Is it possible to rob people with words? Sure! By intentionally giving a business competitor false information, money can be lost. False and misleading advertising is another form of stealing.

The rabbis also established a rule that it is forbidden for someone to ask a merchant the price of something if not interested in buying it, because the hopes of the merchant are raised for a possible purchase when someone asks about the price. Since the customer appears ready to make a purchase, the merchant is thinking about being able to pay the rent and buy some clothes for his children. Thinking that the customer is serious, the merchant spends a great deal of time trying to make the sale. When the customer was never serious, he has stolen the valuable time of the merchant and falsely raised his hopes for a sale. According to this law, it is acceptable to comparison shop and window shop as long as the customer makes his intentions clear.

For those of Christian faiths, Jesus was no less demanding of workers' responsibilities to the people they serve. "There were tax collectors, too, who came for baptism, and these said to him, 'Master, what must we do?' He said to them, 'Exact no more than the appointed rate.' Some soldiers asked him in their turn, 'What about us? What must we do?' He said to them, 'No intimidation! No extortion! Be content with your pay'" (Luke 3:12–14).

➤ "I'll pay when I can."

When someone becomes an employer, whether it is by hiring a gardener or a housekeeper, there are special obligations. Most prominent is the requirement to pay a hired worker in a timely fashion. **"The wages of a hired worker shall not remain with you overnight"** (Leviticus 19:13). It is not for us to assume that the gardener or music teacher can wait an extra week to be paid. When we engage someone in a written or verbal contract, we are obligated to pay that person as soon as he completes the job and submits a bill. Whether it means that we cannot buy new clothes or take that long-anticipated vacation, once we become employers our first obligation is to pay those who work for us.

Basically, this is a form of debt, and we are forbidden to repudiate our debts—**"Neither shall ye deal falsely"** ("Leviticus 19:11)—by any lies—**"Nor shall ye lie one to another"** (Leviticus 19:11)—or other trickery. I get so many calls from folks whose family members borrow money and then, feeling an illicit sense of entitlement, don't pay the debts back. Additionally, there are the folks who cheat each other out of inheritances because they feel emotionally entitled.

All of this is stealing.

➤**"I work here—I earn it."**

Employees also have special obligations to their employers. Chief among them is the issue of trust. When an employer hires an employee, whether in a business or at home, it is essential that he be trustworthy. Aside from stealing through embezzlement, there are other ways of stealing from employers. Many employees think nothing of taking home office supplies. Writing pads, pens, folders, and desk lamps are not kept in stock as door prizes. They can legitimately be taken to do work at home, but otherwise are considered the property of the office.

Playing computer games, surfing the net, or even just personal reading during company time when there is work to be done is obviously stealing. Employers pay employees to do work, not just to look as if they are busy.

Unauthorized giving away of the services or product of an employer is not allowed. Whether it is a waitress giving free food to family or friends or a theater attendant letting people in free, money due the employer is being taken.

According to Rabbi Yisroel Miller, of Congregation Poale Zedeck in Pittsburgh, *"'Don't steal' includes petty theft of office supplies at work, making personal toll calls from the office phone and general goofing off on the job. It also includes stealing other people's time—like thoughtlessly keeping them waiting or showing up late for appointments. It also includes genevat daat (robbing the mind), that is, fooling people and betraying their trust."*

Sadly, according to a major study reported in *USA Today* (April 4, 1997), "Nearly half, 48 percent, of U.S. workers admit to taking unethical or illegal actions in the past year. These include one or more from a list of twenty-five actions, including cheating on an expense account, discriminating against co-workers, paying or accepting kickbacks, secretly forging signatures, trading sex for sales, and looking the other way when environmental laws are violated." The survey of 1,324 randomly selected workers did not ask about unethical or illegal action for reasons such as greed, revenge, and blind ambition. In that regard, it supported the "psych and circumstance" excuse industry by asking the participants only to list violations that they attributed to "pressure" (i.e., long hours, job insecurity, personal debts, family concerns). Fascinating.

➤ **"It's not much."**

Some people justify stealing by saying that things are aren't really big or worth much. According to John, a listener, size doesn't matter: *"I would tell myself things like 'it's no big deal,' 'it's not hurting anybody,' 'it's really just a small thing.' But after becoming a Christian several years ago, I realized there's no sitting on the fence where honesty is concerned. Either you're hon-*

*est or you're not. Just because some forms of stealing don't have
a readily identified victim, such as copying computer software,
it's still against the law, and therefore wrong for someone who
professes to follow the teachings of the Bible which embrace honesty.*

*"The small things really do count. 'The person faithful in
what is least is faithful in much, and the person unrighteous
in what is least is unrighteous also in much' (Luke 16:10)."*

The Bible forbids the stealing of the smallest object. If what
is taken is so small as to have no value, for instance, a splinter
from a fence to use as a toothpick, it is not legally prohibited,
but it still ought not be done. If everyone pulled off splinters,
soon there would be no more fence.

➤**"I couldn't help myself."**

This is part of the new psycho-babble excuse culture we've developed in the last twenty or so years. Therapeutic concepts and
techniques seeped out of the office and became mainstreamed. It
is all well and good to have a judgment-free atmosphere in a therapy session where the individual is comfortable to delve into in-
terpretive associations in order to understand his/her motives
and actions. It does not work when these techniques and therapeutic concepts become the dominant atmosphere of a society so
that accountability is eliminated.

"The former treasurer of the Episcopal Church blamed job
stress and gender bias yesterday in her misuse of $2.3 million
of church funds between 1990 and 1995. Ellen F. Cooke said
that a psychiatrist who evaluated her attributed her behavior
to 'enormous pressures and stress.'" It turns out, as reported in
the *Harrisburg Patriot News*, May 2, 1995, that the money
was used for personal expenses, a house, a farm, school tu-
ition, jewelry, and travel. It is offensive to us that sinful behavior is being passed off as a bad mood. People, even those with

"mental conditions," generally know right from wrong. Most stressed-out people take warm baths, meditate, or pray; they don't steal by misusing their access to other people's property.

➤Miscellaneous.

Under this category, we put folks who justify stealing in one area by proclaiming their morality in all other areas. Tom, another listener, wrote about this excuse: *"Boy, I loved those peanut clusters that the food market had in those candy bins. Every time I went grocery shopping I helped myself to 2 or 3 of them. Dishonest, who me? You are damn right I was dishonest, and a person who did not follow that commandment because I rationalized that since I didn't cheat on my income tax or steal from your mother or embezzle money I was ok in the honesty department. I had to learn that this kind of entitlement and justification would be a demon that followed me around for a long time. It took a store manager to remind me of the Fourth step in AA to become conscious of the dishonest man I had become in many areas of my life. Now I run to the peanut cluster bin, take 2 or 3 out and put them in a plastic bag and check them out like the rest of humanity. And, if I eat one before I make it through the line, I tell the checker and have even handed in an empty plastic bag."*

Stealing More Than Money

➤Stealing someone's ideas.

There are those who plagiarize from other people's *written* efforts to make movies with their plot and character ideas, without affording them credit or compensation. There are those who have casual conversations with creative people and then use their ideas for lucrative projects without compensating or crediting them. They often use as the excuse: "Well, I'm the one who took the financial risks." No matter, it's stealing.

➤Stealing someone's innocence.

One of the most tragic forms of theft is the stealing of innocence. Although the Biblical passage, **"If a man shall seduce a virgin . . ."** (Exodus 22:14) refers specifically to the case where a man has sex with an unbetrothed woman, and has to provide her, if she and her father agree, to a marriage contract, or, if they don't agree, then financial remuneration, rabbinic commentators have called this "theft of the heart." It is the responsibility of adults in our culture to provide safe environments for children. When an adult places a child in an environment that deprives him or her of childlike status, they are guilty of stealing something from the child.

Unfortunately, there are innumerable examples in our own society that such theft of innocence not only occurs regularly but is socially supported. In the case of taking advantage of a child sexually, even if the child agrees to the sexual act, any adult who has sex with a minor (known as statutory rape) has taken away his or her child status by having a child engage in an adult act. I have taken many calls from parents who simply tolerate the new trend toward adolescent sexual intimacies. Society has virtually sent up the white flag of surrender in this arena. Some of that permissiveness is due to parental misbehaviors with drugs and sex when they were teenagers. With their guilt, they feel they have no right to judge or dictate. It is so sad that they can't see past their own embarrassment and false sense of hypocrisy to save their children from the shame and loss they experienced. I have explained to many parents that hypocrisy has to do with their current behaviors, not the old ones they've learned from.

Allowing children to watch inappropriate movies and television shows in which they experience violence, sex, and other behavior inappropriate for their age is another form of stealing a child's innocence. Too many parents abdicate responsibility in monitoring their children's exposure to the media (TV, movies, video games, etc.), because they just don't want to be the salmon fighting to go upstream against the social tide; or they're too busy with their own obsession with money and sex; or because they have become cynical about trying to protect their children from ubiquitous bad input. Not only is monitoring important, but fighting the good fight against the media is also important. Try to find a television program aimed at teenagers that isn't filled with sex or sexual innuendo. I've gotten to the point of fearing PG-13 more than R. R is at least right up front. Too much inappropriate material is hidden behind that PG-13 rating.

I also feel that adult obsession with self-gratification and fulfillment ("We *have to work* for our child's future"), combined with a societal depreciation of the needs of children ("The moments we spend with him/her before bedtime are precious"), has resulted in the institutionalizing of their early care. Having children virtually from birth taken care of by strangers robs them of their early, and necessary, experience with loving, attentive parents, and steals their innocence.

Honesty Training

Bottom line, if you haven't bought it, earned it, been given it, or inherited it—it belongs to someone else and that's where it should stay. That means that such things coming to you by accident, as clothing delivered to you by mistake by the laundry, must not be used and must be returned. That also means that a craftsman must return the balance of any materials given to him to work with. That also means that you must not manipulate, excessively cajole, or exert pressure on people to make them feel guilty in order that they give up to you what you want of theirs. That means that you must return all possessions left in your care for safekeeping, even if you've grown quite attached.

Parents must watch over and teach their children from an early age, so that the sanctity of property becomes second nature to them. Children unwittingly help themselves to sweets and small treasures, feeling that their sense of joy and attachment to the object gives them entitlement. Parents are entrusted by God with the development of the moral character of children. I have been sometimes impressed, and sometimes shocked, by the schemes parents have devised to cure their children of stealing. Some of my callers have wanted to call the police on five-year-olds to teach them a lesson (I have vetoed this one). Others have had their children return the item and apologize in person and/or in writing (I support this one).

None of these techniques will work when the parents are living examples of dishonesty. Doreen's family has trained her children that they can decide who and when to cheat: *"The only type of stealing we do is the movie theater bit and I never considered it stealing. After all, we still pay for the kids—just not the ridiculous amount they want. One of ours is 13 years and yes we do consider him a child and that is why we lie to get him in. Not that it makes it right but we know this can only last so long—until he really looks like a teen—which he doesn't yet."* When children are taught that they are the ultimate authority on whom and when and why they can break a commandment, it increases the likelihood of them expanding the seemingly "ridiculous" to the downright dangerous. Many parents have complained about this truth only when their kid steals the family's car or money because they somehow rationalized entitlement. As one young person once told me on the air, *"I didn't feel so bad stealing from my mom—I grew up watching her be dishonest—so what right did she have to say what I did was wrong?"*

Duke, another listener, wrote about his family's recognition of right and wrong: *"Anytime my wife would take the kids to the movie, she would buy them candy from the grocery store for them to eat while watching. I figure the theaters have rules against bringing your own goodies, but I don't really know for sure and have been too embarrassed to ask—but I always felt a little sheepish about bringing in candy to save money. One time we were headed to the movie, I participated in the buying of the candy beforehand, but I told the kids to not display the candy openly while there as it was against the rules.*

One of my kids spoke up and said, 'Well, if it's against the rules, why are we doing it?' And I have to tell you that neither I nor my wife has ever tried that again."

Point, set, and match.

9

The Ninth Commandment

**"You shall not bear false witness against
your fellow."**

"What a tangled web we weave; we *all* practice to *deceive*," is
the headline for a *New York Times* article (June 7, 1996) that
states that "ninety-one percent confess that they regularly
don't tell the truth. Twenty percent admit they can't get
through a day without conscious, premeditated white lies."
Perhaps even the folks who say they don't lie regularly are
themselves lying?

The report suggests that, as a society, we have moved very
far away from the age when a "man's word was his bond" to a
society in which "people are more accepting than ever before
of exaggerations, falsifications, fabrications, misstatements,
misrepresentations, gloss-overs, quibbles, concoctions, equivo-
cations, shuffles, prevarications, trims and truth colored and
varnished." That acceptance has surely changed the moral
landscape of this nation in everything from the disappearance

of common social courtesies to the prevalence of vulgar and vicious radio and television programming, from disrespect for traditional sexual and marital mores to the ever-growing cynicism about the potential of goodness to survive anywhere.

People *expect* that politicians, lawyers, lobbyists, advocates, journalists, talk-show hosts, and anyone else in the public view will lie if it serves their purpose. It is taken as a given that, if something is not a full-out lie, then it is a partial truth, spin, context, and distortion. Why are we as a society so complacent with this reality? Probably because it lowers the standard against which we have to measure ourselves, and it is difficult to fight a resistant, pervasive malaise that engulfs those around us.

What most people remember from their early school days about George Washington is that he was the nation's first president and that he was reluctant to lie. When we learned the myth, concocted by an ex-preacher named Mason Weems to humanize Washington's "boring" image (*U.S. News & World Report*, March 2, 1998), that George as a small child, caught doing a naughty, owned up immediately with "I can't tell a lie, Pa; you know I can't tell a lie. I did cut down the cherry tree with my hatchet." This happy myth became a standard in the lives of generations of children since then. Honesty and greatness were a package deal.

Lying is part of a larger trend celebrating:

➤Individuality (if it serves *me* it is good).

➤Free speech (stretched far away from freedom to criticize the government without fear to any expression no matter how destructive).

➤Entertainment (commentators in the media say it is the reader's/listener's responsibility to figure out the truth and not to accept what they hear on face value).

➤Free enterprise (exaggerated claims of advertisers are defended as necessary in a competitive market).

➤The blessing of a free state (where rights are valued over responsibilities).

All this "freedom" is not making people feel safer with each other. A February 1990 Harris poll report on Generation 2001, based on a survey of the first college graduating class of the new millennium, dealt with the issue of trust and generations. When comparing the moral integrity and honesty of their generation with that of others, Generation 2001 students trust older people more than their younger contemporaries. They are most likely to trust their grandparents' generation (79 percent), followed by their parents' generation (68 percent). When considering their own generation, the trust level drops to only 25 percent.

Our children are seeing their world become more treacherous. Psalm 12:1–2 speaks to this kind of world: **"Help, O Lord! For the faithful are no more; the loyal have vanished from among men. Men speak lies to one another; their speech is smooth; they talk with duplicity."** How can we have an expectation of abiding friendships, honorable business relationships, fidelity in marriage, and cohesion in families and communities when we can't trust one another? The answer is that we can't. We're all witnessing the breakdown in faith we have with each other and its consequences. People are shacking up instead of marrying because they can't see that there is any difference in outcome between a covenant before God and an agreement to cohabit as long as it seems satisfying. People do not seem to be aware that lack of faith in commitment and truthfulness of vows impoverishes individuals emotionally, children psychologically and economically, and society functionally.

Why Does God Make a Big Deal About Lying?

"There are six things that the Lord hates . . . a lying tongue . . . " (Proverbs 6:16–17) and "Lying lips are an abomination to the Lord" (Proverbs 12:22) give a clear indication that God considers lying a major wrong. Since lying is only about words, it makes one wonder why it's such a big deal. One of the main attributes of God is justice, and truth is a precondition of justice. Only when we have a clear picture of how things are can we discern how to behave appropriately. If we don't have a clear or true picture of how things really are, we are more likely to behave in a way that is ultimately unjust.

In some regards, lying is more serious than stealing. The thief takes material things, while the liar creates injustice and misery. The liar also kills himself spiritually by diminishing in himself the divine glow that raised him above the rest of the animal kingdom through acknowledging his creation as being for the benefit of his neighbor and God.

"I Swear to Tell the Truth, the Whole Truth . . ."

The Ninth Commandment specifically prohibits lying under oath in a court of law. We call it perjury when a person knowingly gives false testimony under oath. Although God defines transgressions and demands punishments, God also dictated that courts and judges administer justice in very specific ways. For example, more than one witness is required for convictions, especially of capital crimes ("A single witness shall not stand up against any man for any iniquity or for error, regarding any sin that he may commit; according to two witnesses or to three witnesses shall a matter be confirmed," Deuteronomy 19:15), probably in part to ensure against intentional perjury or mistaken conclusions leading to unjust convictions.

The truth of the matter is that very few of the very many people who lie in court are prosecuted. In the American judicial system one criterion of perjury is that the false testimony must relate to a significant issue that effects the outcome of a case. In criminal cases, when the issues are far more serious and convictions result in jail time rather than financial compensation, it is natural that perjury would be more of a serious issue. But in civil courts it is quite common for people to lie. Larry Goldman, a criminal defense lawyer in New York, told the *Sacramento Bee* (January 27, 1998) that "As a practical matter, there's a rampant amount of perjury in civil litigation. Both sides commit perjury."

Although the Bible promises perfect justice in such situations (**"The false witness will not go unpunished, no one who utters lies will go free,"** Proverbs 19:5), we must trust that while perfect justice is not always available in our courts, it will be in the Divine Court of final appeals.

You only need watch the *People's Court* to see how people on national television can take an oath to tell the truth and then tell a bold-faced lie. It is amazing how people are able to lie in plain sight on national television without apparent shame. It would seem that the momentary thrill of being on TV and the reward of a few hundred dollars have become more sacred than honor, dignity, and truth.

Just about every case had a plaintiff and defendant with contradictory stories. Sometimes it was just a matter of perception, but other times we know that one and/or the other was lying— generally for revenge and will to win. We just don't know which one is lying about what—especially when they both have something to gain by looking good (even if it requires self-deception). It was up to Judge Wapner, and later Judge Judy, to decide who was telling the truth. We can only hope that with superior powers of deduction and perhaps some specially tuned power of intuition they can tell who is lying.

All this leads us to the most problematic aspect of judges and juries attempting to figure out the truth: If someone has done something wrong, and that person is a good enough actor, he may win the case and get away with the crime. On television's *Law & Order,* a witness often will be telling the truth, which would convict the bad guy, only to be tricked and attacked by a clever defense lawyer into looking less credible. Rather than "may the best man win," sometimes it is "may the best lie win."

"Do You Swear to Tell the Truth . . . ?"

"Do you swear to tell the truth, the whole truth, and nothing but the truth so help you God?" With an affirmative response to these words an individual takes the witness stand to participate in the judicial process and determine the fate of not only the accused but also those who have likely suffered at his/her hand. For the avowed atheist who stands before the judge, there is still the affirmation promising "pain and penalty of perjury."

Even though the vow is made in public and to God, some people feel justified in lying. Perhaps it's the lack of obvious lightning bolts from heaven in response to courtroom lies that lets people imagine they can get away with it. Their motivations include:

➤Protecting themselves (witnesses who fear for their lives if they tell the truth as well as those who don't want to implicate themselves).

➤Hostility by people with "philosophical" bones to pick with the country and the judicial system (which, ironically, protects them in so many ways they don't appreciate).

➤Misguided loyalties, from wanting to feel important by "knowing something" they really don't know, to folks who want to see justice done "no matter how."

One the other hand, there are stories of how after intense preparations for trial, clients have gotten up on the witness stand and completely changed their stories because after placing their hands on the Bible and swearing to tell the truth, they couldn't bring themselves to lie.

Justice Must Be Just

A major impediment to a free society is a dishonest judicial system. Though there are numerous examples of judges who "have been bought" (**"Do not accept a bribe, for the bribe will blind those who see and corrupts words that are just,"** Exodus 23:6), we are grateful for a judicial system that is governed by the Constitution, allows for appeals, and provides protections for the accused. Americans tend to assume that whatever deficiencies our system has, they largely are not a result of corruption, but rather due to judges and juries who are too soft, or racial prejudice, or insufficient concerns for the rights of victims (**"You will not be led into wrongdoing by the majority nor, when giving evidence in a lawsuit, side with the majority to pervert the course of justice; nor will you show partiality to the poor. . . ,"** Exodus 23:2–3). We are grateful because there are many countries that are not governed by these same democratic principles or where pervasive corruption has made true justice unobtainable. It is remarkable that we can be proud of our judicial system in spite of the tendency for people to lie in court.

"... If a Witness Is a Liar ... You Must Show No Pity" (Deuteronomy 19:19–21)

The Bible states that a punishment for perjury is: **"Then shall you do unto him as he had planned to do unto his brother"** (Deuteronomy 19:19). The Jewish legal tradition interpreted this to mean that whatever punishment the defendant would have received based on the testimony of the false witnesses shall be the punishment of the false witnesses.

Are "Bystanders" Ever Innocent?

Not coming forward with relevant truths and evidence, while technically not a form of perjury, is definitely a perversion of justice. According to the Bible: **"If a person will sin: if he accept a demand for an oath, and he is a witness—either he was or he knows—if he does not testify, he shall bear his iniquity"** (Leviticus 5:1). Popular excuses such as, "I mind my own business," or "I just don't want to get involved," don't absolve people of their obligations to each other, justice, goodness, and to God. We are our brothers' keepers. Other than God, we are all we have.

The Real Danger of Lies

Technically, this commandment deals with testimony in a court of law and the impact on the judicial system, but there are clearly vast implications of not telling the truth in our everyday lives. While many of us do not worry about false testimony in a court of law, we should worry about what ramifications there are to the daily lies we tell.

The husband who tells his wife he is working late at night while he is out at a bar drinking with his buddies has told a lie that hurts the marriage, his soul, and his ability to face the realities of his drinking problems. Without trust there is no glue and ultimately no safety for intimacy in any relationship.

Some lies are told about other people for revenge, like false accusations of child molestation in some custody battles. According to a Canadian government study on such false accusations, published in *The Calgary* (May 10, 1998), statistics showed two of three child-abuse complaints were false. The devastation to the life of the innocent parent, the destruction of the parent-child relationship, as well as the confusion and humiliation experienced by the child caught in the middle, are despicable and sometimes irreversible.

Sometimes people tell lies to protect themselves from a deserved consequences. As Jacqueline, one of my listeners, wrote: *"Rather than confronting a problem, I would rather evade it. I find myself being unable/unwilling to speak the truth out of fear of rejection, etc. This phenomenon occurs almost automatically, in a sense that it is more natural for me not to speak the truth than it is to speak it. Also by that I mean by withholding the truth, or not speaking the truth when it is necessary."*

In the case of a child who is accused by his parents of playing with matches, he tells a lie when he claims that he never saw the used matches he discarded and were found by his parents. Like the child who lies about the matches, we mostly lie to cover up guilt. Such lies are not permissible because they allow the individual to avoid responsibility and the possibility of healthy growth and change.

Some lies are told to bring attention so desired by the liar. A recent painful scandal in Los Angeles concerned a medical health-care worker who confessed to the mercy killing of several scores of elderly patients in a well-known hospital. Once the investigation was well under way, he recanted. There was speculation about his wanting to feel important, which the media notoriety gave him, albeit in a sick, sad, twisted way.

There are those lies for personal gain or convenience. Elizabeth wrote, *"My struggle was whether or not to be honest with my employer about not planning to return to work after I give birth. Since I was not returning to work, it didn't seem fair to take the four months benefits paid leave since the benefits are based on my return to work. Since my husband is self-employed, the benefits, if paid by him, would be expensive. The 'friends' I asked counsel of said I should take the four months, 'everybody else was doing it.' I even asked an attor-*

ney friend of mine. He thought that I should lie, too! Guess what? I asked myself what Dr. Schlessinger would say. When the response came back that I would be cheating my employer and that the decision to commit fraud didn't start me or my family out on the right foot, the decision was easy. I will give my notice honestly and fairly—the way I would want to be treated if I were an employer."

Conscience doesn't always have the power to force truth telling; sometimes the Supreme Court has to get involved. In January of 1998, the Supreme Court ruled that an employee who is asked about possible wrongdoing has only two legal choices: tell the truth or say nothing. This ruling resulted in sanctions against five federal workers who denied charges that later were proven true. The Justice Department urged the court to rule that there is no "right to lie" in the Constitution. In a brief unanimous opinion written by Justice William H. Rehnquist, "A citizen may decline to answer the question, or answer it honestly, but he cannot with impunity knowingly and willfully answer with a falsehood."

The current scandals over so-called "recovered memories" of childhood sexual abuse are emotionally and sociopolitically sensitive. The question of whether forgotten memories of childhood sexual abuse can be brought back with the aid of therapy has been bitterly contested since the first cases emerged in the United States a decade ago. Many accused parents claim their family lives have been destroyed by false accusations, from fantasies planted in their adult children's minds by unscrupulous, incompetent, or misled therapists. "False memories can be planted in patients' minds by psychiatrists and there is no evidence that memories can be 'blocked out,'" concluded a report set up by the Royal College of Psychiatrists in England, published in the *British Journal of Psychiatry* (May 1998). The report states, "No evidence exists for the repression and recovery of verified severely traumatic events. There is also striking absence in the literature of well-corroborated cases of such repressed memory through psychotherapy. Given the prevalence of childhood sexual abuse, even if only a small proportion are repressed and only some of them subsequently recovered, there should be a significant number of corroborated cases. In fact, there is none."

When people's lives have become painful or problematic, it is natural that they would seek explanation and solutions. It is also natural that, in this desperate and needy state, they would be sensitive and vulnerable to influence. In reading many of the recantations, such as those published in the newsletter of *False Memory Syndrome Foundation,* most of the women admitted to not really being comfortable with the conclusion of abuse, feeling intimidated by the certainty of the therapist, and often pressured by so-called support groups, but also acknowledged some relief at having a "reason" for their problems.

While in private practice years ago, I witnessed the devastation of a family because of the false accusation of child molestation. An adult daughter, having problems in her life, went into therapy. The therapist informed her that she must have been abused. The vulnerable young woman, depending on the authority of the therapist, charged the father with molestation and terminated all relationships within the family. The father took two lie-detector tests through the police department and passed both without equivocation. Nothing was enough for the therapist to review her "diagnosis." The family was virtually destroyed, along with the father's reputation in his community.

Sinning basically goes hand-in-hand with lying. Few sins are committed without the perpetrator taking some comfort from the expectation that if caught, he has the opportunity to lie himself out of it. Conversely, the more you become familiar and comfortable with a lie, the easier it becomes to lie and branch out into other wrongdoing.

Inner struggles to maintain sincerity and truthfulness are not always rewarded in an external manner with winning or acquisition. A commitment to honesty does build reputation with your neighbor and with God. It may take a while, but when it really counts, you will be the one believed.

Lies Can Kill

On a more apocalyptic scale, "The broad mass of a nation . . . will more easily fall victim to a big lie than to a small one." These words written by Adolf Hitler are living testament to the idea that the bigger the lie the more believable it becomes. Hitler was able to convince the German people that the Jews were responsible not only for their loss in World War I, but also the social and economic difficulties of his time. By constantly distinguishing between the "superior" Aryan race and others, he convinced many Germans of their manifest destiny. How ironic that the German people, who represented the most sophisticated culture in literature, science, and the arts of their generation, were deceived into believing through the science of eugenics that Jews and other non-Aryan races were inferior. Tell a big enough lie and people will believe it.

It is a sad irony that Hitler's theory is still being tested. A group called historical revisionists, as well as several Palestinian leaders and newspapers, expand the view that the Holocaust is a hoax perpetuated by the Jewish people for world sympathy. The testimony of witnesses and survivors, German documents, and Nazi written and film evidence are all fabricated say these revisionists, to exaggerate events. Hate gains longevity through lies.

Divine Truth

We strive for truth is because it is a divine quality: **"A faithful God, never false, true and upright is He"** (Deuteronomy 32:4). God does not lie to people. In fact, when he is about to

pronounce judgment upon Sodom and Gomorrah, He es-
chews deceit: **"Shall I conceal from Abraham what I am going
to do . . . ?"** (Genesis 18:17).

The idea that God is a God of truth is reflected by Jews and
Christians who respond in prayer with the word "amen."
This word may derive from the Hebrew word *emunah,* meaning faith, or as an acronym for *el melech ne'eman,* ("God
trustworthy king"); God is portrayed as being truthful. God's
word is truth; this is demonstrated in a big way when God
promises Abraham that generations to come, when his people
will be enslaved, God will set them free.

Did They Ever Lie in the Bible?

Is the rule against lying absolute, or are there times when we
can legitimately lie? There are a number of biblical examples
where lying appears to be accepted. They generally fall under
two categories: to protect life and for the sake of peace.

The first time Abraham speaks in the Bible, it is to tell his
wife, Sarah, a lie. Because of famine, Abraham went to Egypt.
As they approach Egypt, Abraham begins to worry that
Pharaoh would want his lovely Sarah and, knowing that she
was married to Abraham, have him killed. Therefore he tells
her, **"See now, I have known that you are a woman of beautiful appearance. And it shall occur, when the Egyptians will see
you, they will say, 'This is his wife!'; then they will kill me, but
you they will let live. Please say that you are my sister, that it
may go well with me for your sake, and that I may live on account of you"** (Genesis 12: 10–13).

Jewish teaching has generally held that, even under duress,
no man can intentionally kill or commit a sexual crime on an
innocent person. Remember, though, that this episode occurs
long before the Seventh Commandment is dictated at Sinai. By
"lying," Sarah and Abraham conspire to preserve his life to

give themselves the opportunity to make their way on their divine journey.

In a more clear-cut permissive situation for lying, and one of the strongest statements of friendship, Jonathan is faced with the difficult choice of whether to help his friend (the future king of Israel and progenitor of the Messiah), David. Doing so would require him to tell a lie to his father, King Saul, who had become pathologically jealous and paranoid about David's popularity with the people and troops. Jonathan had to tell a lie to his father to determine whether, in fact, King Saul wished to kill David. When King Saul asked about David's whereabouts, Jonathan said to him **"David asked leave of me** [to go] **to Bethlehem"** (1 Samuel 20:28), knowing full well that David was hiding in the field nearby. King Saul became angry. His desire is to kill David. Jonathan's lie was validated and he sent the future king of Israel away to safety. Clearly, it is permissible and required to tell a lie to prevent a murder.

In another biblical story God actually told the prophet Samuel to lie. When God informed Samuel that He was sending him to find another king (God had rejected King Saul and his heirs for the kingship), he replied, **"How shall I go? For, if Saul hears, he will kill me."** To which God counseled, **"You shall take a heifer with you, and you shall say, 'I have come to slaughter** [a sacrifice] **to the Lord'"** (1 Samuel 16:2). In spite of the fact that Samuel did not "come to slaughter to the Lord," God gave him permission to say so. From God's own lips we learn that telling a lie to save a life is allowable.

An even more dramatic biblical story emphasizes the *need* to lie to save a life is in Exodus (1:15–22). The Pharaoh, having become insecure about the growing ranks of Israelites, ordered two midwives working for the Hebrews to murder all boys born to them. However, **". . . the midwives, fearing God, did not do as the king of Egypt had told them; they let the boys live"** (Exodus 1:17). These midwives chose to disobey an immoral law. When caught, the midwives said, "... the Hebrew women are not like the Egyptian women: they are vigorous. Before the midwife can come to them, they have given birth" (Exodus 1:19). Not only did they not submit to a plot to murder innocents, they recognized that they did not have to tell the truth about the murder and so jeopardize the innocents. They were brave, and righteous, and their weapon against inhuman brutality was resistance and lying.

Trustworthy People

In the Jewish legal tradition, there are certain people like gamblers and "usurers" (today we would call them loan sharks) who are not permitted to serve as witnesses, the assumption being that people who do this for a living are not to be trusted because the professions they are involved with encourage dishonest interactions.

"I do not consort with scoundrels, or mix with hypocrites; I detest the company of evil men, and do not consort with the wicked" (Psalms 26:4–5). Associating and socializing with people who are not prone to tell the truth only encourages us to engage in the same kind of behavior.

It is important that we surround ourselves with friends and business partners we trust so that our personal and business dealings reflect our own values. It is sometimes the case that people will interpret our own values based on the people with whom we associate. It is also true that our need to be included, valued, desired, and feel important might lead us to adopt or at least passively accept the wicked ways of others. It is also true that we pick our friends and groups based upon either healthy or unhealthy aspects of ourselves.

Parents often complain to me that their child would not be misbehaving or getting into trouble if it weren't for those other bad kids. It is difficult for them to accept that their child picked the group specifically for the thrill of acceptance.

It Doesn't Always Seem to Pay to Be Honest

The truth is, it does not always pay to be honest. "Johnny, just tell me the truth and I won't punish you." With statements like these we try to instill in our children the importance of trust. As children struggle with the implications of trust, they must eventually develop an internal motivation that overrides external gratification. A perfect example is the high school student who has been taught that honesty always pays and approaches his teacher to report that she has given him a higher grade than he deserves. When the teacher re-marks the paper to reflect a lower grade and commends the student for his honesty, he responds mouth agape, "What, do you mean I get the same grade? I told the truth!" He was expecting that the teacher would retain the higher grade for his honesty.

Though it is good to give our young children benefits for telling the truth, they must also learn that most often there is a price to be paid. Our children must be taught that the reward for telling the truth is being able to look in the mirror and live with ourselves. They must learn that honesty endears us to others, helps maintain trust in society, and can inspire others to do the same.

Dave, one of my listeners, wrote of the lesson his daughter, Michelle, learned about the "high price" one might pay for being honest: *"My daughter was only days away from high school graduation when the speech and debate club took a trip to a contest. At the debate contest, the kids did some drinking. The debate coach found out the next morning and collected the kids, asking, 'Which of you were drinking?' Despite the fact that at least fifteen kids were involved, only Michelle and one other kid replied in the affirmative.*

The debate coach came down very hard on the two 'honest' students, going to the school administration and getting them kicked out of graduation, and nearly expelled without their high school diplomas. Michelle was the CLASS VALEDICTORIAN, and her commencement speech was subsequently delivered by her best friend, who was threatened by the school administration, lest she make any political statements about how two students who WOULD NOT LIE were treated.

Michelle went on to college to earn a degree from Stanford U. with honors and distinction, a Master's from Oxford on a Marshall scholarship, and a Ph.D. from UNC Chapel Hill. She starts Yale Law school in the fall, and STILL has a tremendous aversion to LYING.

The 'cost' of that honesty back in 1989 has, I am sure, made Michelle even more determined that she will not have paid that price for nothing. Needless to say, I am very proud to be Michelle's father."

Children should not be taught that honesty is a tool to avoid responsibility, consequences, or punishment. But, if they do not compound the infraction or sin with a lie, their behavior should definitely be acknowledged with enthusiasm.

Many religious and military schools have an honor system, where students promise not to break the rules and to report the infractions of others. Officials at Annapolis, reeling from a series of midshipman arrests in the spring of 1996 on charges ranging from drug use to car theft, surveyed students on this issue. According to the *Washington Post* (October 31, 1997), "about 41 percent said they had observed midshipmen lying, and fewer than half of them said they had reported the violation." An academy spokesman said that the declining moral values in the civilian culture in which today's midshipmen have grown up is responsible for this dishonorable conduct and mentality. "In a civilian institution, you don't have the same repercussions. But in the military, when you lie, you may die."

Newsweek reported (June 6, 1994) that many midshipmen caught and kicked out in the worst cheating scandal in naval history stated that many of them were told to lie by their parents. One student recounted that others who cheated told him to "Lie till you die." That student, Brian Pirko, refused to lie and was thrown out for admitting his role. After he confessed, he told the president of the Honor Review Board, "Whatever happens, you know, I feel better from this moment on, just knowing that I've come here and cleared my conscience. I guess that's all I have to say, sir."

He lost his military education and appointment as an officer in the navy; he gained back his soul. That's a good investment for the rest of his life.

Tell the Truth and I'll Sue You!

As a result of our overly litigious society it has now become difficult to give an honest recommendation for employment. Whether it is an accurate negative recommendation for someone who is dishonest or has a poor work ethic, or a less-than-honest positive recommendation for a less-than-admirable worker, these types of recommendations have led to lawsuits. As a result of these lawsuits, many large firms and nonprofit organizations will now only verify whether an individual has worked for them, the length of employment, and the position they held. It is a sad state of affairs when we cannot be honest with potential employers. Although it is generally accepted that people elaborate or outright lie on résumés, it is now almost impossible to ascertain whether the job performance described in résumés is accurate. With the current trend, employers suffer without true evaluations of potential employees, and good workers lose the benefit of positive evaluations in the search for employment. It is our hope that one day honesty can once again play a role in a country that has become successful because good work was rewarded.

Can We Tell White Lies?

A *Peanuts* cartoon (August 1997) asks this question the best. Charlie Brown says to Linus, "We're supposed to write home to our parents and tell them what a great time we're having here at camp." Linus answers, "Even if we're not? Isn't that a lie?" Charlie Brown explains that "Well . . . it's sort of a white lie," to which Linus questions, "Lies come in colors?"

While we are all accustomed to the notion of white lies, it is probably true that we have used "color" as an excuse for too broad a range of excuses and avoidances. The sages provide a great example of the varying perspectives on when it is permissible to tell a white lie relating to the wedding custom of dancing and singing about the bride. The question: "How honest do you get about the bride's looks?"

One rabbinic tradition says we should "[Sing about] the bride as she is" (honest if she is ugly), while another suggests that we "Describe her as a beautiful and graceful bride" (even if she is ugly).

If out of compassion we lie and call ugly by the name of beauty, how it is possible to tell such a lie if the Torah states **"Keep you far from a false matter"** (Exodus 23:7)? The sages answered, "The disposition of man should always be pleasant with people."

In truth, beauty is subjective. After all, "Beauty is in the eyes of the beholder." Therefore, every bride on her wedding day is beautiful. Just as every baby is beautiful. The expression "a face only a mother could love" reflects the fact that not all babies are really beautiful. Ask any parent holding a newborn infant child and that baby is the most beautiful thing in the world. Even if the baby looks like Quasimodo, we abide by the principle "All babies are beautiful."

The biblical language with regard to lying is that one should **"keep far away from lying"** (Exodus 23:7). One should keep far away from lying, as far as possible, but there may be circumstances in which lying would include avoiding *unnecessarily* hurting the feelings of others. The "absolute value" of not lying is modified by the duty of compassion, goodness, and sociability. Social life would be impossible if everyone always told everyone else the truth of their thoughts, feelings, and perceptions.

I distinctly remember the power of one particular *Twilight Zone* program in which an evil man was planning delight in an evening of torturing people via his new find: a player piano that, when playing a selection made by a particular individual, forced that person into revealing truths about himself and others. It was painful to watch the humiliation experienced by each person unwittingly participating in his own agony. All truths are not worth revealing—they can be too devastating, without being constructive. The comeuppance occurred when the evil man was tricked into playing his own music—only to reveal the shallowness, envy, and insecurity behind his meanness.

Often, when a caller wants to reveal a truth because, she protests, "Honesty is the best policy," and I detect either an extraordinary naiveté or pernicious sadism behind the impulse, I challenge the caller with, "Oh yeah? All honesty is worth speaking. Okay, you're ugly and you're stupid and people hate you." This is usually met with immediate, profound silence. "Do you still think all honesty is best spoken?" The naive caller will say no, the sadistic one will agree still.

Honesty means that everything you say must be true, not that everything that is true must be said. Were that the case, no eulogy could be given without upsetting the family.

An example of God's telling a white lie in order to avoid family discord is when God comes to tell Abraham that after a lifetime of childlessness he will become a father. He says to Abraham, **"Why did Sarah laugh, saying 'Shall I in truth bear a child, old as I am?'"** (Genesis 18:12). A close look at Sarah's original comment shows that God made a slight change when quoting her. Sarah had said to God, **"Now that I am withered, am I to have enjoyment with my husband so old?"** Why would God change the part about Sarah calling her husband "too old"? Probably because he didn't want to hurt either Sarah or

Abraham by reiterating something said out of profound emotion. Sarah did not mean to slight Abraham when she made that statement, but, telling Abraham about it might cause pain and damage their relationship. According to Jewish tradition, for the sake of peace, you are allowed to "change" the truth—in fact, it is even a *mitzvah* (divine obligation of good deed).

Many of my callers expressed concern and wonder about their right, obligation, or responsibility to carry such tales: usually about bits of information spoken in a moment, a context, and an emotional state that may not last. We've all said things to be funny, relieve tension, get something aired, or exercise a moment of anger. We know in our hearts that this mood and sentiment is likely temporary and that the overall feeling we have about a person or situation is positive. Would any of us like it if every one of these momentary verbalizations was reported to its subject? Of course not. Yes, we should not have said this in the first place. Now, we should not spread such information and cause destruction and pain unnecessarily. Judgment and good common sense need be employed.

Your Mind Shouldn't Be Like Radio-Free Europe

Though you may be obliged to say the truth, you are not obliged to reveal all your thoughts. Silence is not deception (except in a court of law). If people truly expected perfect candor in all situations, life would become even more rude and hostile. There is the language of courtesy. There are expressions of friendliness that allow for a functioning social life. Social life would be impossible if everyone, with or without being asked, were to tell the truth to everyone else as he sees it. And that is another point, the way we see things is personal perception, and not necessarily objective reality. Your first thought about telling people something should follow Proverbs (10:19): **"When words are many, transgression is not lacking, but the prudent are restrained in speech."** People of goodwill should watch their words, censoring those that will cause embarrassment or hurt.

If, for example, someone were to ask "Do you like this couch?" your response may be influenced by whether you are out shopping with a friend who is buying the couch or whether it is already in your friend's living room. If you are out shopping and your friend is considering buying the couch, while you might not want to say "It is the most hideous couch I have ever seen," it is entirely appropriate to say "It doesn't do anything for me" or "It is not quite my style."

On the other hand, if your friend has already purchased the couch and it is sitting in her living room, while your aesthetic equilibrium might be reeling, it is perfectly acceptable to say "It matches the room perfectly" (which may not say much for the rest of the room) or "It is very nice" (there must be something nice about the couch, like the design, style of the legs, or even the fluffy pillows). In other words, you can always find something nice to say as an alternative to giving a negative, insulting, or hurtful answer.

The problem with calling lies "white" is that you cannot possibly always be sure that it is indeed "white," minuscule, or harmless. Don't imagine that you are able to calculate for sure which lie would be harmless. Even if you feel certain that there wouldn't be any harm, we may seriously underestimate and not anticipate all the ramifications of that seemingly little lie with the limited vision we mortals have. Down the road and around the bend in people and in time, that seemingly little lie might cause much unhappiness or injustice.

We just can't be objective about assessing the good or the harm of our lies primarily because we have a vested interest in our white lies, and in seeing the result of them as being positive—and therefore ourselves as "good." Since, in the final analysis, it is usually that we are most concerned about ourselves, it is self-deception at best, guileful at worst, to pretend to have everyone else's best interest in mind.

Lying About Character and Moral Issues

The case is different if you do not point out moral and behavioral shortcomings to an intimate who asks your opinion; and sometimes, when you see or anticipate great harm being done to innocents, even before they ask for your opinion. I get many calls asking me about the callers' right, responsibility, or obligation to speak up and tell "the truth" about someone's actions, or to, as in the honor system, inform those unknowingly harmed that a problem is occurring. The subjects range from alcoholism, to affairs, to abuse.

The advice we give in these situations is to kindly admonish the individual in private and give them the opportunity to "right himself." If this is unsuccessful, and someone else is at jeopardy, that person must be told. Unfortunately, you can only offer insight and support, you can't force someone to do the right thing. Ultimately, you have an obligation to protect people from the wrongdoing of others.

When you are not truly informed and intimate, it is probably better to stay removed, lest you do more harm than good on little knowledge. I spend a lot of time challenging callers on what they think they know as fact, reminding them of the devastation they will cause if they are wrong. I have been struck by the determination some people have to use bits and pieces of "information" like bullets. The nasty, embarrassing surprise attacks on many of the daytime television talk shows have contributed to this determination to ambush.

Are Secrets a Form of Lying?

Parents must also accept that their children do not tell them everything and that withholding such information is not the same as lying. Children do not want to disappoint their parents. They will make mistakes from which they learn, and this learning process is an important part of their maturity. Children should own up to the more serious mistakes and tell their parents, especially if there are ramifications. A parent should not be upset if he or she finds out something inconsequential that the child has done.

Spouses also withhold revealing fantasies that would upset their partners, as well as commenting about the inexorable changes of aging to the body. These are not lies, they are behaviors of considerate lovingness. For twenty years, pop-psych techniques, supported by stupid articles in mass magazines pretending to lead to greater sexual intimacy for couples, have promoted revealing all sex fantasy. Instead of leading to mutual understanding, I believe these exercises lead to estrangement. When spouses reveal their so-called true desires, the content often offends or intimidates the partner.

Friends do not tell each other constantly about small issues and peccadilloes—that would only serve to hurt and alienate. Every opinion, reaction, perception, and preference is not important, necessary, or kind to reveal. This is not lying. This avoids a universal tyranny of criticism and judgment about things that don't matter nearly as much as goodness, kindness, righteousness, and compassion.

However, withholding information about things that are dangerous or destructive to self or others is wrong, and can prove to be destructive. Children should tell their parents when they've been offered drugs and sex or when they're pregnant, for example. These are issues with profound consequences. Adults should tell each other about current indiscretions, venereal infections, or business and financial problems, because someone else is being jeopardized.

False Flattery

White lies are defined by their benevolent intent and benign nature. Lying for the purposes of false flattery is wrong. Flattery goes wrong when it sacrifices truth and dignity in order to obtain some material advantage—be it objects, money, affection, relationship, or favors. Flattery actually becomes an act of stealing, for which, instead of stealth and weapons, false words of approval are the tools of the theft.

Secondly, anytime you lead a person to believe something that they aren't, or that isn't, you inhibit them from dealing bravely and correctly with the truth. "Flatters," wrote Sir Walter Raleigh, "are the worst kind of traitors for they will strengthen thy imperfections, encourage thee in all evils, correct thee in nothing, but so shadow and paint all thy vices and follies as thou shalt never, by their will, discern good from evil, or vice from virtue."

Of course, it is difficult, but not impossible, to falsely flatter someone who is not already lying to himself. Self-deception is probably our most prevalent form of lying.

Hypocrisy

Hypocrite is a Greek word that describes someone evil within, but showing himself outwardly as being good; *hypo* denoting falsehood, and *krisis,* judgment. If you act or speak in a way to elicit a certain perception or opinion, while in reality your actions are performed *only* for the sake of that opinion or perception, you are being hypocritical.

We are familiar with hypocrisy from very public stories of televangelists who preach godliness on their programs (send money), but who are then caught either misappropriating the money or having trysts with prostitutes in motel rooms.

Joseph Sobran's column for Universal Press Syndicate (April 24, 1997) said it well: "Under the new rules, you can be called a hypocrite for upholding old standards of virtue that you don't exemplify perfectly; but you can't be called a hypocrite for sinking into utter moral squalor, as long as you profess to believe there's nothing wrong with it. So the defender of traditional morality is kept constantly on the defensive, since only he can be accused of hypocrisy . . . and you may look hypocritical when you're only human."

There has been a new phenomenon in our ever more aggressive media—searching for even minor inconsistencies in those who espouse and respect standards. The motive is clear in a society that sees standards as oppressive. Shoot the messenger, and thereby invalidate the message. The reality is that one can believe and live by standards . . . but imperfectly. That is not hypocrisy, that is the reality of the limitations of all human beings to attaining divinity.

Another unfair use of the term hypocrisy is demonstrated by the pain many parents have when they call and ask how they can possibly direct their children away from nonmarital sexual acts and drugs when they themselves, in their younger years, were off track. "Aren't I being hypocritical?" they ask. No, of course not. Never feel guilty for espousing a point of view that has changed over the years due to maturity and morality. Who on the face of the earth would ever be able to give direction or advice if the job requirement called for life-long perfection?

"You will return to God your Lord, and you will obey Him, doing everything that I am commanding you today. . . . God will then bring back your remnants and have mercy on you. . . . God will take you back" (Deuteronomy 29:2–4). It is clear, biblically, that getting back on track is called *repentance* and not hypocrisy—as long as one does not profess perfection.

Lying for Entertainment

With the proliferation and popularity of tabloid television, newspapers, magazines, and radio, it is clear that lying has become a form of entertainment. While many celebrities, like Tom Cruise and Carol Burnett, have successfully sued such publications, it is clearly impossible for people to protect themselves from the vicious and vulgar onslaught of such media outlets, intent upon producing scandal and controversy.

Psalms 10:8 seems to relate to this cruel lying: **"His speech is full of lies and browbeating, under his tongue lurk spite and wickedness. In the undergrowth he lies in ambush, in his hiding-place he murders the innocent."**

Harvard professor Sisela Bok, an expert on ethics, spoke at the Seventy-Fifth annual convention of the American Society of Newspaper Editors. She said, "Among many editors and reporters, there is a sense of looking into an abyss, being drawn into coverage many of you would once have rejected as too sensationalistic, too intrusive, too slipshod, too damaging to individuals and institutions."

Rick Green, a Southern Baptist minister from New Jersey, wrote us that *"Contemporary America thrives upon breaking this, the Ninth Commandment. Daytime talk shows, tabloid magazines flourish with lies and half truths. People love to hear controversy, and in many instances have lost any allegiance to the truth or any ability to search for and find the truth."*

What does it say to our children that each night we watch these tabloid TV shows that misrepresent and damage people's lives and reputations? What does it say to our children that each day we bring home tabloid newspapers and discuss the gossip at our dinner tables?

Teaching Our Children

Young children often make up stories—for them this is fun and creative. It is true also that these young children may blur the distinction between reality and fantasy, which is why we have to be very careful in monitoring what they see in TV and movies, lest they become unnecessarily fearful. A child older than five usually tells lies to avoid doing something or deny responsibility for what they've done. It is very important that parents respond to even isolated instances of lying by talking to their children about the importance of truthfulness, honesty, and trust.

This is where the issue of so-called "white lies" comes in. If children see a lot of lying to friends, relatives, co-workers, service people, and so forth, they learn readily that lying is fine as long as you rationalize it well. We run the risk of the child coming up with his or her own parameters of when it is okay to lie—certainly, neither the parent nor society is going to like that.

An example of turning away from even "white lies" to a healthier style of confronting an embarrassing and potentially hurtful situation concerns what we tell children about receiving gifts they truly hate. Perhaps instead of saying, "Aunt Mae, that is the most beautiful shirt, I love it," we could direct our children to find the blessing and respond: "Aunt Mae, you are so wonderful to think of me and send me a present. You are such a thoughtful and wonderful aunt, I love you." Then, instead of any color lie, the child is directed to consider what is wonderful and important. We think this is a good lesson for life; many tragedies and disappointments are survived by a search for the sometimes well-hidden blessing.

Children are going to be bombarded with messages contrary to your value system all the time. Even something so seemingly neutral as this letter from April indicates how difficult a parent's job is: "*A local Florida TV news program recently advertised a multipart series on how to get out of a speeding ticket. My first response was to think—'Were you speeding? Well then, take your lumps and pay the ticket!' Now, how in the world can we expect folks, much less their children, to accept responsibilities for their actions when we are bombarded with HOW TO programs for shirking? What a strange world we live in today!*"

When my son, Deryk, was about six years old, I caught him in a lie. I had already given him the lectures about trust, honesty, character, hurting the relationship, and punishments.

This day, I tried something different. I told him that he would not know whether I was lying or telling the truth—and that I would be this way for a week (an eternity for a six-year-old). He didn't think much of it at that moment. The next day, while driving him to school, I promised that when I picked him up I'd take him for french fries (a major treat). When I was driving him home from school he excitedly reminded me about the french fries. I turned toward him with a deadpan expression and said, "I lied." He really lost it, yelling and crying at me that this was neither nice nor fair. After only two days of this sporadic lying, he had had enough. He told me "he got it."

I have since described this technique on my radio program a number of times. The parental feedback has been very positive. Children learn the disappointment and insecurity of a relationship with no trust in a controlled manner.

Ultimately, our children need to know that lying is a very serious matter than can undermine our personal, marital, and social relationships. Telling the whole truth can sometimes do the same thing. We should assume that all forms of lying are forbidden, unless it is to save a life, foster justice, or demonstrate profound compassion and goodness. Unless there is specific benefit and without any component of self-service, perhaps we should think twice before moving our lips.

Every attempt to bring honesty into our lives removes the guilt of a false existence and brings us closer to the divine quality of truth. To live a life of lies can create a living hell that is often worse than facing the truth.

10

The Tenth Commandment

"You shall not covet your fellow's house: you shall not covet your fellow's wife, or his man servant, his female servant, his ox, his donkey, nor anything that belongs to your fellow."

A 1995 syndicated cartoon by Jules Feiffer shows a child contemplating "wanting." In the first frame he says, "I want." Then again, "I want." The third time, "I want?" "I want nothing!" "I need nothing!" "I have everything! My mother gets it for me." Next the child screams, "I want . . . TO WANT!"

Contrast that child to seven-year-old Nathan. His mom and dad sent me a copy of his school assignment, which was to write about what a perfect life would be and to draw a picture of the things he would have in that life.

Nathan drew a house and wrote "My home" beneath it. He also drew himself with his dog. Next he drew a checkerboard with faces inside each square, and wrote "my friends" beside that. Next, the essay:

The Perfect Life for Me
By Nathaniel

A perfect life for me is the life that I'm in right now. Because I have a lot of friends and have a big family too. I do not need a perfect life.

"*My wife is a stay-at-home mom,*" writes Nathan's dad, Rob, "*and we have made sacrifices so that may happen. There are times that we wished we could give our kids more materialistic things. It's moments like [reading Nathan's essay] that reassure us that the morals and values we live our lives by far outweigh any materialistic things we could provide.*"

What's So Bad About Wanting?

The impulse for wanting is a very necessary part of being human. Without this particular form of energy, people would be inert, inactive, unmotivated, and ultimately, not useful. Possessions can provide enjoyment, advantages, opportunity for discovery and mastery, an avenue of exchange, a measure of accomplishment, reward, comfort, and security.

It is true that human nature desires more than it needs. Lower animals and plants function automatically to take from the environment what they basically need to survive and reproduce. There are clear limits to their acquisition, and these limits are dictated by instinct. In other words, lower animals are hardwired to stop wanting when their needs are met.

Before you imagine this state of being as ideal, recognize that no lower animals dream of conquering a wilderness, saving children in distant lands, gathering millions for charitable causes, committing their lives to research for a cure for communicable diseases, or cooperating to build an inspirational gathering place to worship and study.

When lower primates raid and kill a neighboring group, it

appears to be for the purpose of survival and reproduction, and involves food, territory for security, and mates for reproduction. When humans raid and kill a neighboring group, it often is for a myriad of nonsurvival purposes—revenge, hate, power, and control, the exhilaration of domination, for the sense of superiority and importance, and greed way out of proportion to need.

We don't hate the lion who runs down, kills, and eats the antelope—we accept that the lion must survive, and has no choice, no free will. We do hate the tyrant, like Cambodia's Pol Pot, who tortured and murdered his own innocent people whom he believed threatened his twisted vision of a good society. Human beings have options and reasoning abilities to find benevolent and fair means to accomplish worthy goals. They have free will to make moral or immoral choices to achieve their ends.

When humans do not set limits on themselves, when their impulse to master and possess goes unrestrained, when they lose the sense that the ultimate good of acts or things resides in their service to godliness, the world then becomes for them too small and limited in resources to satisfy their infinite yearnings. That is a life of torment for the perpetually unsatisfied, and, as you will see, a dangerous world for others in their way.

What Does Coveting Mean?

This is a most interesting commandment. Unlike murdering, stealing, or perjuring, which are concrete acts or behaviors, this commandment concerns the arena of the mind: thoughts, desires, and feelings. In fact, all the commands of God can be put in one of three categories: acts, speech, and heart.

It is very clear throughout biblical Scriptures that God is concerned with our hearts and thoughts. That emphasis is made clear in Proverbs 6:16–19, where it is written that seven things are an abomination to God; one out of the seven is "A mind that hatches evil plots." That God values and judges our hearts is further evidenced in I Samuel (16:6): ". . . a man sees only what is visible, but the Lord sees into the heart."

Why at the end of a list of "dos and don'ts" would there be a prohibition against what goes on in our minds? Isn't it more relevant what we actually do to one another? The answer is that the actual "doing" of a forbidden, immoral, unjust, or unkind act doesn't begin with the act. It begins in the *mind* and *heart* with a sequence of feelings, thoughts, and planning that can and often do lead to the breaking of the first nine commandments. In this commandment, God is reminding us that our evil actions don't emanate from our hands alone but from unpleasantness or petty ugliness from our hearts.

Thought or Deed?

Over the centuries, there have been arguments about the nature of coveting. Some scholars interpret coveting as a type of deed rather than a desire or feeling. An example of this interpretation is stated in Deuteronomy (7:25): ". . . you shall not covet the silver and gold on them and keep it for yourselves. . . ." The notion is that the coveting was an immediate precursor to the forbidden act of theft. In this view, coveting is seen as plotting or scheming.

It is interesting that when Moses reiterates the commandments (Deuteronomy 5:18), instead of using the Hebrew word *tahmod* for coveting, he introduces *tit'aveh*, desiring—"You shall not desire your neighbor's house"—right after "You shall not covet your neighbor's wife." The scholars who interpret coveting as an action utilize the prohibition against desire, because it may lead to coveting, which may further lead to theft or adultery.

Not all scholars agree with this distinction, believing that there is no difference between coveting and desiring. They use Micah (2:2) as an example to differentiate between a deed and a thought: "**They shall covet fields and take them by violence.**" The argument is that first there is covetousness, the feeling in the heart, and then there is the deed, acquisition by force.

You may see these arguments as only splitting hairs because we come right back again to the question as to whether this is a divine commandment applying to inner feelings or a virtual deed (scheming). Why do we imagine that God would not be concerned with our thoughts and hearts when Psalms 15:1–2 suggests that the opposite is true? "**Lord, who may sojourn in Your tent, who may dwell on Your holy mountain? He who lives without blame, and does what is right, and in his heart acknowledges the truth. . . .**"

Not only are we not to murder our brother or sister, we are not "**to hate your brother in your heart**" (Leviticus 19:17). It would seem that God's concern is not only in commanding good deeds but our inner convictions and goodness of thoughts and desires is also required.

Can You Control Your Thoughts and Feelings?

Judaism is primarily a behavioristic religion, and Christianity, derived historically from Judaism, is also concerned with the kind of life one leads. It is obvious that proper thoughts more likely lead to proper behaviors, and improper thoughts to improper behaviors. Thoughts can take on a life of their own. Thoughts of doing wrong things are a blemish on the divine spark within us all.

How can we possibly control our thoughts? And which thoughts are we supposed to control? This commandment involves *wanting something at someone else's expense*—not simply just wanting something. We feel that the goal of this commandment is to stop us from thinking excessively about things that do not belong to us, as well as from loving earthly things in lieu of godliness. When we become obsessed with possessing things, and specifically, others' things, it influences our ability to create a balanced life of meaning and may lead to evil in order to obtain our desire.

Strictly, we transgress this commandment by covetousness, and then obtaining what we want, even legally. For example, I covet your business, and then take it from you with a hostile takeover.

Too much thinking about things generally involves obsessing and misery. When thought exceeds the bounds of what is necessary or good, when your actions are determined only by what you ultimately acquire and possess, then your know you're over the edge.

Of course you can't control every itinerant thought that pops into your head: *All sin begins with thought. I believe it was Martin Luther who said "it is acceptable for a bird to land on your head, but you don't have to let it build a nest"* (Rob Sugg, Elder in the Presbyterian Church USA). How do we not let wrong thoughts "build a nest"? *"We are exhorted to push evil thoughts from our minds by replacing them with good, uplifting thoughts"* (Dr. Robert Kofahl, Presbyterian).

I have gotten many calls over the years from people who harbor what they realize are ugly thoughts, such as resentment, jealousy, envy, or greed. They ask me how they can control those feelings, since they realize that they are behaving badly because of them, or avoiding the person altogether out of fear and guilt. Each time, I have suggested that they do something benevolent. For example, when one woman was envious of her friend's new, great job, I suggested she throw a congratulations party for her, or send her a congratulatory note, or something that would express the exact opposite of what her envy might lead her to do. Each and every time I have made this recommendation, the caller expressed immediate relief from the ugly burden they'd been carrying, as well as a more positive feeling. In contemplating the good deed, their minds returned to good thoughts. Not only do good thoughts usually result in good deeds, good thoughts can resurrect good thinking.

Prayer is yet another avenue to relieve ourselves of negative, ugly thoughts. In reading Scriptures, confession, and personal prayer, we are reconnecting with God. In those moments our hearts and minds shift into a plane that renews our perspective on what is meaningful, valuable, decent, and good.

How Covetousness Creates Evil

About 2,800 years ago, King Ahab wanted the land adjoining his property, but that land belonged to a neighbor. Ahab offered to buy the land for a reasonable price, but his neighbor did not want to sell, because the property had been in the family for a long time. Ahab became depressed over this matter until his wife assured him that she would take care of everything. The wife, Queen Jezebel, had the neighbor falsely accused of blasphemy and treason and put to death (I Kings 21). The king was then able to confiscate the land. From the king's covetousness came bearing false witness, murder, and stealing.

One hundred years before, King David saw a beautiful woman, Bathsheba, on a rooftop and desired her. In spite of knowing she was married, he had her brought to him for a sexual interlude. She later informed him of her pregnancy, and he orchestrated a failed attempt at trying to arrange an "intimate" evening between Bathsheba and her husband, Uriah, in order to make the pregnancy look legitimate. When this failed, because of Uriah's loyalty to his men still in battle, he arranged to have Uriah sent to the front, where he died in the conflict (II Samuel 11). King David's coveting led to adultery and indirect murder. Some rabbinic scholars suggest that because in these ancient times, a temporary divorce writ was always presented to the wife by the husband going off to battle, David didn't "technically" commit adultery. Whether that is true or not, David's actions were an abominable abuse of his kingly power and divine expectations.

King Saul's (I Samuel 18) attempts to murder David years before he was king started with his envy over David's growing popularity with the people. Miriam's curse of leprosy was a result of her jealousy of her brother Moses' special relationship with God (Numbers 12). Her covetousness of his prophet status led her to gossiping.

All of us have stories, we hope not nearly as horrendous as those, of how covetousness, in the form of envy, jealousy, or greed, have taken us off the right path. Irene wrote to us about her story: *"Probably after I had my first baby, I experienced a time in my life when I became envious of all the women who looked like they had it all. You know, a great career, a great husband, a great family, money, and prestige. I was envious of one woman in particular. She was an acquaintance of mine from church. To me she looked like she had it all. Later I found out that she didn't. She had more problems that I did. But at the time I was experiencing these feelings of envy I talked behind her back and took every opportunity to put her down. Thankfully I got through this and I realized that by doing this I was only showing my own insecurities."*

A wealthy business acquaintance enjoys repeating the quip, ostensibly voiced by Andrew Carnegie, who, when asked, "How much money is enough?" offered, "Just a little bit more!" Acquisition can take on a life of its own. Ecclesiastes (5) states that: "No one who loves money ever has enough ...." and (17–19) "So my conclusion is this: true happiness lies in eating and drinking and enjoying whatever has been achieved under the sun, throughout the life given by God: for this is the lot of humanity. And whenever God gives someone riches and property with the ability to enjoy them and to find contentment in work, this is a gift from God. For such a person will hardly notice the passing of time, so long as God keeps his heart occupied with joy."

All that each of us have is a blessing from God. We are to enjoy, be content, and to find meaning in our particular lives.

It is not that someone who seems to have plenty really has more problems; they may have fewer or just different challenges to deal with. The measure of the value of our lives is not from the number of our problems, and not from our possessions or enjoyments. The value of our lives is derived from the purpose we find in acknowledging our blessings.

Marianne wrote about her competitiveness as a search for personal value: *"Greed or envy only get the best of me when I'm competing in a sport. I was raised to perform to the best of my ability and envy gets the best of me when I'm not #1 at what I'm doing. It's a fault that I'm trying very hard to overcome. But, every so often, when somebody beats one of my scores and I'm having a bad bowling night, my frustration mounts and my performance gets even worse."*

There is a world of difference between doing your best and beating everyone else. In the movie *Chariots of Fire*, one runner just had to win; he had much to prove. Another runner, very religious, simply enjoyed the gift of the wind against his face and his feet virtually flew over the ground. For this runner, winning was not the point; the point was appreciating the experience. When we covet someone else's win, we diminish the meaning of the opportunity and experience to participate and appreciate the value inherent in life. Too many people are impressed with what has become the sports mantra, Vince Lombardi's quote, "Winning isn't everything; it is the only thing."

There are numerous warnings throughout Scriptures against catering to the uglier aspects of our inner feelings to have or be what someone else has or is: **"You want something and you lack it; so you kill"** (James 4:2); **"For jealousy inflames the husband who will show no mercy when the day comes for revenge"** (Proverbs 6:34); and **"The life of the body is a tranquil heart, but envy is a cancer in the bones"** (Proverbs 14:30).

Clearly, we need to concentrate our desires on the values

that give us pride, on the values that God cherishes, on the values that lead us to do good. Covetous desires, though apparently natural to the human condition, are to be countered with a recommitment to values outside our ego and selfishness. When this is not done, we are ripe to add to the misery of the world.

Society Wants You to Want

According to an article in the *Educational Forum* (Louis Goldman, vol. 60, Winter 1996), "The typical U.S. consumer is the recipient of 3,000 advertisements daily. The general message in this merchandising is that all of our problems can be solved immediately by the consumption of the proper product."

And from the same report: "Other surveys have shown that, in 1967, 44 percent of college freshmen believed it was essential to be 'very well off financially,' and by 1990 that figure rose to 74 percent. In contrast, 83 percent believed it was essential to develop a meaningful philosophy of life in 1967, but by 1990 only 43 percent did."

We are unaware of any surveys that indicate that people are any happier with more stuff. Stuff without purpose, meaning, and direction in one's life has limited reward. *"A person who does not covet is a person at peace, a person content, a person happy with present circumstances. Of course, such a person would enjoy a new socket set or a bigger house, but these are not consuming ambitions, detracting from the pleasure of simply living."* This quote is from a listener, P. Badham, who also wrote that *"Coveting has become a national pastime; indeed, it is a way of life."*

As Shaunna, one of my listeners, admits: *"The most difficult of the 10 Commandments is the one warning against coveting your neighbor's ... whatever. It's hard to be satisfied with one's own things when there are so many temptations to buy more, get more, own more. I am learning to be content in all things, including when my friends or relatives take those wonderful trips and I stay home with my family. I have come to realize that we make our own choices and set our own priorities, and I am finally comfortable with my life and don't spend the time wishing for what I do not have."*

Rabbi Vogel remembers watching a television interview of people who had become instant lottery millionaires. The interviewer's question, "How many are you happier today?" was not met with a single raised hand. One of the winners replied, "How many new suits can you buy? How many cars can you drive? Every time you get something nicer, it isn't good enough, because you see and want something even nicer." Rabbi Vogel loves to quote the rabbinic teaching, "Who is wealthy? The one who is content with his life."

There is an obvious problem when our focus is more on what we do not have than on what we have. Contentment with our blessings is not laziness. Contentment does not imply a lack of effort of ambition. Instead, contentment means that at every stage of your life your measure is appreciation and gratitude and not an inventory of what is missing or yet to get. This latter concern leads to unhappiness, discontent, feelings of entitlement, frustration, anger, and probably ugly words and deeds because thoughts are the parents of acts. You know you are on the right track in this regard when you can enjoy the success and happiness of others. When, instead of admiration or respect, you suffer from resentment and an enraged sense of entitlement, you know you are on the wrong track.

It is finally a matter of being a master or a slave to things. If you are a slave, you are consumed and held captive by the need to acquire things. If you are a master, you can order and control your desires to include only those things that you decide would bring appropriate assistance, beauty, dignity, or enjoyment.

Want Versus Need

This commandment relates directly to the problem we have today distinguishing between needs and wants. Every adult suffers from this affliction. Many people live beyond their means because they believe they need all those possessions or services. To some, they would be called luxuries; to others, basic necessities. It is the very blurring of these issues that creates overindulgence in our lives and the lives of our children.

Not too long ago, people would not buy anything they could not pay for in cash. They felt tremendous pride from their sense of having earned that which they owned and enjoyed. Today, most Americans live way beyond their means. Buying on credit, incurring large debts and interest bills, is seen as the only way to get all they want. We would venture to guess that buying on credit does not confer the same sense of pride of accomplishment that paying cash earned.

Many of our youth today have very distorted views of what constitutes a basic need. I have spoken to many parents on my radio program who feel guilty about not giving their children everything and anything they want simply because their children say they "need it because everyone else has it." Now need is defined by equity with the adolescent Joneses. I have explained to parents that the necessities of life are needs and have suggested that if their children want a better kind of car, beyond the need for safety and transportation, they inform their children that luxuries are theirs to earn.

Similarly, Rabbi Vogel has spoken to many teenagers who admit that their parents provide them with too much, too quickly. They also admit that, while this is true, they're not about to ruin a good thing. In spite of their lack of adult maturity and experience, many of them recognize that complete gratification is not the way to raise a healthy, self-sufficient adult. Nonetheless, these children become used to having and getting with little contribution. I worry about how they are going to cope as adults when they can't get it without earning it.

Coveting Takes the Meaning Right Out of Living

The fall of Rome is blamed, by some historians, on excessive leisure and prosperity, depriving the society of true meaning. It is an easy trap to fall into in every one of our lives today. As Donna, one of my listeners wrote, *"I think envy has gotten the best of me when I have forgotten my purpose. I am here to make a difference in the world, not to compete for secular glory. When I have rejected my duty and obligation to God I have lost my purpose. Sometimes others will encourage us to play the covet game: who is better than who based on achievements, material goods, and knowledge. I have risen above envy by making God my priority, not my ego."*

Possessions are a gift from God. They are not inherently evil, nor are possessions irrelevant to God—if they were, then why the commandment, "Thou shalt not steal?" Possessions have value by virtue of enhancing our ability to enjoy the gift of life and bring goodness to the world. As goals or ends in themselves, they become idol worship.

There is no more worrisome arena for this concern over success and possessions becoming idol worship than the family. During the last two decades, I have seen the demise of the family primarily based upon a spouse-parent coveting some new love partner, or coveting possessions and power more than child care. David, one of my listeners, wrote to us about his revelation with respect to this latter issue: *"I am 37 years old and happily married with three children. My story starts when my first daughter was born. Both my wife and I were very career oriented and both working, I for an aerospace company and my wife teaching for a school district. We were very comfortable with the lifestyle our double-income family afforded us. My wife was intent on returning to work after our baby was* born and continue in a career outside the home. I not only found her position acceptable but encouraged it.

Our precious little baby came at the end of the school year and my wife spent almost four months of the summer home with our new little Natalie. We worked hard on locating the best possible day care for our daughter. At the end of the summer, our days consisted of getting the new baby up at 5:30 A.M. and taking her to day care, picking her up at the end of the day and then spending a few brief moments at home with her—feeding her and getting her ready for bed only to wake up the next morning and do it all over again.

After about five months of this my wife made a radical milestone change in our lives by deciding to increase her commitment to our child and future children by staying home and being a full-time mother. I was not only surprised by this decision, but opposed it. I respected her decision and felt it was her decision to make, but I was worried about the impact to our lifestyle with the loss of a second income.

You see, looking back, I not only enjoyed her working but I coveted the money she was making. I knew (hoped?) deep down that after a few months of being home my wife would get bored and then return to work so we could return to the days of spending and selfish living.

With my wife's continued resolve to be at home, we then made significant changes to our lifestyle by moving into a smaller, more affordable home, we drove older vehicles, and we got rid of the adult toys that a double income had afforded us.

I can now say, four years later and with tears in my eyes, that I am the happiest person/man/father in the world and the proudest husband of a wife who decided to stay at home to be a real mother to her children. I am a convert to the importance of children being able to have their mother home all day with them to love them, to hold them, to play with them, and nurture them. I am a convert to what is really important in life and where all of my time, effort, and ability need to go: our children.

We now have the 'finer things of life': we have each other, a loving home, and a full-time mom."

It's All About Perspective

What has always moved and touched us is the ability some people have so beautifully developed to appreciate their lives and find the blessing. Perhaps this is even the ultimate divine goal of this commandment. For example, this comment from Susan: *"I recently toured a friend's brand new home, cathedral ceilings, white carpet—very elegant. I genuinely felt so happy for her. Not even a twinge of envy. I came home and looked at my 30-year-old avocado green countertop and realized—I waited long enough and now avocado is BACK in style! Life is good."*

And this letter from Harvey: *"I had quadruple bypass surgery two years ago and now I have undergone my third surgery involving glaucoma. I am telling you all this because of a statement I want to make to you, Dr. Laura. You helped me turn the emotional corner from depression. You showed me that I HAVE TO BE THANKFUL OF WHAT I HAVE, AND NOT FEEL BAD OF WHAT I LOST. It seems to me that we must deal with what is given to us and not just make the best of it, but make it better. Some people just are not happy unless they are miserable and let other people know it. I consider myself a wealthy person—not in material things, but a loving and CARING wife (Helene), five wonderful children (I count my son-in-law as a son), terrific friends, a company that has stayed with me through my ordeals and co-workers who helped."*

Anne wrote of her appreciation of the bittersweet aspects of life: *"Everybody has something in their lives that I would not want. I learned not to envy them their lives but rejoice in mine. My life isn't perfect; life is bitter-sweet. But I am so lucky. Life gives you some sweet things and some not so sweet things. You learn to make wiser decisions. You learn to deal with each situation based on your strengths and moral character not from wishing you had some possession your friend has. Envy creeps in on occasion but I count my blessings instead of my friend's new diamonds, weight loss, or vacation home—and I am the richer. I also then am able to rejoice in their happiness. I learned to live my life according to the principles of my religion, my own convictions, directions, and love.*"

A hilarious example of a lack of perspective comes from a syndicated cartoon by Leigh Rubin, published in 1997. It shows two giraffes calmly following two disgruntled elephants out of Noah's ark. One of the elephants is complaining, "What a lousy trip . . . it rained the *whole* time!"

There will never be satisfaction in our lives if we cannot find the immediate blessing or feel purposeful in our efforts. Blessings and meaning do not come from things but from what we do with or in spite of those things. Most of the true pleasure in life comes from our own efforts and relationships. How can we appreciate our potential place in this time when we devalue our own lot, lack gratitude, have unrealistic expectations, constantly compare our lot to those of others and either feel arrogant triumph or resentful failure, when we believe that each desire must be fulfilled? The answer is that we can't, and we've built ourselves a living hell.

And How Do the Children Learn?

Sandie wrote us that, "*I really like the Islamic version of the Golden Rule: He is not a true believer who does not desire for his brother what he desires for himself.*"

Colleen wrote me about her nephew's first understanding of this commandment: "*Two years ago my nephew learned the lesson of 'thou shalt not covet' with grace and aplomb. You see, his little brother's birthday is one week ahead of his birth-*

day. At the time of the incident they were turning three and six. While the younger brother was opening his birthday gifts, the older brother was sulking and brooding about not being allowed to open them. His parents explained that even though it was very difficult to be a spectator to his brother's gift-opening, it was rude and wrong to be such a stinker about it.

He thought about that for about a week. When it came time for his own birthday, the younger brother was a little upset about not being able to open presents. Rather than snatching away the gifts and telling his little brother where to go, he said, I know how hard it is to watch someone else open gifts, so you can help me if you want. Even though he was not passing along the same lesson about not being a stinker, he learned a tremendous lesson about being a gracious big brother and decent human being."

Children desperately need to learn compassion as a way to teach them how to control greed and wants. They will learn first and best from their parents' behaviors how much emphasis, emotion, arguments, conversation, time, and effort go into things versus family, charity, true self-improvement, education, the arts, prayer, and religious observance. They learn also from the effort parents put into teaching them to distinguish between wants and true human and spiritual needs. Parents must not overindulge children with objects of fads and trends out of proportion to books, sports, music, school, and charity work. Parents should also involve their children in activities of generosity and selflessness, so that from an early age, children can learn the joy of giving in addition to the fun of receiving.

What Is Success?

Ultimately, this chapter is about measuring our success through things. Shannon sent us this poem (author unknown) from her church bulletin. She said that she carries it around with her because of its inspiration and how it keeps her grounded on those things that are truly important in life. She thought that this would be a nice, modern Ten Commandments:

Success

Success is speaking words of praise
In cheering other people's ways,
In doing just the best you can
With every task and every plan.
It's silence when your speech would hurt.
Politeness when your neighbor's curt.
It's deafness when the scandal flows,
And sympathy with others' woes.
It's courage when disaster falls,
It's patience when the hours are long,
It's found in laughter and in song,
It's in the silent time of prayer,
In happiness and in despair.
In all of life and nothing less,
We find the thing we call success.

Nowhere does this poem on success name possessions as the means. Don't get us wrong, we both love our things, but we strive to love God more. It is in that striving, and not from the things, that we ultimately find peace and joy.

If one were to follow commandments one through nine perfectly and with great control of our behaviors, according to the Tenth Commandment, we would not be out of the woods spiritually. We are not saints just because we've avoided committing commandments one to nine if we are filled with resentment against others for what they do or have, or feel empty for what we don't have. Our potential godliness is sullied by the rotting in our souls of envy, greed, and jealousy. Controlling our desire to have makes us wholesome and nicer and decreases the potential for doing wrong or evil.

When Coveting Is a Good Thing

Can anything positive come out of a "covetous" reaction to some aspect of thy neighbor's life? The answer is yes. When you look upon someone with respect for what they are or do, you can want to be like that person. You can feel inspired, motivated, and elevated by their example to demonstrate compassion, discipline, piety, courage, effort, persistence, sensitivity, charity, and a search for knowledge. In other words, you can and should envy the goodness of others by becoming like them.

God wants us to desire or covet some things with a passion. According to Psalms (19:11), God's judgments are to be desired more than gold. Those who hunger for the eternal aspects of character, spirituality, and the determination to bring goodness and beauty into the world will not easily be sidetracked from what is important to what is superficial and fleeting. **"One thing I ask of the Lord, only that do I seek: to live in the house of the Lord all the days of my life, to gaze upon the beauty of the Lord, to frequent His temple"** (Psalms 27:4). This is the kind of coveting that helps make a life worthwhile.

Distinguishing between right and wrong kinds of coveting isn't difficult. The Tenth Commandment warns against coveting someone else's possessions and life. Wrong coveting ends up in one person, the covetous, gaining, though losing his soul, at the expense of the other. Right coveting, that is, growing in spirit, wisdom, knowledge, and goodness, does not take from, nor diminish, anyone else—in fact, it benefits each of us and the world.

Finally, in Jewish law, you are permitted to have material desires—for a nice house, car, and so forth. You are not allowed to desire someone else's house. The difference is not only in the potential for theft. In desiring someone else's possessions, you are questioning God's apportionment: "Why do they have this and not me?" This shows a lack of faith and trust in the Lord. The Tenth Commandment is the final exclamation point on the first commandment—to believe in and trust God.

Epilogue

"Ship me somewheres east of Suez, where the best is like the worst," Rudyard Kipling wrote, "Where there ain't no Ten Commandments, an' a man can raise a thirst." Geography notwithstanding, England might be the place! The British newspaper *The Sunday Times* (November 16, 1997) reported that the Church of England's liturgical commission decided to remove the commandments from the holy communion service in the new millennium prayer book. "Philip Gore, a synod member for the Manchester diocese, said the decision reflected the church's fear that any kind of religious challenge will alienate congregations. Earlier this year, it emerged that the church had suffered its biggest drop in attendance for more than twenty years. 'Many in the church do not want a God who makes too many demands of them,' he said. 'Therefore, they want to dismiss the commandments as *irrelevant to our modern age.*'"

This astonishing conclusion reminds me of a *Toles* syndicated cartoon, in which a defendant in a courtroom proclaims, "Your Honor, we've come to the highest court because the law in question is over *100 years old*—written before the

telephone was even invented—at a time very different from
the one we live in today." In the next frame we see God, the
Ten Commandments behind Him, divine gavel in hand, saying, "Irrelevant!"

I once asked an audience of almost three thousand if they
thought the Ten Commandments were out of date. Many
hands went up. When I asked, "Which ones specifically?" no
one moved. Yet, I could see the discomfort in the room. It was
as though they were trying to justify their original proclama-
tion of the commandments' obsolescence, but realized that
there was nothing to back up that notion—nothing but moral
ennui.

The Ten Commandments are the first direct communication
between a people and God. Even for Christians, who believe
that salvation is not found just in obedience to God's law but
also in faith in Jesus Christ, their religion demands that they
put that faith into practice through the laws.

God's moral laws are still binding. They are the blueprint of
God's expectations upon us and His plan for a meaningful,
just, loving, holy life. Each of the Ten Commandments asserts
a principle, and, as this book elaborates, each principle is a
moral focal point for thousands of real life issues, including relating to God, family, our fellows, sex, work, charity, property,
speech, and thought.

Unfortunately, ignorance or dismissal of the commandments has taken such a hold in society that fewer and fewer
people have a clear idea of the difference between right and
wrong. Worse still, as long as they think they have what they
want, many don't care.

Rebecca, a listener to my show, wrote me about the issue of
archaic commandments: *"In regards to your comments on
contemporizing God, I had an interesting experience while living in Belgium, serving a mission for my Church. I was attending a religious meeting where a speaker was giving a talk on the
Ten Commandments. He was a professor of religious studies at*

the local University, and was constantly being told by his students that the Ten Commandments were outdated, not applicable to today's society, and should be changed. He said the Ten Commandments did not need to be 'op nieuw geschreven,' but 'op nieuw gelezen,' which means that they don't need to be rewritten but rather reread."

I agree. People may feel intimidated by God's laws because they just see them as a list of rules that one must live by *or else,* but underlying these rules are the most important concepts of love, honor, and respect. Rabbi Yosef Ber Soloveitchick's June 22, 1972, lecture to the Rabbinical Council of America included this important spiritual understanding: "Most of our sages distinguished between *chukim* and *mishpatim.* They declared the compliance with *chukim* to be a gesture of pure obedience and subordination to God. Conversely, adherence to *mishpatim* is a result of an inner moral need that God implanted in man, when the latter was created in His image. The mere fact that man carries God's image within himself suggests that morality is characteristic of human nature, and that doing good is an indispensable necessity, no less than food or air."

Although we believe that is true, man does still exert free will to choose between good and evil—between the spirit of the commandments and the pull away toward spiritual chaos. This book is an attempt to influence that choice toward God.

In conclusion, I remember a *Non Sequitur* cartoon by Wiley, which shows Moses, after having presented the Commandments to the Israelites, saying, "Hmmmm ... good question. I'll go back and find out." After a long walk back up and down Sinai, with a stormy, fiery interlude, Moses reappears, singed and exhausted, with the following message: "He says, 'Yes. You have to obey ALL of them ALL of the time.' And this concludes the %@#%&!# question and answer period. . . ."

Sounds clear to us.